JAMGÖN MIPAM

JAMGÖN MIPAM
His Life and Teachings

Douglas Duckworth

Shambhala
Boulder
2011

Shambhala Publications, Inc.
2129 13th Street
Boulder, Colorado 80302
www.shambhala.com

Printed in the United States of America

Shambhala Publications makes every effort to print on acid-free, recycled paper.

Shambhala Publications is distributed worldwide by Penguin Random House, Inc., and all its subsidiaries.

Designed by Daniel Urban-Brown

Library of Congress Cataloging-in-Publication Data
Duckworth, Douglas S., 1971–
Jamgön Mipam: his life and teachings / Douglas Duckworth.—1st ed.
p. cm.
Includes translations from Tibetan.
Includes bibliographical references.
ISBN 978-1-59030-669-7 (pbk.: alk. paper)
1. Mi-pham-rgya-mtsho, 'Jam-mgon 'Ju, 1846–1912. 2. Buddhist philosophy.
I. Mi-pham-rgya-mtsho, 'Jam-mgon 'Ju, 1846–1912. Selections. English. 2011.
II. Title.
BQ972.1637D83 2011
294.3'923092—dc22
2011012950

CONTENTS

INTRODUCTION

THIS BOOK REVOLVES around one of the most extraordinary figures in the history of Tibet, Jamgön Mipam (1846–1912). Mipam (commonly written as *Mipham* but pronounced "Mipam") shaped the trajectory of the Nyingma school, a Buddhist tradition from Tibet that traces its history back to its early transmission from India in the eighth century. Mipam is a major figure in this tradition, and in terms of the breadth and depth of his writings, he is in a class of his own. His works live today as part of the curriculum of study at several contemporary monastic colleges in Tibet, India, and Nepal. Thus, Mipam is not simply a towering figure of historical importance; he continues to hold a central place in a flourishing Buddhist tradition. Although he lived quite late in the long history of Buddhist development in Tibet, his influence on the Nyingma school has been enormous.

This book is an introduction to Mipam's life and works. It is organized into three main sections: the first provides some general background; the second presents an overview of some of the main themes in his work; and the last offers translated excerpts from his writings. Using this framework, I hope to give a sense of who Mipam was and present a survey of the rich heritage he has passed on.

Part One gives a context for understanding Mipam and his writings. Not a lot of biographical information about Mipam is available—which is surprising, considering the contribution he made to Buddhist thought and monastic education—but what we do know about his life and particularly from his works reveals that he was an extraordinary genius. He spent most of his life in meditation retreat, yet he was also actively involved in Buddhist scholarship. Mipam wrote extensively and not just on a few areas of Buddhist thought. He wrote on an incredibly wide range of scriptures and traditions, and his works address topics that extend well beyond the classic Buddhist scriptures. In addition to surveying these topics, Part One touches on some important features of Buddhist traditions in India and Tibet, providing a background for the tapestry of Mipam's texts and allowing us to better appreciate his contribution.

Part Two gives an overview of Mipam's interpretation of Buddhism. This section looks at major themes in his corpus to discover how he presents Buddhist theory and practice. In particular, this section looks more deeply into Mipam's interpretation of emptiness, a central issue in Buddhist philosophy, and contrasts his interpretation with those of other prominent Tibetan figures.

Part Three contains a sample of his writings. Each of the excerpts includes a short introduction to provide a context and help the reader appreciate significant elements of the passage. The selections draw from a wide range of Mipam's writings to illustrate the eloquent way in which he articulated the key issues explained in Parts One and Two. References to a number of these translations are provided in several chapters in Part Two, so the reader can immediately jump to the relevant selections to further explore the issues raised in the text.

Mipam was a sophisticated thinker who, in a grand synthesis, took on a number of difficult points in Buddhist thought. While this is an introductory book aimed at a general audience, it also deals with some tough issues in Buddhist philosophy, which is inevitable when dealing with someone like Mipam. For this reason, a person new to Buddhist philosophy may want to read slowly and even read some sections more than once. Taking time to assimilate ideas is crucial to the process of integrating the significance of philosophical texts, Buddhist or otherwise. Understanding Mipam's works is certainly not easy, but to glimpse even part of the beauty of such a master's compositions is well worth the effort. Given that he spent so much of his life in meditation retreat, his philosophical writings are deeply rooted in an experiential orientation and can be read as quintessential instructions for Buddhist practice.

PART ONE

Life and Context

ONE

Mipam's Life

Mipam was a descendent of the Ju (*'ju*) clan. Clans and family lines are an important part of Tibetan identity, and they occupy a central place in Tibetan culture. Mipam's father, who was a doctor, belonged to this clan, which is said to have a divine ancestry. The Ju clan gets its name from the word *ju,* which is interpreted to mean "holding on to the rope of the luminous deities who descended from the sky." His mother was also of high status; she was a daughter of a minister in the kingdom of Degé, where Mipam was born. His homeland was a region at the center of intellectual culture in eastern Tibet in the nineteenth century.

His name, Mipam Gyatso, (which literally means "undefeatable ocean"), was given to him by his uncle.[1] From a very young age, he is said to have had a natural connection with the Great Vehicle of Buddhism; he was replete with innate qualities such as faith, renunciation, wisdom, and compassion. He is even said to have been able to recall everything that had happened since he was an infant![2] As is the case in the life stories of most prominent lamas in Tibet, Mipam is presented in his as a child prodigy. Yet given the momentous influence of such a recent figure as Mipam, we are left with relatively few details of his life.

His studies began when he was about six years old, and he memorized *Ascertaining the Three Vows,* an important Nyingma text on Buddhist vows.[3] Committing texts to memory is a common practice in Tibet when studying classical texts in depth. The fact that Mipam first studied this text in particular is significant because the three vows (those of individual liberation, bodhisattva, and Secret Mantra) comprise the training of moral discipline—the foundation of all Buddhist practices. Further, this text covers a wide range of Buddhist teachings—from the Lesser Vehicle all the way to Secret Mantra—and shows how they all can be integrated without contradiction, which is a major theme throughout Mipam's works.

When he was only ten, Mipam was said to be "unobstructed in reading and writing," and he began to compose a few short texts. Some traditional Tibetan scholars claim that among his earliest compositions, at the age of seven, no less, was his famed *Beacon of Certainty,* a masterwork of philosophical poetry. This would be an amazing feat and is a testament to the high regard in which Mipam's scholarship and intellect is held.

Mipam's creative intellect was not restricted to mainstream Buddhist topics. While Gendün Chöpel (1903–1951)—the famous Tibetan author, rebel, and iconoclast—is known for his commentary on the *Kāma Sutra* (the famed "sex manual" of ancient India), Mipam was actually the first Tibetan to write a commentary on it.[4] This shows both his originality and the eclectic character of his literary works.

According to his biography, he became a novice monk when he was twelve, following the local tradition of his homeland. He entered the monastery of Jumohor, which is a branch of the Nyingma monastery of Zhechen. There he came to be known as "the little scholar-monk."[5] Early in his life, when he was about fifteen or sixteen, he did a retreat on Mañjuśrī in a hermitage at Junyung for a year and a half. Mañjuśrī is a deity associated with wisdom, and throughout his life, Mipam had a special connection with this deity. Through successfully accomplishing this practice in his youth, it was said that he knew the Buddhist scriptures, as well as the arts, without studying. From then on, he did not need to study texts other than simply receiving a "reading transmission" (*lung*). A reading transmission involves the formal authorization to study a text when a teacher imparts the blessings of the embodied meaning of the words by reading it aloud to a student. Oral transmission from teacher to student is an important part of the Buddhist tradition in Tibet.

When Mipam was about seventeen, his homeland of Degé was taken over in the midst of a regional conflict, which eventually led to the government of the Thirteenth Dalai Lama in central Tibet sending troops to quell the insurgence. During the fighting, Mipam, accompanied by his uncle, went on a pilgrimage to Lhasa in central Tibet. He was around eighteen or nineteen at this time.

On the trip, he stayed at a Geluk monastery near Lhasa for about a month.[6] Although his stay was not long, his time at this monastery was significant. Here he was exposed to the Geluk tradition of scholarship, which is famous in Tibet for setting the standard of monastic education. He quickly gained fluency in dominant features of the Geluk tradition's interpretation of Buddhist thought, as well as the procedures of debate.

A large part of why Mipam's work became so influential can be attributed to the fact that he was able to formulate a viable alternative to the dominant Geluk interpretation of Buddhist thought, which had come to monopolize intellectual traditions of Buddhism in central Tibet since the seventeenth century. As an articulate voice of Nyingma scholarship, his works directly challenged the Geluk hegemony on monastic education. While his writings contested central aspects distinctive to their interpretation, he also incorporated significant features of Geluk thought into his own work, as we will see later.

STUDY

When we look at Mipam's scholarship across a range of diverse topics—logic, poetics, the Middle Way, medicine, astrology, and tantra, among several others—we might think that he spent all his time writing. But despite his voluminous literary output, the story of his life reveals that he spent most of his time in meditation retreat and composed texts on breaks from those retreats. Moreover, he does not appear to have devoted much time to formal study, and the way he did study was quite extraordinary.

For instance, it is said that when he received teachings on Candrakīrti's *Introduction to the Middle Way* with a Geshé (professor), he told his teacher that he need not bother with a detailed commentary. He asked him only for the reading transmission of this scripture. *Introduction to the Middle Way* is a text on the profound view of the Middle Way, and like most other Sanskrit verses composed in India more than a thousand years ago, it is exceptionally difficult to understand without commentary. Nevertheless, after hearing the teacher read the text just once, Mipam explained it all from the beginning. The teacher then responded, "Although I have the title of 'Geshé,' I don't have even a fraction of the intellect of this one!"[7]

He received reading transmissions of important Buddhist scriptures from teachers in both the early school of translation (Nyingma) and the later or "new schools" (Sarma).[8] In the Tibetan tradition, a lineage of teachers has an all-important place. Receiving teachings from qualified teachers—a connection to a living lineage—marks the authenticity of those teachings. Based simply on these reading transmissions, Mipam composed elaborate commentaries on the texts.

In his early career, Mipam studied the *Way of the Bodhisattva* with Patrul Rinpoché, the author of the famed *Words of My Perfect Teacher.* The teaching took five days, but apparently this was enough for Mipam to fully comprehend the words and meaning of this classic. He later composed an important commentary on the ninth chapter of this text, the Wisdom Chapter.[9] This chapter is particularly important because wisdom is what makes a bodhisattva's practice unique: it is wisdom through which emptiness is realized. Thus, it is wisdom, or insight, that makes the practices of a bodhisattva what they are, the *transcendent perfections*—generosity, discipline, patience, diligence, concentration, and wisdom. These comprise the practices undertaken by a bodhisattva to bring all beings to enlightenment. Among these six, wisdom elevates the other five virtues to the status of being "transcendent" or sublime, because it realizes the empty nature of reality and thus sees the illusory nature of all things.

Mipam studied a wide range of Buddhist scriptures with a number of prominent teachers of his day. He received instruction on the fundamentals of the Buddhist path and what are known as the common arts, such as grammar, from the famous scholar-practitioner, Jamgön Kongtrül (1813–1899). *Jamgön,* literally "gentle protector," is an epithet for a consummate scholar who embodies wisdom. Mipam, along with two of his teachers, Jamgön Kongtrül and Jamyang Khyentsé Wangpo (1820–1892), came to be known as "the three Jamgöns of Kham." Mipam's main teacher, his "root guru," was Jamyang Khyentsé Wangpo.

Mipam is said to have served his teacher in three ways: with material offerings, with service, and with practice. According to Jikmé Püntsok

(1933–2004), an extraordinary devotee of Mipam and holder of his lineage, Mipam gave his teacher all his belongings seven times. This was his material offering. As for service, he humbly served his teacher like an ordinary attendant, serving food and cleaning up. His offering of practice, the supreme offering a student can give a teacher, was also exceptional given that he spent most of his life in meditation retreat.

On one occasion, Jamyang Khyentsé Wangpo had Mipam sit on a high throne in front of several volumes of Buddhist scriptures. He presented him with extensive offerings and said, "I entrust these scriptures to you. From now on, uphold these teachings through exposition, debate, and composition. You are to illuminate the Buddha's teachings in this world for a long time!" His teacher thus empowered him and gave him the name Mipam Jamyang Namgyel Gyatso (which literally means "undefeatable ocean, gentle melody, victorious over all"). Later, he is reported to have said that there was no one on earth more learned than Mipam.[10]

Mipam's knowledge did not always come without effort. The first time he read the *Vinaya Sutra,* a central text outlining the essentials of Buddhist ethics, he had difficulty with some passages, but he then read the entire thirteen volumes of the Vinaya section of the Buddhist canon of scriptures. After that, there was nothing in the *Vinaya Sutra* that he did not understand. The Vinaya has an important place in monastic education in that it lays out the fundamentals of moral discipline, particularly for the monastic community. It is one of three sections of the Buddhist canon, the others being the Sutra, which comprises discourses attributed to the Buddha, and the Abhidharma, which contains systematic philosophy. Throughout his life, Mipam is said to have read the entire collection of the translated words of the Buddha (108 volumes) seven times.[11]

We are also told that in the beginning of his studies, Mipam found the texts of the new translations easy to understand, but that the texts of the old translations—his own Nyingma school—were difficult for him. Later, when he was able to comprehend them, he attributed this to the fact that he never doubted the profundity of these texts, crediting himself and not the texts as the source of his failed understanding.[12]

Mipam studied not only his own Nyingma tradition, but other traditions as well. After all, engaging with other traditions is a prerequisite for someone to be called *nonsectarian,* a term with which he is commonly associated. It is significant that Mipam is reported to have said that he came to discover all the profound points to be found only within the lineage of the old translations, that is, the Nyingma lineage.[13] Undeniably, we can find a strong sense of sectarian identity in his works. After all, it is not necessary to see all traditions as equal to be nonsectarian; we can respect other traditions but still must have a special relationship with the tradition in which we directly participate. While Mipam showed respect for the different sects in Tibet, he certainly did not gloss over differences.

Following his teacher's request, Mipam wrote commentaries on classic Buddhist texts based on his Nyingma tradition. He stated clearly that he was not motivated by sectarianism in doing this, but rather by the feeling that most of the Nyingma followers were merely imitating the scholars of other traditions. He felt that the teachings of his tradition were on the verge of becoming "like a painted butter lamp"—an artifact without much power. He said that few people even wonder about the philosophy of the Nyingma, much less ask about it. For these reasons, he composed texts to elucidate the Nyingma view.[14]

By emphasizing a uniquely Nyingma interpretation, Mipam's works sparked criticism from other schools, particularly from Geluk scholars. On several critical points of interpretation, Mipam diverged markedly from the prevailing interpretation given within the Geluk tradition, which had come to dominate institutional scholarship in Tibet. In particular, his commentary on the Wisdom Chapter from the *Way of the Bodhisattva* drew sharp criticism that spawned a polemical exchange with a number of prominent Geluk scholars. Mipam took up correspondence with one of his most perceptive critics from central Tibet, and they soon became friends, exchanging gifts along with arguments. The rich exchange between these two exceptional scholars came to be known as "the meeting of the Sarma tiger and Nyingma lion."[15]

DEBATE

There is a clever quote attributed to Mipam that is a pun on his name, which literally means "undefeatable" (*mi* being "un" and *pam,* "defeat-able"): "The undefeatable one (mipam) being undefeatable (mipam), I am Mipam (the undefeatable). If sticks and stones don't defeat me (mipam), I cannot be defeated (mipam) by words!" As both a strong debater and an elegant author, he certainly lived up to his name.

Debate is an important part of the way Tibetan monastic traditions define and refine their philosophical views; opposition provides contrast and a way for scholars to stake out the boundaries of their traditions. Indeed, dialectical exchange is at the heart of scholarship, and one way a scholar is defined in Tibet is as someone who is an expert in exposition, composition, and debate.

A significant moment in Mipam's life came in a debate in which Patrul Rinpoché acted as moderator. Mipam and his opponent debated about the famously difficult Wisdom Chapter of the *Way of the Bodhisattva*. When the debate between the two appeared to be even, someone asked Patrul Rinpoché who was winning. Since Mipam was his student, he said, "A son is not praised by his father, but by his enemy; a daughter is not praised by her mother, but by the community!" Instead of answering, Patrul Rinpoché suggested that they turn to a topic concerning the Great Perfection, the highest Nyingma view and practice, upon which Mipam's opponent had written a commentary. It was during the debate on this topic (discussed in the next section on meditation) that Mipam won.[16]

It is significant that Mipam won the debate on the Great Perfection, as it testifies to his skill in engaging this subject within a rational, dialectical exchange. It also underscores that the view of the Great Perfection is not naive anti-intellectualism; rather, it involves a subtly profound view that, at least in Mipam's presentation, incorporates reason and transcends it. Central to Mipam's writing is the prominent place given to reasoned inquiry as a means to arrive at the view of the Great Perfection. This feature distinguishes the character of his works, and it is where we find his significant contribution to Nyingma philosophy. Indeed, the interplay and transcendence of reason is a central theme in his writings in general.

The story of Mipam's debate carries a particular significance because his opponent was learned in the Geluk tradition. This debate between two great scholars of the Geluk and Nyingma schools, based solely on a topic related to sutra, at first appeared to be even. This is not surprising because each school's system of interpretation has a sophisticated version of how the philosophy of sutra should be understood. However, when tantra is brought into the picture, we can see how the tide changes. For the Nyingma tradition, the Great Perfection embodies the culmination of tantra, and significantly, tantra is held to have a unique philosophical dimension that contrasts with the way it is considered in the Geluk school.

In general, Buddhist tantras are scriptures attributed to the Buddha or another enlightened being that involve extraordinary teachings in mythological settings. *Tantra* usually refers to a class of texts, like sutras, but it is used here as a synonym for the Vajrayāna (in contrast with the path of sutra), which is a direct path to enlightenment.[17] It is significant that the Geluk tradition holds that the distinction between sutra and tantra relates only to methods of meditation and not to a philosophical view, as the Nyingma school believes. For this reason, a Geluk scholar does not typically relate to tantra in the same philosophical way that he would to sutra. For Mipam's Nyingma tradition, in contrast, the difference between sutra and tantra involves an important distinction in the philosophical view as well as method. Marking a critical difference, the Nyingma tradition considers the view in tantra to go further than sutra through a distinctive approach to the nature of experience and subjectivity, which will be addressed later. Besides his exceptional genius, this could have been a factor that tipped the scale for Mipam to win the debate.

Another story from Mipam's life illustrates his mastery of the subject matter of both sutra and tantra. Once his teacher, Patrul Rinpoché, was asked, "Who is more learned, you or Mipam?" Patrul Rinpoché replied that they were about even in sutra, but that Mipam was much better in tantra.[18] This reply is noteworthy, because while Mipam wrote a considerable amount on sutra, he also wrote extensively on tantra. Significantly, his commentaries on sutra topics, such as the Middle Way, integrate aspects of tantra. In an important way, his writings on sutra and tantra draw from each other such that each illuminates the other.

Mipam's writings on sutra (and the Middle Way in particular) sparked controversy not only from the Geluk school but from within his own tradition as well. He often emphasized the importance of logic and epistemology, topics that were generally not stressed in the Nyingma tradition. Some

Nyingma followers were skeptical of the role, if any, that logic and Middle Way analyses had in the practices of tantra, which had historically defined their tradition. Since Mipam had explicitly stated that one must understand the Middle Way to understand the Great Perfection,[19] those who were not inclined toward this kind of scholarship were apparently indifferent to his work or even regarded it with suspicion. Others in the Nyingma tradition who were actively involved in scholarship on sutra topics did not always agree with Mipam's particular exposition of the Middle Way.

It is important to understand that before Mipam, there was no orthodox corpus of Nyingma commentaries on sutra topics. Also, monasteries had come to dominate the Tibetan landscape, and the subject matter of sutra had a central place in monastic education. As a result, many in the Nyingma tradition had adopted an interpretation of sutra topics from the Geluk (or Sakya) tradition for their new monastic institutions, while maintaining a Nyingma tantra practice. Mipam, however, advocated a uniquely Nyingma view of sutra. In his writings on the Middle Way and other works, he developed a platform for Nyingma monastic education by formulating a systematic presentation of sutra drawn from an interpretative framework based in the Great Perfection. This was his unique contribution to the Nyingma, but not everyone in the Nyingma tradition was ready or willing to adopt his interpretation. It did not take long, however, for this interpretative framework, forged for the Nyingma monastic colleges, to dominate the curriculum in these schools in Tibet, India, and Nepal. Mipam's works continue to be widely studied in such institutions up to the present day.

MEDITATION

One of the greatest Tibetan scholars of the twentieth century, Gendün Chöpel, was reportedly asked who he thought was more learned, Mipam or Tsongkhapa (1357–1419), the renowned forefather of the Geluk tradition. He replied,

> I have thought about this a lot. They both were emanations of the Buddha's mind and had visions of Mañjuśrī. If they were both here

now, since Tsongkhapa had spent a lot of time around monks, he would probably win in a debate. Even so, Mipam's force of reason, power of understanding, and manner of expression is more awesome. If others hear this, they may think it to be a contradiction, but I am serious.[20]

This statement highlights how debate is a major part of the curriculum in the Geluk tradition in which Gendün Chöpel was trained. It is noteworthy that Mipam was also learned in debate, but he often criticized a merely intellectual approach. He consistently emphasized the importance of overcoming theoretical understanding through meditative experience. While he certainly took part in debate and the scholarly traditions of the monastic colleges, he frequently appealed to meditative wisdom that is not confined to conceptual understanding.

Mipam valued meditative wisdom as the means to gain comprehensive understanding. His main meditation deity was Mañjuśrī, the embodiment of wisdom. As mentioned earlier, from the time he was a young boy, he was said to have had a special connection to Mañjuśrī, in both the

Mañjuśrī

peaceful form as well as the wrathful form of Yamantaka, who embodies wisdom's vigorous activity. Meditations on various forms of Mañjuśrī were a central part of Mipam's meditation practice throughout his life. It is thus not surprising that many of his compositions begin with an invocation of praise to Mañjuśrī.

As already noted, Mipam spent much of his life in meditation retreat, as is evident from his life story and the numerous colophons of the texts he composed while on breaks from these retreats. He spent thirteen years in meditation retreat in a cave known as the "tiger den," near the monastery of his teacher. Long meditation retreats follow a time-honored Tibetan tradition established by yogis like Milarepa. Far away from the distractions and hustle of ordinary life, the natural beauty and simplicity of a mountain retreat is an ideal place for cultivating the mind in meditation.

Once when Mipam came out of a retreat, Jamyang Khyentsé Wangpo asked him how his practice had gone. Mipam responded that when he studied, he tried to see if he could reach the completion of analysis, and when he practiced the generation stage of visualizing the deity, he did so with great diligence to see if he could perfect that practice too. His teacher replied, "This is difficult. Longchenpa said to rest naturally without doing anything. By doing so, I never saw any natural face of mind with a white complexion and rosy cheeks, but if I were to die right now, I would not have the slightest fear. Ha!" He laughed, and Mipam took this to be a practical instruction from his teacher.[21]

Although all of one's root teacher's words are to be taken as practical instructions, the exchange between Mipam and his teacher is particularly significant. We can see how Jamyang Khyentsé Wangpo's words, taken as an instruction for practice, point to the uncontrived style of meditation in Great Perfection practice. In contrast to a gradual approach that seeks out conclusions through logical analysis or an approach that is focused on meditation practices of the generation stage that contrive a deity by visualization, the practice of the effortless and natural Great Perfection is the direct way to recognize the nature of mind. Mipam's writings are permeated with the flavor of the natural Great Perfection, the highest practice in the Nyingma tradition. His teacher's words here may have touched him deeply, because they accentuate the heart of Great Perfection practice.

The Great Perfection affirms that the nature of the mind is presently the Buddha and offers a direct means to actualize this reality. Since in a fundamental sense everyone is always already a buddha, no contrived effort is necessary to alter this natural state to produce some other buddha at some other time. In the end, contrived effort only gets in the way of actualizing our own true nature. Wisdom in the Great Perfection dawns from within; it springs forth naturally when let be. Wisdom and compassion shine forth as the natural outflow of the empty and aware ground of being, without the need for forcible creation or contrivance. Importantly for this tradition, anything forced by effort cannot possibly compare with the qualities of the natural state, because the natural is unrivaled; the natural is divine.

The Great Perfection, which was such an important part of Mipam's life and work, embodies a textual and meditative tradition at the heart of his Nyingma lineage. In a significant way, the Great Perfection is the guiding principle of Mipam's works. His writings were not ordinary compositions; they were inspired works that came to be considered "mind treasures." He attributed the source of his natural revelations to the blessings of his meditation deity and his teacher. His will to write dawned naturally; he is reported to have said, "I have no choice but to write."[22] It is interesting to note that the rich depth and evocative beauty conveyed in his works, as well as the manner of their composition, reflect the style and content of the effortless Great Perfection. The view and practice of the Great Perfection is an important part, one could even say the *most* important part, of understanding what Mipam was up to in his life and work.

Mipam is a unique figure among prominent Tibetan Buddhist leaders, because he was not endorsed as an incarnate lama, a *tulku*—at least, not while he was alive. Also, unlike many other important figures of his day, he did not actively promote the new traditions of textual treasure revelations, known as *terma*. While these revelations gained widespread popularity in Tibet, particularly in the Nyingma tradition to which Mipam belonged, he neither discovered treasure texts publicly nor wrote extensive commentaries on them. Rather, he focused on elucidating the teachings that had been transmitted directly to Tibet from India.

Though he was not endorsed as an incarnate lama while alive, at the end of his life, he is said to have admitted to one of his students that he was not an ordinary being, that he was actually a bodhisattva. Mipam is also reported to have said that he would not take birth again in impure realms.[23] Nevertheless, the continued recognition of his subsequent incarnations, which is a long-lived Tibetan Buddhist tradition, has continued. Given this, we may wonder how the tradition interprets Mipam's statement that he would not be born in an impure realm. Was it a lie or a joke, or were those who recognized his subsequent incarnations mistaken? After all, how does his statement that he would not be born again in an impure realm concur with his being a bodhisattva, a being who vows to take birth in the world until all beings are completely free from suffering? Perhaps we may resolve this using the traditional device of pure perception: there are no impure realms, so Mipam's incarnations would always be welcome here.

TWO

Background of Buddhism in India

TIBET LOOKS TO INDIA as a source of the authentic teachings of the Buddha. To understand Mipam's view and the contribution he made to Buddhist thought in Tibet, it is important to be familiar with the background of Buddhism in India. We should at least be aware of some central points concerning the way Indian Buddhism is generally understood in Tibet. After all, Mipam said that his Nyingma tradition of early translations "is nothing but the stainless word of the Buddha and the scriptures of the six ornaments and their followers."[24] The "six ornaments" refer to six prominent Indian commentators on Buddhist scriptures. This chapter introduces significant features of the works of these figures as they are relevant for understanding Mipam. First we will look at the words of the Buddha.

WORDS OF THE BUDDHA

It is widely held in Tibet that the Buddha "turned the wheel of Dharma" three times, which means that he taught in distinct settings for different audiences of varied capacities. The first turning of the wheel of the Dharma is the teaching of the four noble truths: the truth of suffering, the truth of the origin (of suffering), the truth of the cessation (of suffering), and the truth of the path. The main emphases of these teachings are the principles of impermanence, suffering, and selflessness. In terms of the conduct of moral discipline, which is the foundation of the Buddhist path, the main principle of practice in these teachings is nonviolence, to bring no harm to others. The first turning of the wheel of Dharma comprises the scriptures common to the Great Vehicle (Mahāyāna) and the Lesser Vehicle (Hīnayāna). The middle and last turnings, however, are not accepted as the words of the Buddha by the traditions demarcated as the Lesser Vehicle. Thus, the last two turnings of the wheel of Dharma contain sutras unique to the Great Vehicle of Buddhism.

The main distinction between the Great Vehicle and the Lesser Vehicle is *bodhicitta*, "the mind of awakening," which can also be translated as "the enlightened mind" or "the spirit of enlightenment." Bodhicitta is the resolve to become a buddha for the benefit of others. From this main distinguishing feature of bodhicitta comes a distinction in view: the Great Vehicle conveys emptiness in a more comprehensive way than the Lesser Vehicle. There is also a distinction in the path of practice: in contrast to the paths of the Auditors (*śrāvaka*) and Self-Realized Ones (*pratyekabuddha*) in the Lesser Vehicle, the Great Vehicle engages the bodhisattva path, which is inspired by bodhicitta. Since the paths are different, so are the results: the Lesser Vehicle does not result in the practitioner becoming a complete buddha; rather, the aim is to achieve a personal nirvana that is the total extinction of existence. The Great Vehicle, however, does result in becoming a complete buddha. A buddha remains actively engaged in enlightened activity to liberate beings for as long as samsara remains. Thus, those who accomplish the Great Vehicle do not abide in samsara due to their wisdom that sees its empty, illusory nature. Further, unlike those who attain the nirvana of the Lesser Vehicle to escape samsara, they do not abide in an isolated nirvana due to their compassion. For these reasons, in an the Great Vehicle, nirvana is said to be "unlocated" or "nonabiding" (*apratiṣṭhita*), staying in neither samsara nor nirvana.

While the fundamental topics of the first turning of the wheel of Dharma (the subject matter common to the Great and Lesser Vehicles) did not provoke that much controversy in Tibet, the relationship between the middle and last wheels of Dharma and how to interpret the meaning of these scriptures are central issues of dispute around which the lines between various schools are drawn. The middle turning of the wheel of Dharma is exemplified by the Perfection of Wisdom Sutras, in which the Buddha speaks of the emptiness of all things "from form up to omniscience." The explicit topic of the middle wheel is emptiness, and its meaning is central to the Great Vehicle, although "emptiness" has been interpreted in various ways in India and Tibet.

The last turning of the wheel of Dharma pertains to the Buddha-Nature Sutras, as well as the so-called Mind-Only Sutras.[25] The last wheel primarily delineates a topic of utmost concern, the ultimate truth, which is also the subject of several different Tibetan interpretations. Instead of emphasizing the impurity depicted in the first turning of the wheel, the last wheel describes the pure nature of mind. While the middle and last turnings of the wheel of Dharma may differ in the way they represent the view of the ultimate truth (as emptiness or the natural purity of mind, respectively), they do not differ in their teachings on ethical conduct. Both wheels of Dharma prescribe the practices of a bodhisattva, the development of compassion, and the six transcendent perfections. These actions aim at benefiting others (in addition to simply avoiding harm) and are embraced by an understanding of emptiness; they are guided by bodhicitta.

In Tibet, commentarial treatises (Tib. *bstan bcos,* Skt. *śāstra*) on sutras, rather than the canonical sutras themselves, have become the principal topics of study. There are more than sixty volumes of sutras in the Tibetan canon, and the commentarial texts serve to systematically organize the complex range of views found in the various sutras. While these treatises are numerous (3,626 texts!), a select few have become principal texts in the curriculum followed by Buddhist monastic colleges in Tibet. Additionally, tantras play an important role in the life of Tibetan Buddhist culture. Yet like the sutras, the canonical tantras generally are not studied very much. As with sutras, the commentaries and the practices they inspire play a more dominant role.

Before looking into the Tibetan commentarial tradition and into Mipam's interpretation in particular, we will first examine some of the main texts and traditions in India that came to shape Buddhist thought in Tibet. Let us now turn to the major commentaries of Buddhist texts from India and touch on some of the important themes in these texts that have come to hold a central place within Tibetan Buddhist monastic education. These works form the backdrop of Mipam's thought and will help us understand it better.

NĀGĀRJUNA

A number of Buddhist treatises from India have risen to prominence in the Tibetan Buddhist world. The works of Nāgārjuna (circa second century) are of particular importance. Nāgārjuna is the earliest commentator on the Great Vehicle Sutras and is famous for systematizing the view of *Madhyamaka,* or the "middle way." From early times, the middle way has been a recurring theme in Buddhism. After breaking a fast with rice milk and sitting under a tree, Śākyamuni (the historical Buddha) became enlightened, having taken the Middle Way by renouncing both the extreme of hedonism in his father's palace and the extreme of asceticism in the forest. The philosophy of the Middle Way took shape through the works of Nāgārjuna.

Notably, Nāgārjuna laid out the Middle Way between the extremes of nihilism and eternalism by clearly delineating two truths: the ultimate truth and the relative truth. He showed how everything is empty, because no phenomenon has an independent or inherent essence. This emptiness is the ultimate truth. The relative truth, on the other hand, is the dependent arising of all things. Nāgārjuna's celebrated text, the *Root Verses of the Middle Way,* brings together emptiness (the ultimate truth) and dependent arising (the relative, or conventional, truth) to show that whatever dependently arises is empty and that whatever is empty is dependently arisen. Since the meaning of the two truths form a central background for Mipam's presentation, let's explore it in some detail.

EXCURSION INTO THE MIDDLE WAY

The ultimate truth is emptiness, and it is important, first of all, to understand what this means. Emptiness is a fundamental topic in Buddhist thought and one that distinguishes a uniquely Buddhist view. In a significant way, emptiness is the most important topic for a Buddhist because, according to the Buddhist worldview, correctly understanding emptiness sets us free. That is to say, we suffer as a result of misapprehending reality, taking it to be solid and fixed. When we interpret reality to be something it is not (that is, taking what is impermanent to be permanent and becoming attached to its enduring existence), we suffer as a result of this misinterpretation. To see emptiness, however, is to see reality for what it is. Thus, the topic of emptiness is of vital importance. Since it is also a topic that is difficult to grasp and easily misunderstood, we will spend some time with this crucial point before going further into Mipam's unique interpretation.

There are many ways to arrive at emptiness by analyzing things. Mipam says that the simplest reason to understand why things are empty, and the easiest to bring to mind, is the reason that things are neither singular nor plural.[26] The reasoning can be stated simply as follows: other than conceptually designating something to be "one thing," nothing is truly singular because everything has parts; therefore, nothing is plural either because without "one," there can be no "many." Let's explore the implications of this analysis with a few examples.

When you look at any phenomenon, such as your hand, you can see that it seems to be singular and real. However, upon analysis, you find that it is composed of parts: four fingers, a thumb, and a palm. Each of those parts also has parts: each finger has an upper, lower, and middle part, the nail, and so forth. When you look further into what comprises the particular parts of your finger, you eventually get down to the lines of your fingerprints; you may then use a microscope and go down further to find smaller components like the constituents of each skin cell, molecule, and so on.

While we can stop at any part of the hand and say, "palm," "index finger," "thumb," and so forth—or at any level of analysis and say, "hand," "finger," "joint," or "cell"—the words we use and the concepts associated with these words are simply designations. There is nothing truly singular about these objects apart from what we impute to them with our words and thoughts. When we attribute a singular, independent reality to something that we have derived from a label, we fix the world in a way that conflicts with how it actually is. Although these labels help us to organize and make sense of our world, attributing true reality or independent existence to our projections (particularly the false conceptions of "me" and "mine") leads to suffering. This is why the understanding of emptiness, that nothing is independent and singular, is so important in the Buddhist tradition.

Furthermore, without any singular thing, which is the basis of what is plural, there can be no plurality. What is singular is singular only in dependence on its (multiple) parts, and nothing, when carefully analyzed, can be found that is independently singular separate from its parts. Moreover, singular things are not only dependent on a plurality of parts; they are also dependent on their designations—the labels we give them. Other than the designations of words and thoughts, nothing truly singular can be found anywhere. When we think about the reality of these designations and see that there is no innately real boundary for any single object we perceive, we can see how our words and thoughts function to abstract objects from a dynamic matrix of interrelations in which they exist.

Examining the nature of phenomena in this way allows us to loosen our fixation on the reality of the world and helps us to get a sense of the meaning of emptiness and the two truths. When we stop to think about it, we can see how there is no clear boundary for anything singular in the world. We can see this in anything. For instance, extend the analysis to a consideration of the dimensions of a hand. When looking for what it is that defines a singular hand, even if you set out to measure the outline of your hand completely and accurately, you will fail to find any "real" measurement. This is because of the simple fact that you will get a different measurement whenever you use a different measuring device, like a ruler, tape measure, magnifying glass, microscope, and so on. The finer the instrument used, the longer the measurement you come up with will be—two feet, two yards, two miles . . . Which is the right measurement? It is relative. It depends on the tool you are using to measure.

You may think that using the conventionally accepted "standard" tool for measuring whatever we want to measure will give the right result—in this case, the standard tool of hand measurement. What might the standard of hand measurement be? You may defer to science and think that a scientific tool would give you the *real* measurement. However, when you look scientifically into the actual dimensions of an object like a hand and get into all the grooves in your skin, the grooves within the grooves (there are no straight lines in nature), the grooves within those, and so on, and so on, you find that the boundaries of the hand become harder and harder to determine. The harder you look into an object, the more elusive its boundaries, and thus the more difficult it is to distinguish precisely what the exact dimension is of the thing being delimited.

When we consider the hand in light of modern physics, we cannot find a clearly defined line separating the hand from that which is around it. We simply find the fuzzy boundaries of subatomic particles. When determining boundaries around entities in the physical world, it is as if we are zooming into a fractal in which we endlessly find contours within every contour and continuously smaller contours within those. When there is no end in sight—no indivisibly small particle, ground, or limit around which to base our dimension of size—we have good reason to say that the contour of the hand is literally infinite! We can think of the ultimate truth as this infinite boundary or, better yet, as the lack of any real circumference. Conversely, the relative truth is the context-dependent boundary of the hand—that is, the hand for which a particular size depends on the particular tool of measurement. Alternatively, we can say that the relative truth is the hand that is generally called a "hand" in the world. In either case, we can understand the relative truth as the undeniable appearance and context-dependent boundary of the world and the ultimate truth as the open, infinite dimension of the world, its emptiness.

By reflecting on this example, we can get a sense of the meaning of emptiness and the two truths. An important part of Mipam's view is that emptiness is the nature of everything, because everything—without exception—lacks a true nature; nothing has an independent essence. Anything we analyze in terms of its ultimate status lacks essence and is empty: hands, chariots, and cars, as well as wisdom and nirvana, are all empty. Through understanding emptiness, our sense of self as a bounded entity, separate from others, withers away.

Before moving on, let's look further into the compatibility, or unity, of the two truths. Unity is a major theme in Mipam's work and particularly relevant in the context of discussing the two truths. A phenomenon traditionally used to illustrate the lack of self, or emptiness, is a chariot. A chariot is not found in its parts—the axle, wheels, seat, and so on. If you look at each part separately, they are not the chariot; the axle is not the chariot, and so forth. Yet the chariot is not found separate from its parts either. Therefore, the chariot is empty just like the self is empty. The meaning of emptiness can also be seen in a simple aggregate or heap, such as a pile of sand. The parts of a heap are all similar grains of sand, none of which constitute the whole.

Consider the nature of a heap of sand in what is known as the sorites paradox (*sorites* is derived from the Greek word for "heap"). If you start with a heap of sand, and throw it into the ocean one grain at a time, at what point do you no longer have a heap? If one grain of sand is not a heap, what about two grains? Or three? Is there a dividing line between "heap" and "no heap" such that one grain of sand makes the difference? If not, then what is the defining boundary of "heap," and where does it go when all the sand is in the ocean? Stop to consider this; it is a simple and important question.

The Buddhist answer is that the heap is merely a designation; it is a product of mind and imputed by thought and language. With this example, we can see the two truths as follows: the ultimate truth is the lack of any real heap, and the relative truth is the appearance of a heap when not analyzed in terms of a true nature or ultimate status. In the case of a heap, this is clear and straightforward. It is more difficult to see in more complex objects like chariots, cars, and the self. The important point, however, is that when analyzed, nothing with an independently real essence can be found—emptiness applies to anything and everything. Also, an essential point to understand is that emptiness does not mean nihilism, as if there were nothing at all. And it is not relativism either, as if the world existed however we wanted it to be. Rather, the world is empty, and it undeniably appears; just because there is no real heap, this does not invalidate the fact that there is a heap that appears to us, and that when we can call it a "heap," people know what we are talking about. In fact, according to Nāgārjuna and Mipam, the lack of any real "heap"—its emptiness—is the necessary condition for its relative existence.

When we attribute an independent identity to things (like a heap) in the world, thinking that they come in and out of existence, we make a mistake. This notion of independent entity is a product of a deluded mind and is the source of attachment, aversion, and hence, suffering. Therefore, acknowledging emptiness (accepting that nothing is independently real) is an important step in the process of overcoming our mistaken habits of attributing an independent reality to what is not independently real. Through reflecting on the dependent nature of things, we can begin to glimpse the meaning of emptiness and learn to see how emptiness is compatible with dependently arising phenomena. Thereby, we can understand an important facet of the two truths: that to exist is necessarily to exist dependently, or in other words, to exist is to necessarily be empty.

LINEAGE OF THE PROFOUND VIEW

Nāgārjuna's works have enjoyed unprecedented influence in Tibet and East Asia and continue to attract the attention of philosophers worldwide. He is best known for the texts known as the Collection of Reasonings,[27] which comment on the explicit teaching of the middle wheel of Dharma (that is, emptiness). He also wrote the Collection of Advice,[28] which pertains to the first wheel of Dharma, as well as the Collection of Praises,[29] which explains the meaning of the last wheel of Dharma.

His treatises are known as the "original scriptures" of the Middle Way because they predate the development of competing streams of interpretation. Later commentaries on Nāgārjuna's work triggered considerable discussion and debate about the meaning of the Middle Way and how best to convey it. Candrakīrti's commentary, *Introduction to the Middle Way,* became a particularly influential text in Tibet. Candrakīrti (600–650) is a pivotal figure around whom the two main streams of interpretation of the Middle Way are identified in Tibet: the Consequence School and the Autonomy School. The Consequence School gained popularity after the twelfth century, when Candrakīrti's texts were first translated into Tibetan.

For most all Tibetan traditions, the Consequence School (*Prāsaṅgika* literally means "one who uses consequences") is held to be the highest view of the Middle Way. The Consequence School contrasts with the Autonomy School (*Svātantrika* literally means "one who uses autonomous reasons"). The meaning of the Consequence School is complex, and several ways of interpreting its meaning have been offered by different Tibetan traditions. The source of the dispute concerns Candrakīrti's criticism of a critique of Bhavaviveka (circa sixth century). Focusing on Nāgārjuna's

Root Verses of the Middle Way, Bhavaviveka had criticized an earlier commentary by Buddhapālita (470–550), claiming that it had failed to frame Nāgārjuna's statements of absurd consequence in the form of an autonomous argument that stands alone. In other words, Bhavaviveka said that the earlier commentator had failed to use the principles of logic to formulate reasons that clearly proved the assertion that phenomena are empty. Rather, Buddhapālita left the statement as an absurd consequence, simply showing the absurd implication of a position that maintains that phenomena are not empty.

Candrakīrti responded that there was an important reason for Buddhapālita's style of commentary, which did not reformulate the consequence into an autonomous argument that would logically affirm that all phenomena are empty. By restating the assertion as one's own claim and not just leaving the consequence as an instructive device to teach others, one introduces a faulty representation of ultimate truth. That is, since all assertions are constructions of distorted thought, any assertion taken as representing one's own position concerning the status of ultimate reality is always a flawed representation. On the other hand, nothing need be affirmed in a consequence aimed at undoing another's wrong view, so leaving the statement as a consequence is preferable.

For example, in the case of an autonomous argument taken as one's own assertion, such as "The table is empty because it arises dependently," there is the presumption of something that is a "table" that exists on its own. In terms of the ultimate nature of reality, however, such an underlying presumption is an unwanted implication entailed by a statement taken to represent one's own position. On the other hand, simply stating an absurd consequence of an opponent's view, without taking it as one's own claim, is preferable (such as "It absurdly follows that the table is not a product because it is permanent"). This is because pointing out an absurd consequence of a belief can show another that the belief is unsound (for example, the belief that the table is permanent) without thereby committing oneself to any unwanted claim or fault.

With these few words, I have tried to highlight a principal feature of the Consequence School. While my simplified explanation does not do justice to this complex tradition, what is important is that the Consequence School of the Middle Way, as it is known in Tibet, was spawned from Candrakīrti's arguments and draws on a radically deconstructive form of argument to shred any and all notions regarding what reality is. A central insight of this school is that any attempt to pin down or determine reality is always only a conceptual construction. We will return to the Consequence School later to see how Mipam characterizes this complex tradition with simplicity and elegance.

LINEAGE OF VAST ACTIVITY

Another influential figure who systematized Great Vehicle thought was Asaṅga (circa fourth century). Asaṅga was instrumental in the transmission of the "five treatises of Maitreya,"[30] an important set of commentaries on Buddhist sutras. The traditional legend about these works conveys that they were taught by Maitreya (the future buddha) to Asaṅga in Tuṣita Heaven after Asaṅga had spent twelve years meditating in a cave. These texts comprise what have come to be the most influential commentaries on the last wheel of Dharma. Several of the texts expand on important themes in the Yogic Practice School (*Yogācāra*) and highlight the significant role that mind plays in constructing reality. Among several other central topics, they shape an elaborate discussion around the workings of the mind and the relationship between the mind and ultimate truth. One of the five treatises, the *Sublime Continuum,* which is a commentary on the Buddha-Nature Sutras, played a major role in Tibet and in the works of Mipam in particular. It is known as a text that bridges sutra and tantra and so has a special significance among the five treatises.

In addition to the Middle Way tradition developed by Nāgārjuna, the other "chariot tradition" from Asaṅga unleashed a complex system of philosophy known as the Yogic Practice School. Its Sanskrit name, *Yogācāra*, is a word that literally means "one who practices yoga." The etymology reflects this tradition's emphasis on meditative and contemplative experience as opposed to dry intellectual analysis and sophistry. The traditions of the Yogic Practice School are thus experientially oriented and offer a sophisticated technical vocabulary for describing the process of experience. Rather than focusing solely on breaking down conceptual constructs, followers of this school also emphasize what experientially remains when thoughts no longer structure the way we relate to the world.

Nāgārjuna and Asaṅga are known in Tibet as the "chariots of the two traditions" and are respectively associated with "the lineage of the profound view" and "the lineage of vast activity." Although Asaṅga's tradition is associated with activity, we can understand his tradition of the Yogic Practice School as primarily dealing with *the way things appear*, or how we experience reality. Nāgārjuna's tradition, on the other hand, primarily concerns *the way things are*. Mipam's writings bring these two traditions together. We will see that an important dimension of his work is his keen ability to synthesize seemingly diverse strands of thought. Not only does he synthesize the works of Nāgārjuna and Asaṅga, as well as other Indian figures we will meet in the following pages, but he brings together several competing voices in the Tibetan commentarial tradition as well. Further on, we will look at how he weaves all these threads together.

ABHIDHARMA

Along with transmitting the famed five treatises of Maitreya, Asaṅga wrote extensively on the Abhidharma, a foundational system of Buddhist philosophy. To appreciate the Yogic Practice School, it is important to know something about the Abhidharma, where the roots of the Yogic Practice School lie. A fundamental part of the philosophical tradition of Abhidharma is an analytical style that breaks things down to their component parts. Such a dissection targets the objects of common sense and the notion of a singular, enduring self in particular. By reducing the objects of ordinary experience to their constituents, one comes to see that they are not solid or real.

According to the Abhidharma, ultimate reality is that which is *not* extended in space and time, as opposed to extended objects (that have spatial dimensions and endure through time), which only exist as imputations of thought and language. Accordingly, objects that we normally experience, such as a pot or a pan, are not held to be real. Rather, what is generally held to be real for the Abhidharma schools are the simple elements of matter and mind that compose these objects. These components are twofold: (spatially) indivisible material particles and (temporally) indivisible moments of consciousness.

The Abhidharma presents what is ultimately real as irreducible elements; for instance, a river exists only as an imputation, whereas in reality there is only a constant flux of water (particles). Similar to the pixels on your dad's old television set or the scene that Georges Seurat created with dots of color in his famous painting *Sunday Afternoon on the Island of La Grande Jatte*, what is really there are only particles (red particles, blue particles, and so on) and not people hanging around with parasols and the like. Through the principle of reductionism—that something complex can be more accurately explained in terms of something else more fundamental—the Abhidharma claims that only irreducible components of mind and matter constitute reality.

In a Buddhist context, an important function of this analysis is to overcome mistaken notions of reality, particularly the mistaken concept of a self. The self is a misidentification of what we really experience, because what we interpret to be a self is actually the five aggregates: forms, feelings, perceptions, formations, and consciousnesses. Upon investigating experience, there is no self to be found; there are only these aggregates. Each of them is also multiple and momentary. Since our body, feelings, and mental states are constantly changing, there is no singular and lasting self within this effervescent flow of experience. Thus, a singular and enduring self, or anything like it, does not exist other than as a mere imputation.

While according to Mipam and other Tibetans' presentations, a prototypical Abhidharma school—the Great Exposition School (*Vaibhāṣika*)—takes the place of the "lowest" Buddhist philosophy, we can also see that there are important insights to be taken from this school when we reflect on the reality of our own perceptions. For instance, when we look at a chair, what do we really see? We don't see the whole chair; we only see parts of it. When we think about it, we only ever see one side of it, the front or the back, at any given instance. When we investigate the nature of perception in this way and examine the content of just what it is that we really see, we find that we never perceive a whole "chair." This flies in the face of our commonsense way of thinking, "I see a chair." Upon analysis, the "wholes" that make up the objects of common sense cannot be said to really exist in the way we uncritically experience them. So what is it that we perceive? For the Abhidharma schools, what is really there are the irreducible *components* of these whole objects. It is the elements (*dharmas*) that constitute the objects of experience; these are the fundamental building blocks of reality.

While these fundamental elements constitute reality according to Abhidharma, they are only momentary, fleeting instances of matter and temporary mental events. The view that these elements are ultimately real substances with discrete essences was a central target of Nāgārjuna's Middle Way commentaries. The Yogic Practice School then followed the Middle Way's critiques of substance to elucidate the mind's role in constructing the lifeworlds we inhabit. While the Yogic Practice School developed after the Middle Way's critiques of Abhidharma, it also essentially continued an Abhidharma project. Thus, there is a significant continuity between the traditions of Abhidharma and the Yogic Practice School; both traditions are involved in the similar projects of (1) breaking down our distorted constructions of reality and (2) presenting a theory of what really is so that we may come to experience reality without distortion, just as it is.

YOGIC PRACTICE SCHOOL

The Yogic Practice School describes the world in terms of our experience of it. After all, all we can ever know of the world comes through our experience. A characteristic claim in the Yogic Practice School is that nothing is independent of mind. Although things certainly appear to be external and separate from mind, in reality they are not. A common example used to support this view is the dream. In a dream, we think we encounter a world that is really out there when, in fact, we are only dreaming.

While the idea that there is nothing outside the mind may sound as if it comes straight out of science fiction, we cannot actually be certain that extramental matter is real, because perceptions of matter always occur with a perceiving mind. After all, why do we perceive water the way we do (as a liquid to drink) and not like a fish does (as a home) or like a hell-being supposedly does (as molten iron)? Why do we perceive tables and chairs as we do and not as particles on a subatomic scale or galaxies on a cosmic scale? According to the Yogic Practice School, it is not due to a world "out there"; rather, the mind plays a fundamental role in shaping our experience. We perceive what we do because of our mental predispositions. To put it another way, it is due to our instinct, our habits, and our karma that we perceive things the way we do, and in turn, these perceptions reinforce our habits.

Importantly, the Yogic Practice School unpacks the implication of the fact that we have access to the world only insofar as it is known to us. Since all objects of knowledge are necessarily *known,* if we want to provide the most accurate account of knowledge, we cannot speak of perceived objects without taking account of a perceiving subject. In other words, the mind is an indispensable part of any account of reality. The problem with the assumption that matter exists separate from mind lies in the fact that an instance of matter alone, without mind, can never be found, because *conscious experience necessarily precedes any reflection on the nature of the objective content of experience.* Mind is primary; the very possibility of investigating objects entails the presence of a mental event, the phenomenal experience of objects. This is a general feature of Buddhist philosophy. In Tibet and for Mipam, what has come to be known as the philosophical system (*grub mtha',* Skt. *siddhānta*) of Mind-Only, however, goes on to draw the conclusion that mind is the only reality.

What we find in the Mind-Only system is similar to what is called "idealism" in Western philosophy (as opposed to materialism). One of the main proponents of idealism in Europe was the Irish philosopher George Berkeley (1685–1753), who famously stated that "to be is to be perceived" (*Esse est percipi*), meaning that nothing exists outside of perception, or there is nothing outside the mind. While idealism is relatively new in the English-speaking world and has not gained prominence here, it has remained an important part of Buddhist traditions for millennia. Attempts to provide a rational account of experience tend to end up in some form of dualism (mind/matter), materialism (mind is matter), or idealism (matter is mind).[31] In the case of the Mind-Only philosophy, in the end, it turns out to be something like idealism.

In contrast to the two truths presented in Nāgārjuna's Middle Way, which describe the *objects* of experience, the Yogic Practice School speaks of three natures to describe experience *as such*. The three natures address the way we know or how we experience; thus, they do not so much concern what reality is, but rather, the way we experience it. The three natures are the imagined (Tib. *kun btags*, Skt. *parikalpita*), the dependent (Tib. *gzhan dbang*, Skt. *paratantra*), and the thoroughly established (Tib. *yongs grub*, Skt. *pariniṣpanna*) natures. The imagined nature consists of the objects of dualistic experience and the subjective cognition that perceives duality; the dependent nature is the causal flow of consciousness; and the thoroughly established nature is the emptiness of duality (the imagined nature) within that causal flow of consciousness (the dependent nature). In addition to emptiness (of duality), the ultimate truth in the Yogic Practice School includes pure consciousness devoid of dualistic, conceptual, and linguistic construction.

Vasubandhu (circa fourth century) was another influential exponent of the Yogic Practice School. Like Asaṅga (who is said to have been his half-brother), he wrote an important Abhidharma commentary and also composed several key works central to the Yogic Practice School. Notably, Vasubandhu extended an analysis from the Abhidharma tradition to argue that the existence of a material world composed of irreducible atoms is incoherent. He did so by contesting the Abhidharma claim of a material world composed of partless atoms. He built up the Yogic Practice School's position that denies the existence of extramental objects and concluded that a material world external to mind is nothing but a mental construction.

We might think that the issue of whether or not a world exists outside of our experience is not a primary concern for Buddhist philosophy. After all, Buddhism is concerned with the problem of suffering and how to overcome it. Since all we have to go on is what we are capable of experiencing, mere metaphysical speculation about a world beyond our capacity to experience it cannot really help us achieve our goal of eliminating suffering. Nevertheless, Mipam pointed out that the claim that there are external objects is only based on inference, since we can never have access to the perception of an object outside of our perception of it. On the other hand, he stated that the view that there are no external objects is supported by inference and, further, that we can also directly experience that our perceptions are mind (for instance, we can see a case of mistakenly attributed external objects in the example of a dream). Thus, he claimed that the view that there is no external world, that all experience is mental, is strongly supported by reason.[32] Denying the reality of an external world forces us to acknowledge that the mind plays a fundamental role in shaping the world in which we live. This can help us to play a more active role in taking responsibility for our world, and it empowers us to transform it, which comes to play a particularly important role in the practice of tantra.

VALID COGNITION

Dharmakīrti (600–660) was another important exponent of the Yogic Practice School and an influential figure for Mipam. When Mipam studied Dharmakīrti's *Commentary on Valid Cognition,* a famously cryptic and technical text, he had a dream in which he saw the renowned scholar of the Sakya tradition, Sakya Paṇḍita (1182–1251), who is famous for his classic work elaborating Dharmakīrti's system. In the dream, Sakya Paṇḍita asked Mipam, "What is there to know from the *Commentary on Valid Cognition*? It is affirmation and negation!" He then split the text in two and told Mipam to put them together. When Mipam did this, the text became a sword, and he saw all phenomena arrayed before him. When he swung the sword once, he cut through them all without any obstruction. Henceforth, there was not a word in the *Commentary on Valid Cognition* that he did not understand.[33]

Dharmakīrti articulated a sophisticated system of knowledge known as "valid cognition" (Tib. *tshad ma,* Skt. *pramāṇa*), which became highly influential in Tibet. In a way akin to how Candrakīrti brought a level of rigor to the Middle Way critiques, Dharmakīrti gave the Yogic Practice School the support of a rigorous system of decisive analysis. The Buddhist tradition of valid cognition draws heavily on the traditions of Abhidharma and the Yogic Practice School. In particular, this tradition develops a complex system of epistemology (the means of knowledge) for understanding how we know and also what distinguishes true knowledge from misconceptions. An important part of this tradition is a distinction between language and reality, or universals (Tib. *spyi mtshan*, Skt. *sāmānyalakṣaṇā*) and particulars (Tib. *rang mtshan*, Skt. *svalakṣaṇā*).

When we use concepts and language, we necessarily think and speak in terms of general, universal properties. A central insight to be taken from this tradition is that concepts distort reality. For instance, we use the word *fire* to convey the meaning of a common property of that which is hot and burns. But such a universal property, distributed across all particular instances of what we call fire, does not exist out there in the world. We use the word *fire* to refer to something that is extended in time and space (yesterday's "fire," the forest "fire," the kitchen "fire," and so on are all fire), but when analyzed, no such singular object really exists outside our imputation. A concept, or universal, only exists in our thoughts and language, not in the real world. That is, we don't get burned by the singular "fire" that we impute with our thoughts and words; we get burned by the particular instances of fire that are hot and burn.

To further illustrate this important difference between universals and particulars, consider the following: When I ask you for a pen, I ask to borrow "a pen," which could be any pen. Yet nothing in particular is "any pen." Such a thing as "any pen" is simply an idea that exists in our heads, not in the world. That is, you cannot write with "any pen" or with that which is held to be the common property of "penness" that is distributed across all instances of particular pens. Thus, what I ask you for is a universal. What you give me—that is, the particular pen that can be used for writing—is what we call a particular.[34]

Mipam likened these two (real particulars versus constructed universals) and the distinctive way in which the mind knows them to "the heart and eyes of the treatises of valid cognition"; he said that "a deep understanding occurs" when these are known.[35] Understanding this distinction is essential to fully appreciate the system of valid cognition. In a significant way, making the distinction between universals and particulars, or language and reality, helps us to undo the confusion that occurs in the process of thinking and using language. From a Buddhist perspective, our suffering is a result of believing our distorted concepts to be real. That is, we suffer by mistaking what is not the self as the self, what is impermanent as permanent, and what is suffering as happiness. A fundamental part of loosening the grip of a distorted conceptual framework is to distinguish reality from its mistaken conceptual construction.

SYNTHESIS OF TRADITIONS

Tibet is unique in the Buddhist world in that both traditions of valid cognition and the Consequence School took root there. It is hard to underestimate the significance of this fact and the enormous influence this convergence had on the unique forms of philosophical and contemplative practices that flourished in Tibet. Southeast Asian traditions did not share in these developments of Great Vehicle Buddhism. Although the tradition of the Great Vehicle came to dominate Buddhist thought in China, since Buddhist texts had been translated there long before Dharmakīrti and Candrakīrti lived, their works did not gain prominence in China. As a result, they were not transmitted in Korea or Japan either. In Tibet, however, the intersection of valid cognition from Dharmakīrti and the Consequence School from Candrakīrti led to a vibrant philosophical tradition. The synthesis of Dharmakīrti and Candrakīrti, the "two famous ones" (*kīrtis*), plays a fundamental role in Mipam's comprehensive interpretative system in particular.

The deconstructive critiques of Nāgārjuna's Middle Way and the constructive system of Dharmakīrti's Yogic Practice School had already come to a synthesis in India as well, in the works of Śāntarakṣita in the eighth century. As one of the first Buddhist scholars to visit Tibet, Śāntarakṣita was particularly important in the early transmission of Buddhism in the Land of Snow. His tradition of the Yogic Practice School of the Middle Way (*Yogācāra-Madhyamaka*)—which presents the conventional truth in accord with the Yogic Practice School and the ultimate truth in accord with the Middle Way—was a powerful synthesis that he brought to Tibet in the formative era of the assimilation of Buddhism. This synthesis was particularly significant for the Nyingma tradition as well.

INDIAN BUDDHIST COMMENTATORS WHO
WERE PARTICULARLY IMPORTANT FOR MIPAM

Name	Specialty	Chronology
Nāgārjuna	Middle Way	Second century
Asaṅga	Yogic Practice School	Fourth century
Dharmakīrti	Valid cognition	Seventh century
Candrakīrti	Consequence School	Seventh century
Śāntarakṣita	Yogic Practice School of the Middle Way	Eighth century

Mipam shows how these five voices can be heard in harmony, not monotone.

The systematic philosophy of the Yogic Practice School of the Middle Way contrasts sharply with the Consequence School. Candrakīrti, who is renowned in Tibet as a proponent of the Consequence School, argued against central positions of the Yogic Practice School that we will discuss further later—namely, that there could be minds without objects and that awareness was reflexive (self-aware) by nature.[36] Once Candrakīrti came to be widely accepted in Tibet as the definitive interpreter of Nāgārjuna, the Yogic Practice School of the Middle Way, despite its importance, tended to take a backseat to the Consequence School in most Tibetan hierarchical rankings of philosophies.

The classic texts authored by the Indian figures mentioned in this chapter have taken a central place in the curriculum of monastic colleges in Tibet. Mipam commented on the works of all these figures. Significantly, he did so in a unique way that integrates them into a single and systematic whole. We have touched on some of the issues that come up in these texts so we can better appreciate this important feature of his works. His commentarial texts continue to have a major place in the curriculum of Tibetan monastic colleges, particularly those of the Nyingma school. Before we look into the contents of these texts, however, we will turn to Tibet to provide some further background.

THREE

Buddhist Identity in Tibet

M IPAM BELONGS TO THE NYINGMA (literally the "old school") tradition. The Nyingma school identifies itself with the early transmission of Buddhism to Tibet in the eighth century, in contrast to the Sarma or "new schools." This was the era when the Dharma King, Trisong Detsen, invited Śāntarakṣita and Padmasambhava to Tibet. Śāntarakṣita, who was a proponent of the Yogic Practice School of the Middle Way, played a central role in shaping the form of Buddhism in Tibet. He was a great scholar, but his tradition of sutra scholarship was not sufficient to tame the wild land of Tibet, so the master of tantra, Padmasambhava, was called on. This interplay of sutra and tantra, a prominent element in Mipam's works, has been an important theme in Tibet since early times.

The debate at Samyé, the first monastery established in Tibet, was a paradigmatic event that came to define the identity of Buddhism there. The debate supposedly took place between Hvashang, representing China and a path of sudden enlightenment, and Kamalaśīla (circa eighth century), representing India and a gradual path to enlightenment. Hvashang advocated the rejection of all mental engagement and reasoning, whereas Kamalaśīla argued for the importance of careful analysis. According to Tibetan accounts, Hvashang lost the debate. After all, it is not surprising that someone who rejects reason lost a debate based on reasoned arguments! Nevertheless, a sudden path to enlightenment was not lost in Tibet; this path continues to have a place in Tibetan meditative traditions. In particular, the Nyingma tradition of the Great Perfection shares prominent features with Hvashang's path of nonthought. An important difference, however, is that in the Nyingma path laid out by Mipam, mental engagement (such as reason) is not rejected from the beginning, as it is portrayed to have been in Hvashang's tradition. For Mipam, analysis is not rejected; it is transcended.

The Samyé debate represents a tension between two competing approaches to enlightenment: one based on study and another on meditative practice. Is enlightenment the product of study, or does it come about through meditation? The polarization of these two paths tends to be a recurrent theme in Buddhist rhetoric. The two approaches are entrenched in the Buddhist culture of Tibet, with the monastics in institutions of study on one side and the meditators in retreat on the other. A large part of Mipam's work was bringing these two traditions together. Even today in the West, we can see how a polarization of scholar and practitioner lives on in the stereotypes of "the Buddhist scholar who does not practice" (and inhabits a university) and "the Buddhist practitioner who does not think" (and inhabits a Dharma center).[37] Since these polarities are so resilient, Mipam's integration of scholarship and practice carries a lot of weight.

OLD AND NEW SCHOOLS

The Nyingma tradition that Mipam inherited identifies itself with the golden age of the early translations of Buddhism in Tibet from the eighth century, through the work of enlightened figures like Padmasambhava, Śāntarakṣita, and a host of extraordinary translators with access to scholars from the living tradition in India. After the imperial age of Buddhist Tibet, the support for institutionalized Buddhism was withdrawn (in the wake of King Langdarma's reign). Tibetan Buddhist traditions generally depict this period as a "dark age" of Buddhism; however, some scholars have characterized it as precisely the time when Buddhism took root in Tibet in creative ways, outside of centralized political and institutional structures. In any case, it was during this time that the traditions of the early translations thrived.

In the eleventh century, centers of regional authority took shape in Tibet, as did institutional support for Buddhist translations. This period marks the beginning of what came to be known as the Sarma traditions, or new schools of translation. The traditions that had flourished up until this point (such as the Nyingma) were now viewed with suspicion. Early Nyingma apologists, like Rongzom (circa eleventh century), made an effort to defend the authenticity (and superiority) of the Nyingma. Central texts of the Nyingma tradition, such as the *Secret Essence Tantra* (*Guhya-garbhatantra*), were said to be Tibetan creations without Indian originals. This eventually led to the Nyingma tradition publishing its own canon of tantras to supplement the Buddhist canon compiled by the new schools, which omitted central Nyingma texts like the *Secret Essence Tantra.* Eventually, a Sanskrit manuscript of the *Secret Essence Tantra* was found, dispelling doubts that it was a Tibetan creation.

The *Secret Essence Tantra* is the most important tantra in the Nyingma tradition. It comes from a group of eighteen tantras known as the *Māyājāla* ("the magical net"). The metaphor of the net is significant; it is also used in a sutra where we find the famous image of the jeweled net of Indra, which is said to extend across the universe. It has a jewel at each point where the threads cross, and each jewel reflects each and every other jewel in the entire net. The net is a metaphor for the universe: the whole universe is contained within each single part. The finite is part of the infinite, while the infinite is constituted by and reflected within the finite. The metaphor aesthetically illustrates an important theme in Great Vehicle Buddhism in general and in tantra in particular, namely, the inseparability or unity of nirvana and samsara. Nirvana is not held as somewhere else *out there,* separate from samsara, like a separate and transcendent infinity apart from the finite. Rather, nirvana is to be discovered *within* the nature of samsara. Likewise, the ultimate truth is not to be found separate from the relative truth but within it.

In addition to containing the metaphor of the net, the *Secret Essence Tantra* also extends a theme of universal buddha-nature—the doctrine that all beings have the innate potential to become buddhas—to embrace a view that everything is already the buddha. Thus, the *Secret Essence Tantra* reveals an important turn within Buddhist thought: a shift from Buddha-nature (*tathāgata-garbha*), the universal potential for enlightenment, to the secret-nature (*guhya-garbha*), the affirmation of universal enlightenment right now. This turn toward an immanent absolute is a major feature of the tradition of tantra in Tibet, as well as in Buddhist traditions across East Asia.

As early as the eleventh century, Rongzom associated "essential nature" (Tib. *snying po,* Skt. *garbha*) with the meaning of the Great Perfection.[38] Self-existing wisdom (*rang byung ye shes*), as a fundamental core of being and matrix of reality, remains an important part of the Nyingma tradition. The role of this embodied, immanent reality contrasts with the abstract and transcendent ultimate truth (emptiness) that is emphasized in other (non-tantric) forms of Buddhist philosophy. The dynamic interplay between two modalities of ultimate truth—transcendent in sutra and immanent in tantra—is a central theme in Tibetan Buddhism that we will discuss further.

Rongzom wrote a commentary on the *Secret Essence Tantra* and also composed an influential text, *Establishing Appearances as Divine,* that incorporates logic with a view of tantra. This work exemplifies the distinctive role that logic plays in establishing the view of tantra in the Nyingma tradition. Such reasoning comes to play an important role in Mipam's works too. In particular, Mipam appropriates Rongzom's use of reason in what he calls the "valid cognition of pure vision" (*dag gzigs tshad ma*), which he uses to legitimate a view of appearances as divine.

Mipam also incorporates Dharmakīrti's system of valid cognition into his presentation of conventional truth, into what he calls the "valid cognition of confined perception" (*tshur mthong tshad ma*) in particular. In contrast to pure vision, confined perception concerns ordinary modes of being in the world, those that are distorted and dualistic. Pure vision and confined perception are two perspectives Mipam uses to delineate the validity of appearances, that is, how things *appear* (which is the conventional truth) as opposed to how things *are* (which is the ultimate truth). While there is a degree of validity to ordinary experience, like seeing a rope in front of you as a rope and not a snake, in the end, even your ordinary perceptions of a rope do not remain valid. That is, an ordinary experience of the world (such as a separate self interacting with an external world) is only true as long as we sustain the working assumptions of samsara—namely, ignorance. According to Mipam, when our ignorant perspective, or confined perception, gives way to a divine world of pure vision, the ordinary world will no longer be ordinary or valid for us; rather, we will inhabit a world that is divine, a world that is pure.

In laying out two approaches to conventional truth, confined perception and pure vision, we find an important feature of Mipam's work. Indeed, it is the central means by which he brings together sutra and tantra within a single system of interpretation. We will return to this topic later, but first let us continue to look at some of his other noteworthy predecessors.

BUDDHIST SECTS IN TIBET

The era of the fourteenth and fifteenth centuries was a watershed for Tibetan Buddhist traditions. This was the classical age of Buddhist thought in Tibet, an age that witnessed an unprecedented flourishing of Buddhist scholarship. Significantly, the distinct interpretations of the main Buddhist sects in Tibet were forged during this creative and dynamic time. In important ways, the predominant features of the traditions of interpretation articulated in this era have largely passed on to the present without major modification. It was during this period that Tibet hosted the exceptional genius of Buddhist scholar-practitioners like Longchenpa (1308–1364), Dölpopa (1292–1361), Tsongkhapa (1357–1419), and Gorampa (1429–1489). Since all these figures are important for Mipam, we will briefly look at each one, beginning with Longchenpa, who was the single most influential Tibetan figure for Mipam.

In a significant way, Mipam's works can be seen as an extended commentary on Longchenpa's writings. Longchenpa is famous for his lucid works on the Great Perfection. In particular, he is well known for bringing forth an unprecedented systematization of the Great Perfection in three multivolume masterpieces: the "Seven Treasuries," which outline the philosophy of the Great Perfection; the "Heart Essence in Four Parts," which elaborates the practice of the Great Perfection; and the "Trilogy of Rest," which beautifully integrates the theory and practice of the Great Perfection. His poetic verses weave together philosophical acumen, mystical insight, and contemplative practice in a powerfully evocative and aesthetic way that is unmatched in Tibet.

Mipam's works were inspired by those of Longchenpa. He used Longchenpa's texts as an interpretative framework through which to formulate a uniquely Nyingma style of commentary on sutra topics like the Middle Way. Mipam was able to carry on the tradition of Longchenpa's visionary works on the Great Perfection by putting them into conversation with the dominant analytic traditions that had developed in Tibet over the five hundred years that separated the two authors. In an important way, he modernized Longchenpa; that is, he rendered Longchenpa's visionary works in a way that spoke the language of the monastic institutions of his day.

Another towering figure, Dölpopa, laid out what would come to be one of the most influential and controversial interpretations of Buddhist thought in Tibet. Dölpopa, who was born in what is present-day Nepal, is known as the forefather of the Jonang tradition. This tradition is known for Dölpopa's famous claim that the ultimate truth is not empty of itself; it is "other-empty." For Dölpopa, what is other-empty exists within reality; it is real and empty of what is other—the unreal. In this way, the ultimate truth is not empty because it is the true ground of reality; it is only empty in the sense that it lacks all relative phenomena. He went on to claim that all phenomena of the relative truth are "self-empty"; that is, they are utterly absent in reality. Relative phenomena are self-empty because they are empty of their own respective essences and not because they are lacking with reference to something extrinsic to themselves.

Dölpopa drew heavily on the topics of the last turning of the wheel of Dharma (that is, buddha-nature and the Yogic Practice School) to affirm his unique view of ultimate reality. Mipam, like Dölpopa's Jonang tradition, also describes the Buddha-Nature Sutras of the last wheel of Dharma as the definitive meaning (Tib. *nges don*, Skt. *nītārtha*), saying that they represent the ultimate truth. Similar to the Jonang interpretation of buddha-nature, Mipam affirms that buddha-nature is replete with the qualities of the buddha when one still has the experience of an ordinary sentient being. Later we will see further similarities with the Jonang interpretation in Mipam's discussion of the two truths and in his portrayal of the ultimate truth in the Yogic Practice School as "authentic experience."

Tsongkhapa, who came to be known as the forefather of the Geluk tradition, criticized Dölpopa's interpretation as realist by arguing that it misrepresented the genuine meaning of the ultimate truth of emptiness. He said that the ultimate truth is not to be understood as one thing being empty of another but must be known as a mere absence of true existence. Significantly, Tsongkhapa laid out a distinctive interpretation of the Consequence School and distanced himself from the Yogic Practice School. He said that the Consequence School alone had the correct interpretation of the Middle Way and argued that other Buddhist philosophies fell short of the authentic view. A prominent voice for the Consequence School in Tibet, Tsongkhapa marks an important line between the old and new schools of interpretation of the Middle Way.

Tsongkhapa's work was influential for Mipam and played an important part in shaping the latter's formulation of the Middle Way. Much of Mipam's work directly challenges the Geluk interpretation of the Middle Way initiated by Tsongkhapa. Nevertheless, Mipam shares Tsongkhapa's emphasis on the central role of analysis in discerning the correct view. Even while the authentic view of reality is beyond analysis and conceptual construction, rather than rejecting reason, Mipam makes use of conceptual analysis to transcend conceptual frameworks. For him, analysis plays an instrumental role in clearing away the mind's habit of reification and thus makes way for wisdom, the nature of mind, to shine forth. We will see how some features of Mipam's Middle Way interpretation are shared with the Geluk and the Jonang traditions. However, he also distinguishes his own school's interpretation from these traditions in significant ways.

Before we turn to Mipam's works, we will briefly examine one more important figure from the fifteenth century, the Sakya scholar Gorampa. Gorampa vehemently criticized Tsongkhapa's interpretation of the Middle Way. In contrast to Tsongkhapa, he argued that the Consequence and Autonomy schools use different methods, but that these methods do not necessarily imply that they have different views on the nature of ultimate truth. Notably, Gorampa argued against Tsongkhapa's claim that the ultimate truth must be held as a mere absence. Instead, he argued that the ultimate truth is free from all conceptual constructs of affirmation and negation, presence and absence. In his portrayal of the Middle Way, Gorampa firmly rejected Tsongkhapa's characterization of what is existent as the relative truth and what is nonexistent as the ultimate truth. He made robust arguments that the Geluk tradition was nihilistic and that the Jonang tradition was eternalistic, while positioning his own Sakya tradition as the genuine Middle Way, the alternative to these two extremes.

Mipam shares Gorampa's view on the importance of understanding the ultimate truth as nonconceptual. He is thus in accord with a significant feature of the Sakya tradition's interpretation of the Middle Way (namely, the empty aspect of the ultimate truth beyond conceptual constructs). He also draws on Gorampa's juxtaposition of the Geluk and Jonang as extremes to forge a middle way between. However, he does not follow Gorampa in his harsh critiques of Tsongkhapa and Dölpopa. Rather, Mipam harmonizes aspects of both these traditions' interpretations, while at the same time distinguishing his own uniquely Nyingma view.

MONASTICISM IN THE NYINGMA

An important development occurred within Buddhist monastic institutions in the five hundred years that separated these luminaries of the fourteenth and fifteenth centuries—Longchenpa, Dölpopa, Tsongkhapa, and Gorampa—from Mipam in the nineteenth century. Under the dominance of the Geluk tradition, large monasteries with considerable political influence had spread throughout Tibet. The institution of the Dalai Lamas, initated by support from the Mongols, came to embody the religious and political authority of the Geluk tradition in Tibet. As the dominant power in Tibet, the Geluk tradition was able to advance a particular style of dialectical philosophy and an institutional structure that together set the standard for systematic Buddhist education.

The fact that the Nyingma tradition lacked a centralized institutional structure was one reason why the school was particularly well suited to play a major role in what came to be known as the "nonsectarian movement" (ris med) in the nineteenth century. Also, prior to the Geluk hegemony, the Nyingma tradition had not been a major contender for political power in central Tibet, so it fared better than other schools (the Geluk's rivals like the Kagyü and Jonang) that were suppressed under the new Geluk regime. The Fifth Dalai Lama had, in fact, been an avid supporter of the Nyingma tradition. Due in part to this relationship, two Nyingma monasteries were established in central Tibet at the height of Geluk power in the seventeenth century. In eastern Tibet, the other four of the six main Nyingma monastic traditions were also founded during this era. With the exception of Kaḥtok monastery (which originally dates to the twelfth century and was revived in the seventeenth), Nyingma monastic institutions were relatively new establishments. Aside from the Nyingma, most other non-Geluk monastic traditions did not fare as well during this time of Geluk supremacy, and several monasteries were forcibly converted to Geluk institutions.

Near the end of his life, Mipam is reported to have said that had he been born during the time of the two renowned Nyingma masters of the seventeenth century (Terdak Lingpa and Lochen Dharmaśrī), he would really have been able to benefit the teachings and beings, but there was no point in him taking birth again now.[39] This is significant because these two brothers—and the Nyingma monastery the elder brother established in central Tibet—had a close relationship with the Fifth Dalai Lama. Perhaps Mipam felt that he could have encouraged a harmonious relationship between the Geluk and Nyingma traditions, which tended to be hostile in the years that followed when the Geluk tradition came to dominate Tibet. Mipam's works, particularly on the Middle Way, were taken as attacks on the Geluk tradition, even though he himself expressed immense respect for Tsongkhapa and, in significant ways, drew on important aspects of Tsongkhapa's thought in his interpretation. Mipam might have felt that the sectarian animosity that had festered in the wake of a dominant Geluk tradition had become too deep-seated. Perhaps he felt there was no longer the same opportunity for fruitful and transformative dialogue as there had been in the seventeenth century, before the suppression of non-Geluk monastic traditions.

In any case, Tsongkhapa's legacy of the Geluk tradition changed the face of monasticism in Tibet. Large-scale monastic communities with celibate monks, closely following the Geluk model, came to play a prominent role in Tibetan cultural history. Soon after the Geluk rise to power, large monastic institutions took a central place within the Nyingma tradition too. With a move toward a formalized curriculum and increased focus on sutra topics, the Nyingma monastic colleges that developed in the nineteenth and twentieth centuries bore a certain resemblance to Geluk institutions. Yet at the same time, these colleges posed a challenge to the authority of Geluk scholarship as the sole legitimate interpretation of Buddhist thought and practice.

MONASTIC COLLEGES AND THE NONSECTARIAN MOVEMENT

What came to be known as a nonsectarian movement developed in the eastern Tibetan province of Kham in the nineteenth century. Alliances had formed across the region following the political ascendancy of the Geluk tradition in central Tibet. This turbulent and creative era of Tibetan history witnessed an enormous intellectual and literary renaissance. We find a wave of doctrinal syntheses and movements that sought to formalize monastic education in new institutions among the Sakya, Kagyü, and Nyingma traditions. The Nyingma tradition came to play a particularly influential role, and Mipam was a primary architect of this era.

Before the nineteenth century, the Nyingma tradition was mainly defined by its interpretation and practice of tantra, in particular, the *Secret Essence Tantra*. The institutional transformation of the Nyingma tradition that began in the seventeenth century and continued into the nineteenth and twentieth centuries was a complex process of the systematization, or domestication, of the tantric vision of divine unity. Before this time, the Nyingma tradition was more of a meditative, ritual, and contemplative tradition centered on the mystical vision of tantra. Mipam's work is a product of the synergy between the wild, divine world of tantra and the rational, analytic rigor of the newly founded monastic colleges in his tradition.

In the beginning of the twentieth century, Mipam and one of his students founded a monastic college at Kaḥtok monastery. Another student of Mipam's came to be the first professor to teach at the newly established college there.[40] Extending from this college, twenty-five monastic colleges were soon founded. Many such institutions were inspired by the work of Mipam and by another influential figure of the era, Khenpo Zhenga

(1871–1927), who was a contemporary of Mipam's and credited with founding eighteen monastic colleges. We will say a few words about his role to provide some contrast with Mipam.

Khenpo Zhenga began teaching at the monastery where Mipam's teacher, Patrul Rinpoché, had lived. Shortly after the turn of the twentieth century, he was invited to be a professor at the monastic college at Dzokchen, where he taught for about seven years.[41] He was later invited to Pelpung, a Karma Kagyü monastery near Degé, and founded a monastic college there. There is some controversy regarding Khenpo Zhenga's tenure as a professor at Pelpung monastery. Unlike Jamgön Kongtrül, one of Mipam's teachers who was there in the previous century, Khenpo Zhenga did not teach a view of "other-emptiness." He reportedly preferred self-emptiness to other-emptiness. Dilgo Khyentsé (1910–1991), who was one of Khenpo Zhenga's students and seems to have been the last contemporary teacher to have met Mipam personally, related an account of Khenpo Zhenga saying that the bad karma of a hunter is better than that of someone who holds a view of other-emptiness.[42]

The doctrine of other-emptiness was an important means by which Jamgön Kongtrül unified diverse Buddhist doctrines. The language of other-emptiness—which portrays the ultimate truth in affirming language—directly contradicts the orthodox Geluk formulation of the ultimate as a mere absence of inherent existence. Some Nyingma monastic traditions, such as the Nyingma monastery of Kaḥtok, explicitly embraced an other-emptiness view. Other Nyingma monasteries adopted a Geluk interpretation regarding topics of sutra, like the Middle Way, while maintaining a tradition of tantra distinctive to Nyingma.[43]

There is a story that is particularly relevant here, a story of an exchange between two of Mipam's students. They were discussing what was studied in the curriculum at three prominent Nyingma monasteries. In a paraphrase of this dialogue, one said to the other, "At Dzokchen monastery, Khenpo Zhenga only teaches Indian treatises and at your Nyingma monastery, while commentaries on tantras are taught according to the Nyingma tradition, commentaries on sutras are taught according to the Geluk. Therefore, only Kaḥtok monastery maintains a pure Nyingma tradition!" The other responded with a question: "For the *Ornament of*

Clear Realization, which commentary are you using at Kahtok monastery?" The first student answered, "Gorampa's (Sakya) commentary."[44]

This dialogue illustrates an important point: before Mipam, the Nyingma did not have its own authoritative corpus of commentaries on sutra topics, which had come to play a predominant role in the curriculum of monastic colleges. Mipam composed several commentaries—within an interpretative framework based on the works of Longchenpa and Rongzom—on many of the central Buddhist scriptures studied in monastic colleges. This was a major part of his contribution to the Nyingma school. He gave his tradition its own interpretation of sutra topics (like the Middle Way) that were unique and distinctive to the Nyingma and that continue to have an important place in the curriculum at Nyingma monastic colleges.

Khenpo Zhenga also composed commentaries on several Buddhist classics that came to be used as textbooks for the newly founded monastic colleges among non-Geluk traditions.[45] However, the way he did so contrasts with Mipam's works. Mipam had drawn on the works of Rongzom and Longchenpa to articulate a distinctively Nyingma interpretation of Buddhist scriptures. Khenpo Zhenga, however, commented directly on the Indian sources, without taking on any specific Tibetan layer of commentary.[46] Without relying on a specific Tibetan interpretation, his commentaries can be seen as a move to circumvent sectarian disputes by appealing to Indian originals rather than some distinctive strand of nearly one thousand years of Tibetan commentary.[47] His work contrasts not only with that of Jamgön Kongtrül, who embraced an explicit other-emptiness interpretation, but also with that of Mipam. Mipam's works have a stronger Nyingma sectarian identity.

Despite the distinctive interpretative styles of Jamgön Kongtrül, Khenpo Zhenga, and Mipam, there is a tendency to fuse them together within what has been called the "nonsectarian" tradition. We should keep in mind that the term *nonsectarian,* as applied to diverse positions in this way, is multivalent. It certainly does not refer to a single system of interpretation. Also, it does not mean that all traditions are necessarily taken as equal on all levels. Rather, a general quality of what it means to be nonsectarian in Tibet is an attitude of respectful engagement with a broad range of competing Buddhist traditions of interpretation. Such attention to a plurality of interpretations does not necessarily involve a coercive amalgamation of others' views with one's own. Rather, a gesture in the direction of inclusiveness, an ecumenical approach, contrasts with a more insular model of scholarship that frames the boundaries of discourse within one's own narrowly delineated tradition of interpretation. Thus, we can understand what came to be known as the nonsectarian movement as a broad set of traditions, stemming from eastern Tibet in the nineteenth century,

TIBETAN BUDDHISTS WHO WERE PARTICULARLY IMPORTANT TO MIPAM

Name	Main Sect Affiliation	Chronology
Rongzom	Nyingma	Eleventh century
Longchenpa	Nyingma	1308–1364
Dölpopa	Jonang	1292–1361
Tsongkhapa	"Geluk"	1357–1419
Gorampa	Sakya	1429–1489
Patrul Rinpoché (Mipam's teacher)	Nyingma (nonsectarian)	1808–1887
Jamyang Khyentsé Wangpo (Mipam's root teacher)	Sakya (nonsectarian)	1820–1892
Jamgön Kongtrül (Mipam's teacher)	Kagyü (nonsectarian)	1813–1899
Khenpo Zhenga	Nyingma (nonsectarian)	1871–1927

Several of Mipam's prominent Tibetan inspirations, teachers, and contemporaries.

that developed a common interest in preserving a variety of Buddhist traditions as a response to the singular dominance of the Geluk school.

With the renewed interest in Buddhist intellectual traditions in Tibet (as exemplified in the revived scholarship of non-Geluk traditions), the works of several scholars from previous generations were compiled and printed during the fertile era of the late nineteenth and early twentieth centuries.[48] The works of Longchenpa, which were so influential for Mipam, were newly edited and printed during this era. Mipam wrote the catalogs for the publishing of the "Seven Treasuries" of Longchenpa, in addition to writing catalogs for the collected works of Rongzom, another of his influential Nyingma predecessors.[49] Such catalogs for the volumes of an author's collected works outline the contents contained therein and represent an important means by which Tibetans frame a body of literature.

The works of Gorampa, the fifteenth-century Sakya scholar, were also published in the early twentieth century, as were the works of the Eighth Karmapa, Mikyö Dorjé (1507–1554).[50] Mikyö Dorjé played an important role in formulating the commentarial tradition on sutra topics for the Karma Kagyü. The publication of these texts, along with the new compositions of Mipam and Khenpo Zhenga, contributed to the development of the monastic colleges that were forming across eastern Tibet at this time.

TRANSITION

Before concluding this chapter, we should take into account the political turmoil in eastern Tibet during this era as well, at least as it is relevant to Mipam's life and legacy. Mipam's homeland of Kham is a wild and rugged area in eastern Tibet. It is a contested land sandwiched between the dominant forces of China and central Tibet. In the middle of the nineteenth century, following a famine, there had been some fighting in Nyakrong, a district in Kham. The fighting would eventually escalate into a war and an attack on Degé, where Mipam lived, around 1862. During the conflict, in which many lamas were killed or kidnapped, Mipam fled to a nearby nomadic area and also took the opportunity to go on a pilgrimage to Lhasa.

When Degé was conquered and the queen of Degé taken hostage, the ministers of the court fled to Lhasa for support. The government of the Thirteenth Dalai Lama intervened and dispatched a militia to conquer the rebel leader and his armies of Nyakrong.[51] The administration in Lhasa seized the opportunity to put both Nyakrong and Degé under its own jurisdiction. Previously, the Geluk authority in Lhasa had not wielded such influence in Degé. Even so, coming under the rule of central Tibet would not be the least of their problems, for China would soon become the source of another struggle.

From the east, China led a rigorous military campaign into eastern Tibet in the first decade of the twentieth century. The army took control of most of the areas of Kham and placed them under Chinese administration.[52] China's military exploits in Tibet were motivated simultaneously by dreams to colonize Kham and fears of the long imperial arm of Britain in the wake of that country's venture into Lhasa in 1904; the humiliation of the Opium Wars at the hands of the British was still fresh in the minds of the Chinese.[53] China's power in Tibet reached an unprecedented height between 1910 and 1911, during which time it had taken control of much of Kham and marched troops into Lhasa. In October 1911, however, things changed dramatically.

China's Qing dynasty fell in 1911, one year before Mipam's death. That year marked the end of more than two thousand years of imperial rule in China. At that time, resolving internal conflict and transitioning were the primary agenda items for the Chinese government; Tibet was no longer a priority. In the years that followed, there was a window of time in which Buddhist monastic colleges flourished on the Tibetan plateau. It did not last long, however, for Mao Zedong brought the land under the control of the People's Republic of China in 1950. The Mao years culminated in the Cultural Revolution, which—unfortunately for Tibet and China—brought unprecedented destruction to religious institutions and traditional cultures across both regions. Fortunately, most of Mipam's texts survived the devastation. Not only are his works preserved, but they continue to be taught, discussed, and debated actively within a vibrant living tradition.

FOUR

Survey of Mipam's Works

M IPAM'S COLLECTED WORKS are voluminous. There is only one Tibetan author with a larger volume of work, Bodong Choklé Namgyel (1375/6–1451), to whom more than a hundred volumes are attributed. The most recent redaction of Mipam's collected works (Kaḥtok edition) fills thirty volumes. An early catalog of his works recounts that there are thirty-two volumes, corresponding to the thirty-two major marks of the body of a buddha. However, some of his works have been lost, and not all of his writings made it into the collections. After his death, Mipam's writings were assembled by his main students. Some of the texts included in his collected works were compiled posthumously from his notes and outlines.[54]

Mipam's most extensive treatment of the Middle Way is his commentary on Śāntarakṣita's *Ornament of the Middle Way*. In this commentary, he shows the compatibility of the Middle Way (in particular, the Consequence School) and the Yogic Practice School. This text not only exemplifies an important statement of his central views on the Middle Way, but it also treats several key points of Buddhist philosophy in general. He wrote it when he was only thirty-one years old and completed the work in just three weeks.[55]

While a classic in India, the *Ornament of the Middle Way* had received scant attention in Tibet since Candrakīrti's *Introduction to the Middle Way* rose to prominence. Candrakīrti had argued against foundational positions of the Yogic Practice School that are taken up in the *Ornament of the Middle Way* (namely, reflexive awareness), and seemingly for this reason, the text fell out of favor. Mipam revived this important work of the Yogic Practice School of the Middle Way and made a strong argument—contra Tsongkhapa—that in the end, the view of the ultimate is the same in the Yogic Practice School of the Middle Way as it is in the Consequence School. A Nyingma scholar objected to Mipam's commentary on the *Ornament of the Middle Way*. His critique came from his Geluk-influenced understanding of the authentic Middle Way view, which treats the Consequence School as incompatible with the Yogic Practice School. Mipam responded to this criticism in a short text entitled *Eliminating Doubts*.

Another important source for Mipam's Middle Way views is his commentary on the Wisdom Chapter of the *Way of the Bodhisattva*. In this text, he elucidates the meaning of ultimate emptiness, nonconceptuality free from all constructs. This commentary also drew criticism, this time directly from two prominent scholars in the Geluk school. Mipam responded to each of their critiques in two provocative texts that delve deeply into several important issues of the Middle Way.[56] These three texts unpack his view of the meaning of emptiness and the Middle Way. A compilation of short instructions on the general points of scriptures, entitled *Difficult Points of Scriptures in General,* is another excellent source for his views on the Middle Way. The content in this collection notably contrasts with central features of the predominant Geluk interpretation of the Middle Way, such as its way of representing the ultimate truth as solely a negation—a lack of true existence.

Another significant statement of his Middle Way view is the *Beacon of Certainty,* which is arranged around responses to seven incisive questions. In this short, beautiful work of philosophical poetry, Mipam illuminates the Nyingma view on the Middle Way and the Great Perfection. In the beginning of the *Beacon of Certainty,* Mipam distinguishes an understanding that comes from genuine certainty from mere belief that comes from following what others have said. His emphasis on certainty reflects his commitment to analysis and self-reliance with regard to a firm grounding in personal experience (not simply relying on the dry words of another) on one hand and the Nyingma tradition (not simply relying on other traditions' interpretations) on the other. Indeed, certainty (*nges shes*) is a prominent theme in his works. In particular, he emphasizes a twofold certainty: (1) a certainty in which you do not rely on something else and (2) a certainty that cannot be taken away by something else.

Among the five treatises of Maitreya, Mipam wrote complete commentaries on three of the texts: "the two that distinguish"—*Distinguishing Phenomena and Suchness* and *Distinguishing the Middle and the Extremes*—as well as the *Ornament of the Great Vehicle Sutras*.[57] These three texts elaborate the Yogic Practice School's view of the three natures and explain the ultimate truth as nonconceptual wisdom free from duality. Significantly, Mipam presents these texts in a way that is compatible with the Middle Way. It is notable that he wrote a massive, 760-page commentary on the *Ornament of the Great Vehicle Sutras*. Structured around the process of an individual's engagement in the Great Vehicle, this text is an encyclopedic work that lays out the distinctive qualities of the path of a bodhisattva, such as the unique commitment and practice. While Mipam says that this text is a Mind-Only treatise, he emphasizes that it can also be understood as a text on the Great Vehicle in general, compatible with the Middle Way.

Later we will look at how Mipam articulates the relationship between Mind-Only and the Middle Way, but one of the main points to the *Ornament of the Great Vehicle Sutras'* placement in one of these two Great Vehicle philosophies—Mind-Only or Middle Way—is the issue of whether all beings are held to be potential buddhas or not. One place where this issue is addressed is in the fourth chapter of the text, the chapter on heritage (Tib. *rigs,* Skt. *gotra*). Heritage, which also carries the connotations of "lineage," "potential," or "family," is the cause or potential within sentient beings for enlightenment. A verse from the *Ornament of the Great Vehicle Sutras* states that some beings lack the cause, or heritage, of liberation. According to Mipam, if this verse is held to mean that such beings will never be free from samsara, then it represents an inferior, Mind-Only position. If a being's lack of heritage is held to be only a temporary circumstance, however, and not eternal damnation to samsara, it reflects a position compatible with the Middle Way by endorsing the view that all beings become buddhas because all beings have buddha-nature, the innate qualities of a buddha.

Mipam lays out his view of buddha-nature in a short text called *Lion's Roar: Exposition of Buddha-Nature,* which draws on another of the five treatises of Maitreya, the *Sublime Continuum.* Here he presents three main arguments showing why all beings have buddha-nature. He also distinguishes his view of buddha-nature, which he portrays as the unconditioned unity of emptiness and appearance, from other traditions' views. Namely, he contrasts his view with traditions that maintain buddha-nature as truly real and not empty (Jonang), traditions that hold buddha-nature to be simply the mind's absence of true existence (Geluk), and traditions that maintain that the cognitive quality of buddha-nature—the element that is in unity with emptiness—is impermanent (a Sakya view). Mipam's other "lion's roar"—his *Lion's Roar: Affirming Other-Emptiness*—shows the way he establishes an other-emptiness view that affirms the existence of the ultimate truth as not empty of its own essence.

As with the works of most scholars in Tibet, most of Mipam's do not directly address the canonical sutras but focus on the commentarial treatises. However, he did write a few commentaries on specific sutras as well.[58] Indeed, he wrote on all three sections of the traditional Buddhist canon: Sutra, Vinaya, and Abhidharma. Mipam's works relating to the Vinaya include an interlinear commentary on the *Individual Liberation Sutra.* Additionally, he composed an interlinear commentary on a text that discusses vows for laypeople.[59]

Mipam also wrote a short text on the three vows—the vows of individual liberation, the bodhisattva vow, and the tantric commitments—entitled *Establishing the Three Vows as Essentially One.* The relationship between monasticism and tantra has played an important part in forming the contours of Buddhist Tibet, so harmonizing the practices of tantra with monastic vows continues to be a central concern for Buddhist traditions. Establishing this harmony has been particularly important for followers of the Nyingma tradition since the seventeenth century, such as Mipam, because before then the Nyingma tradition was primarily defined by its adherence to particular tantras and was not so strongly tied to celibate monastic institutions. With the rise of Nyingma monasteries in the seventeenth century, the integration of tantra and monasticism became a central concern.

Mipam wrote on the two main classics of Abhidharma that reached Tibet: the *Treasury of Abhidharma* by Vasubandhu and the *Compendium of Abhidharma* by Asaṅga. The latter treatise presents the Abhidharma in accord with the Great Vehicle. Another important work he composed on Abhidharma is his popular *Gateway to Scholarship*, an encyclopedic textbook that draws from both Vasubandhu's and Asaṅga's presentations. The *Gateway to Scholarship* has come to be widely studied, not only in Nyingma monastic institutions, but also in Kagyü and Sakya monasteries. Moreover, Mipam wrote commentaries on the *Compendium of Valid Cognition* and the *Commentary on Valid Cognition,* the two central texts by the main Buddhist scholars of valid cognition from India, Dignāga and Dharmakīrti. His commentary on Dharmakīrti's influential *Commentary on Valid Cognition* is more than nine hundred pages.[60]

In addition to writing on topics of sutra, Mipam wrote several volumes on tantra as well. In particular, he wrote two important texts on *Mahāyoga,* which has a significant place in the Nyingma tradition; it is likened to the ground, or foundation, of the "inner tantras." For the Nyingma, the inner tantras correspond to what is known as "Highest Yoga Tantra" in the new schools of translations (Sarma), so they represent the pinnacle of the tantras. Mipam's two texts on Mahāyoga expound on its two main subdivisions: the accomplishment section and the tantra section. His *Discourse on the Eight Commands* addresses the accomplishment section of Mahāyoga, which deals primarily with the generation stage of visualizing deities, particularly the eight Mahāyoga deities. These eight deities play a significant role in Nyingma ritual and meditative practices. His *Essential Nature of Luminous Clarity,* which is an overview of Longchenpa's commentary on the *Secret Essence Tantra,* addresses the tantra section of Mahāyoga. This text is a key statement of his theory of tantra, the view. It has a significant place in his corpus because it is the main place where he presents his outlook on the fundamental principles of tantra. Mipam also wrote an interlinear commentary on Padmasambhava's *Garland of Views,* which is based on the thirteenth chapter of the *Secret Essence Tantra.*

The *Secret Essence Tantra* is the most important tantra in the Nyingma school. Mipam's commentary explains eleven main topics regarding this tantra—as well as the threefold ground, path, and fruition—in accord with the Great Perfection. He says that his commentary accords with the way that both Rongzom and Longchenpa explain the tantra. He termed this manner of commentary the "Rong-Long" tradition (Rongzom and Longchenpa) in contrast to the Zur tradition that explains it as strictly a Mahāyoga text. As we have seen, Rongzom and Longchenpa were Mipam's primary Nyingma sources.

Mipam's main influence, Longchenpa, drew extensively from sutras to establish the legitimacy of the contested Nyingma tantras in general and the tradition of the Great Perfection in particular. Mipam also drew from sutras in his works, but it was apparently for a different reason than Longchenpa's. Longchenpa primarily focused his work on the Great Perfection and used sutras to support his view of the Great Perfection as a legitimate expression of the meaning of Buddhist sutras. Mipam, in contrast, primarily focused on commentaries of sutra topics (like the Middle Way) and used the Great Perfection as the guiding principle of his interpretation. In other words, whereas Longchenpa directly elucidated the tradition of the Great Perfection and used sutras to support his claims, Mipam elucidated the Great Perfection within sutra itself. A predominant feature of Mipam's commentarial style in general, across sutra and tantra, is his keen ability to interpret texts through the lens of the Great Perfection. He drew heavily from Longchenpa to articulate his uniquely Nyingma interpretation of Buddhist scriptures.

Among Longchenpa's numerous works, Mipam commented directly on his *Wish-Fulfilling Treasury*. In particular, he wrote specific commentaries on the twelfth and eighteenth chapters of this text. That he chose to write on these chapters is noteworthy; it gives us an idea why this text, among all of Longchenpa's works, may have been so significant for him. Chapter 12 of the *Wish-Fulfilling Treasury* treats the ascending views of the philosophical systems according to the Nyingma tradition—showing how each higher view enfolds the lower ones in a way that integrates their insights while going beyond them. These philosophical systems culminate with the inner tantras and the Great Perfection. This is significant, because here we find not only a typical structure of ascending views in the four philosophical systems that culminate in the Middle Way (Consequence School), but ascending views within the four classes of tantra as well. It is a distinctive quality of the Nyingma to continue the ascension of views beyond the Middle Way and associate each class of tantra (or Vajrayāna) with a higher philosophical view. An important feature of this structure is that the insights of the lower systems are contained within the higher ones; they build on and integrate each other up the scale. By acknowledging this central feature of the Nyingma view, we can better understand Mipam's presentation of the Middle Way in context, as well as appreciate the overarching structure of the larger system of interpretation within which it is contained.

The other chapter of the *Wish-Fulfilling Treasury* that Mipam focused on, the eighteenth entitled "Coming to Know Reality," is also significant in that it highlights a shift from an analytical approach of study to the embodied wisdom of meditation. In contrast to just a dry, abstract analysis, the experiential dimension of meditative practice is central for Mipam. For his Nyingma tradition, meditation integrates philosophical analysis while transcending it; meditation proceeds from where analysis leaves off. In this, we see the time-honored process of unfolding insight in Buddhism: first through study, then through reflection, and finally culminating with meditation. To illustrate this, consider the opening words of the chapter: "Having completed reflection in this way, you should generate the wisdom of meditation in your mind-stream . . ." Longchenpa's commentary on this first verse is also noteworthy:

Having come to understand the ultimate ground in the general context of what is to be known in the philosophical systems through the wisdom of study, now is taught the uncommon teaching of the inconceivable nature of luminous clarity, buddha-nature, which is the spontaneously present mandala that is the ground of the paths of the Vajrayāna, Secret Mantra . . .[61]

We can see that the tradition of tantra, or Vajrayāna, is particularly important for the Nyingma. In a fundamental way, tantra discloses the practical application of the doctrine of buddha-nature, which is a key element in practice that bridges sutra and tantra. Moreover, it embodies the common ground for buddhas and sentient beings, samsara and nirvana. Indeed, buddha-nature, the Great Perfection, and the synthesis of sutra and tantra are all dominant themes in Mipam's works.

Mipam elaborates the distinctive view and practice of the Great Perfection in his momentous compilation known as *Trilogy of Innate Mind*, a collection of his oral instructions compiled posthumously by his students.[62] He regarded what would have become his *Trilogy of Innate Mind*, had he completed it, as the essential life force of the nonsectarian teachings.[63] It is significant that he attributed such importance to these texts, because what he did complete of the trilogy describes the nature of mind, the "innate mind," which has the same meaning as buddha-nature. This compilation contains his most extensive treatment of the Great Perfection, and even though he did not finish it, it is filled with brilliant insights that elucidate the unique features of the Great Perfection.

In addition to his extensive writing on Nyingma material, Mipam also wrote on several major texts of the Sarma tradition, or the new schools. For instance, he wrote a commentary on the *Song of the View* by a Geluk scholar.[64] The text on which he chose to comment is particularly interesting, because it attacks a view that negates inherent existence as something separate from phenomena, a stereotypically Geluk view. While Mipam draws on central aspects of Geluk thought, like the author of the *Song of the View*, he is willing to critique what he finds as problematic within dominant strands of the Geluk tradition's interpretation, namely, the tendency to preserve the reality of the ordinary world in the wake of insight into its ultimate nature. In other words, he argues against the interpretation that insight into the empty nature of things leaves the ordinary experience of the world unscathed.

Mipam is also credited with a commentary on Tsongkhapa's *Three Principal Aspects of the Path*,[65] which is a pithy text summarizing the essential points of the Buddhist path in three aspects: renunciation, the altruistic intention of bodhicitta, and the authentic view of emptiness. Additionally, he wrote a commentary on the famous *Treasury of Reasoning* of the Sakya tradition, a Tibetan classic on valid cognition.[66] He also composed a short supplication to masters of the Jonang lineage.[67] Drawing on the Bön tradition—a heterodox tradition that claims its roots in pre-

Buddhist Tibet—he wrote an eight hundred–page treatise on a system of divination based on knots.[68] Here, we can see that his interests were not limited to simply articulating the views of his own Nyingma tradition.

Significantly, Mipam wrote a massive two-volume exposition on *Kālacakratantra,*[69] as well as texts on the practices of other Sarma tantras such as *Hevajra, Guhyasamaja, Cakrasaṃvara,* and *Vajrayoginī,* among others. He also composed an interlinear commentary on Saraha's *Treasury of Songs.*[70] Saraha is a renowned master of the *siddha* tradition of accomplished meditators in India and known for his evocative poetry. Mipam authored several of his own songs on the view of the Great Perfection, in addition to short compositions of quintessential instructions on meditative practice.

He wrote several devotional texts as well, including an invocation to Śākyamuni Buddha entitled *Treasury of Blessings,* which is supplemented by a massive composition in one thousand pages that expounds on the Buddha's former lives.[71] Additionally, he wrote a beautiful commentary, called *White Lotus,* on the famous seven-line supplication to Padmasambhava; it draws out how these seven lines simultaneously resonate with several levels of meaning, including the Great Perfection.[72] Among his supplication texts, he even composed a guru-yoga practice for evoking Dharmakīrti.

While Mipam is known for his commentaries on sutra and tantra, his writings are not limited to these topics. For instance, he wrote a text of advice to the king of Degé.[73] Mipam had served as an advisor to the king and had received patronage from the royal family. He wrote on all of the traditional ten arts, which include (in addition to the "inner art" of Buddhism): linguistics, poetics, material arts (e.g., painting and sculpture), healing, logic, astrology, and drama, among others. His works include a commentary on the famous fourfold medical tantra, as well as several short works on medicine that address pulse-reading, urinalysis, and even the concoction of aphrodisiacs.[74] He wrote a long commentary on the *Mirror of Poetry,* a classic of Indian poetics, and compiled a Sanskrit-Tibetan dictionary that includes a lexicon of words related to the Great Perfection. He also composed a divination system based on the mantra of Mañjuśrī[75] and a short treatise on letter-writing.[76] In his *Treasure-Trove of*

Material Arts, he describes the crafts of painting, sculpture, jewelry, knitting, and carpentry, in addition to the process of making such things as incense, ink, herbal pills, and fireworks.

Furthermore, he compiled and edited the popular Gesar epic, which had hitherto been mainly an oral tradition. The epic recounts the exploits of King Gesar, who is acknowledged to be an incarnation of Padmasambhava, in a classic tale that unfolds in a struggle of good versus evil. Mipam composed his own prayers and praises to Gesar, and he also arranged a theatrical dance depicting Gesar and his retinue, which continues to be a popular performance at Nyingma monasteries.[77] It is remarkable for such a prominent scholar as Mipam to take such an active role in promoting a folk tradition. This illustrates the unceasing dynamic of his creative intellect and the stunning breadth of his vision.

PART TWO

Overview of Mipam's Buddhist Works

FIVE

Unity

A CENTRAL THREAD THAT RUNS through Mipam's interpretation is the interplay of conceptual, dualistic mind and
nonconceptual, nondual wisdom.

MIND AND WISDOM

Mipam makes a critical distinction between mind and wisdom and also
puts forward a powerful way in which they can be integrated. We can see
these respective domains play out in the approaches of (1) analytical traditions of study and contemplation and (2) meditative traditions of quintessential instructions. We will see again and again how Mipam calls on
these two approaches in his works—one based on analysis and the other
on uncontrived meditation.

We can say that the analytical path is a "bottom-up" approach to wisdom
in that it begins with an ordinary, conceptual mind and uses concepts as a
means to eventually transcend concepts. A strictly meditative path can be
called a "top-down" approach in that it jumps directly to wisdom's nonconceptual experience of reality. In contrast to the gradual path of study
and reflection, it is a direct path that involves meditating according to the
quintessential instructions received from a teacher. In this approach, a lot
of analysis is not necessary because, according to an important feature of
Mipam's tradition of the Great Perfection, wisdom is already present in a
fundamental way within the nature of mind. Therefore, all we really need
to know is how to access it and let our true nature manifest. This approach

involves transmission from a qualified teacher, someone with experience and connection to a living lineage of wisdom's realization. This wisdom can be experienced directly through a transmission from a qualified teacher to a qualified student.

As we look broadly at Mipam's works, we will see a recurrent tension, or resonance, between two perspectives: (1) a conceptual, or gradual, perspective of reason and (2) a direct, nonconceptual perspective of wisdom. These two perspectives reflect a distinction between consciousness, a realm of discursive reason determined within a conceptual framework, and wisdom, an open horizon of intelligence beyond concepts. Recognizing the distinction between conceptual mind and nonconceptual wisdom is important to understanding Mipam's work. He defines the ordinary mind, or consciousness (*rnam shes*), as "that which is clear and aware with the nature of conceptuality"; in contrast, he defines wisdom (*ye shes*) as "the naturally luminous clarity that is the nonconceptual, reflexive awareness of reality."[78] We will see this distinction at play throughout his works, as he brings these seemingly incompatible perspectives into conversation. Such a dialectical tension is a prominent feature of his Nyingma tradition.

On one side of this dialectic, we have the Great Perfection, and on the other side, the framework of conceptually driven analyses and rational approaches to truth. The Great Perfection is a textual and meditative tradition that affirms that the nature of mind is intrinsically the buddha. It offers a radically direct approach to actualizing this reality by cutting through conceptual elaborations and directly experiencing wisdom. An important feature of the view of the Great Perfection is that it consistently evades systematic analysis; in a fundamental way, it is antithetical to abstract conceptual thought. Nevertheless, the Great Perfection is not simply an anti-intellectual meditative practice that rejects reason, and Mipam supports its view with rational arguments. Time and again, he emphasizes the role of reasoned analysis as a means to clear the way for the direct experience of the Great Perfection. While his writings address a wide range of Buddhist doctrines from sutra to tantra, the Great Perfection is the guiding principle throughout his works.

Mipam has a keen ability to synthesize diverse strands of Buddhist thought and practice. His synthetic interpretation responds to centuries of debate about how best to understand the Buddhist view, communicate it, and put it into practice. An important point to keep in mind is how Mipam's system of interpretation spans the genres of sutra and tantra. He incorporates a wide range of different texts and perspectives into the all-embracing structure of his interpretation (see translations 1, 2, and 28).

Two Models of the Two Truths

A key to comprehending Mipam's interpretation of Buddhist thought and practice is to understand the two truths—the ultimate and the relative. He clearly outlines two models and shows how the two truths should be understood in two distinct ways. [79] In one model, he represents the two truths as emptiness and appearance; in his other model, he depicts them as two modes of experience. In the first model, emptiness alone is the ultimate truth, and any appearance is the relative truth. This model primarily relates to the domain of deconstructive analysis, that is, analysis that seeks to determine the ultimate nature of reality. When the nature of a phenomenon is analyzed in terms of its ultimate status, how it really is, nothing whatsoever is found. This is the ultimate truth. In contrast, the appearing mode of things—any phenomena that may appear—is the relative truth. Thus, in this model, appearing phenomena are necessarily the relative truth in contrast to the ultimate truth, which is exclusively emptiness.

Within this first model, the ultimate truth is not qualitatively different from the relative truth. In fact, the two truths are actually inseparable; they are not really different, but are only conceptually distinct. The relationship is something like two sides of the same coin; whatever appears is empty, and whatever is empty necessarily appears. [80] In this way, being empty and appearing are just two aspects of what is an inseparable unity in reality. This unity cannot be directly known by analyzing the two truths separately, where appearance and emptiness are mutually exclusive. Nevertheless, a conceptual semblance of this unity can be brought to mind as a means to evoke the experiential insight of unity, which is disclosed in the nonconceptual experience of meditative equipoise.

In his other model of the two truths, Mipam represents the ultimate truth as authentic experience and the relative truth as inauthentic experience. In this model, authentic experience—or more literally, perception that accords with reality (*gnas snang mthun*)—is ultimate, and perceptions that do not accord with reality are relative. In contrast to the former model in which *only emptiness* is the ultimate truth and *all appearances* are relative, in this latter model, the experience of meditative wisdom (that is, unity) is ultimate. Rather than being driven by a deconstructive analysis to establish that phenomena are empty, this model concerns the process of experience. Significantly, both the content of wisdom's vision and wisdom itself are ultimate in this context, not just the negation of distortion. As such, both the subjective cognition of wisdom (*yul can ye shes*) and the objective expanse of phenomena (*yul chos kyi dbyings*) are ultimate; and conversely, distorted perceptions of reality and the mind that perceives dualistically are relative truths.[81]

Moreover, the two truths in this latter authentic/inauthentic model have a different relationship than in the case of the two truths as appearance/emptiness. In this latter model, the two truths are such that the ultimate truth is reality experienced without duality or reification, while the relative truth is reality experienced within a distorted framework. We can see that the ultimate truth here is thus something positive, and the relative truth is something negative; they are two qualitatively different ways of experiencing reality. That is, the experience of the undistorted nature of reality (nirvana) is ultimate in contrast to mistaken modes of being (samsara). Therefore, the ultimate truth in this context is not simply emptiness (the lack of true existence in things), because here the experiential presence of reality, known as it is, is the ultimate.

We can see how Mipam lays out both of these models of the two truths based on two different ways of arriving at the ultimate truth. The ultimate truth in the first model of appearance/emptiness is arrived at by ultimate analysis, which seeks to identify the true nature of things. With this type of analysis, the mind does not find any essence whatsoever in any phenomena. That lack of essence is the ultimate truth. In contrast, the ultimate truth in the authentic/inauthentic model highlights an experiential dimension. When reality is perceived without distortion in the context of meditative experience, this authentic experience of wisdom is the ultimate truth. According to Mipam, these two models need not conflict; they represent different contexts, or perspectives, for relating to the two truths. These two perspectives correspond to (1) when the two truths (appearance and emptiness) are divided in postmeditation and (2) when there is no division of two truths (unity) in meditative equipoise.

Mipam describes the two truths in his latter model based on a distinction between the domain of conceptual consciousness (inauthentic experience) and the domain of nonconceptual wisdom (authentic experience). It is significant that, in this model, he affirms that wisdom is ultimate in contrast to consciousness. The distinction between wisdom and consciousness, or awareness (*rig pa*) and mind (*sems*), has a central place in the tradition of the Great Perfection. Also, the division of authentic/inauthentic experience is the way the two truths are represented in traditions that affirm other-emptiness,[82] in contrast to the two truths as appearance/emptiness, which is primarily associated with the view of self-emptiness.

"Other-emptiness" refers to a phenomenon's lack (its emptiness) with respect to something else, like wisdom's lack of defilements. It is empty of what is other. In contrast, "self-emptiness" can be understood as a phenomenon's lack with respect to itself, like a chariot's lack of real existence. It is empty in and of itself. Traditions that affirm other-emptiness, such as the Jonang, tend to emphasize the experiential dimension of meditative equipoise and hence highlight the model of the two truths based on authentic and inauthentic experience. On the other hand, the predominant way in which the two truths are set forth in traditions that emphasize a deconstructive analysis of reality, like the Geluk, is through the appearance/emptiness model, in which the ultimate is simply emptiness and the relative is appearance. Mipam brings both of these traditions together by showing how both models and both approaches to experience (in meditative equipoise and postmeditation) are important means of relating to the two truths in Buddhist scriptures.

Moreover, both of these models of the two truths play a key role in the way Mipam brings together the middle and last wheels of Dharma. The primary way in which the two truths are expressed in the middle wheel of Dharma (such as in the Perfection of Wisdom Sutras) is through the appearance/emptiness model, in which emptiness is the ultimate truth and any appearance is necessarily the relative truth. In contrast, the primary way in which the two truths are expressed in the last wheel of Dharma (in the Mind-Only and Buddha-Nature Sutras) is through the authentic/in-

MIPAM'S TWO TRUTHS AND THREE WHEELS OF DHARMA

Buddhist Sutra	Vehicle	Distinctive Teaching		Meaning	Primary Two-Truth Model
First Wheel of Dharma	Lesser Vehicle	four noble truths (suffering, impermanence, no-self)		provisional meaning	imputation/ substance
Middle Wheel of Dharma	Great Vehicle	emptiness (absence of true existence)		provisional meaning	appearance/ emptiness
		emptiness (non-conceptual unity)		definitive meaning	
Last Wheel of Dharma	Great Vehicle	Buddha-nature	pure nature of mind		authentic/ inauthentic experience
		Mind-Only		provisional meaning	

Mipam shows how an internal provisional/definitive distinction can be made within each middle and last wheel of Dharma.

authentic experience model, in which nondual experience is the ultimate truth and dualistic experience is the relative truth. Unity's empty aspect is the primary subject matter of the middle wheel of Dharma, while its aspect of appearance, or clarity, is the primary subject matter of the last wheel of Dharma.

While the middle wheel is the definitive meaning according to the Geluk tradition, the Jonang tradition emphasizes the last wheel as the definitive meaning. In general, the definitive meaning (Tib. *nges don,* Skt. *nītārtha*) represents the ultimate truth, distinct from the provisional meaning (Tib. *drang don,* Skt. *neyārtha*), which is only considered to be true provisionally or as an expedient means to reach an understanding of the ultimate truth. In contrast to the Geluk and Jonang traditions, Mipam emphasizes the way that *both* the middle wheel and the Buddha-Nature Sutras of the last wheel of Dharma are the definitive meaning. Such a synthesis is an important part of understanding his tradition (see translations 3 and 13).

Synthesis

We can see how the ultimate truth, as an experiential presence, might easily be misunderstood in Mipam's two-truth model of authentic/inauthentic experience: saying that nonconceptual awareness is ultimate could lead to fixation on that awareness as an inherently existent reality, conceptually construed to be real. In this way, awareness would not be seen as it is—empty. Without acknowledging emptiness, the mere *idea* of the ultimate truth as a pure experience of nonduality can easily be confused for the *actual* ultimate truth. Also, attachment—which includes fixation on an experience of nonduality—is a major factor that obstructs realization. Thus, experientially, such fixation can be particularly dangerous for the Yogic Practice School, which attributes the experience of nondual wisdom to the ultimate, because fixation on this wisdom confines it to the relative.

We can see this type of danger in the example of meditation. Based on achieving a certain degree of success in sustained attention through calm abiding (*śamatha*) meditation, for instance, as is said in the training manuals, we can expect that experiences of bliss, clarity, and nonthought will occur. When we hold on to these experiences, however, this not only prevents them from occurring but hinders us from deepening our meditation practice. Holding on to authentic experience as something truly real can function in the same way, effectively hindering the experiential insight of the ultimate truth.

Additionally, as is the case with the thought of nonthought, it is easy to fixate on an idea of nonduality, thinking "nonconceptual wisdom" and mistaking this idea for the real thing. If we are not careful, the habits of attributing reality to misguided notions easily transfer into a habit of attributing reality to a misguided notion of authentic experience. Holding fast to the idea of an ultimate nonduality does not allow its authentic meaning to unfold; rather, it prevents any genuine insight into the ultimate truth from happening at all. For these reasons, emptiness (the ultimate in the former two-truth model of appearance/emptiness) is also an integral part of Mipam's representation of the two truths in the Middle Way.

Emptiness—as a lack of true existence—is an important corrective for the tendency to fixate on the ultimate truth as a real presence when approaching meditative experience. However, emptiness alone, as an absence of true existence, can also become objectified into a mistaken idea about the nature of reality. Thus, the experiential dimension of the ultimate—authentic experience—also serves to correct the tendency to hold on to emptiness in the two-truth model of appearance/emptiness. In this way, the presence of the experiential ultimate serves to prevent the ultimate truth from remaining a stale, abstract concept of emptiness. As Mipam consistently emphasizes, emptiness as a lack of true existence (in the two truths as appearance/emptiness) is only part of the story of the ultimate truth. Emptiness and appearance are known as a unity in authentic experience, so relating to the ultimate in both models is important for a comprehensive understanding. In fact, a full understanding of emptiness—distinct from a partial one that does not include the empty essence of wisdom—distinguishes the authentic view of Middle Way from the inferior view of Mind-Only, as we will see. In this way, we can observe how both models of the two truths—emptiness/appearance and authentic/inauthentic experience—have a significant role to play in Mipam's presentation of the Middle Way. In an important way, neither model is complete on its own; rather, each model entails the other.

Through these two models, Mipam brings together two polarities of Buddhist thought: (1) a scholarly approach that emphasizes conceptual analysis and (2) a meditative approach that emphasizes nonconceptual experience. While analysis into the true nature of phenomena results in seeing the empty nature of things, a meditative approach facilitates bringing insight into experience. Indeed, seeing the empty nature of things is authentic experience, and both approaches, which accord with meditative equipoise and postmeditation, have an important place in different contexts. Moreover, failing to cultivate one of these approaches—that is, neglecting either critical analysis or meditative practice—can easily lead to a misunderstanding of the nature of reality. This is why an integrated approach can be a reliable way to proceed. Without meditation, theory easily becomes dry words, and emptiness can be misunderstood as a dead, intellectual idea of "no-thing." Without analysis, undirected meditation can easily lead to a simplistic misunderstanding of emptiness as some sort of "thing." Both approaches, taken on their own, have a tendency to stray from the middle path into the extremes of nihilism (in analysis directed at emptiness) or essentialism (in meditation directed toward the experiential presence of mind). For these reasons, it is important to integrate theory and practice, and Mipam does an excellent job of conveying this integration in his works.

These two approaches to truth can also be understood as (1) the way of study and contemplation and (2) the way of quintessential instructions. The way of study and contemplation involves a thorough process of analysis; it is referred to as the analytical meditation of scholars (*paṇḍita*) in contrast to the resting meditation of hermits (*kusāli*). Analytical meditation is a progressive approach to realization, unlike the sudden or instantaneous approach of hermits. An important part of Mipam's work was bridging these two approaches and bringing the meditative insight of the Great Perfection into conversation with analytical traditions of monastic scholarship.

According to Mipam, both of these paths wind up at the same place in the end, the stage of a buddha. One style may be better than another at a certain time; that is, one approach may be more effective to evoke or represent truth for a certain person in a particular context. Nevertheless, both have a legitimate place in the path to becoming a buddha, so taking either approach in a genuine way does not need to involve contempt for the other (although a healthy degree of polemical exchange can serve to refine understanding and safeguard against sidetracks). Indeed, the lively debate between "scholars" and "meditators" can remind us of the potential shortcomings of each path.

We can see that unity is a predominant theme throughout Mipam's works. It is particularly important in his presentation of the two truths. He consistently emphasizes that there is no emptiness apart from appearance and no appearance apart from emptiness; they necessarily occur together. For Mipam, to be only empty without appearing is merely a negation, a conceptual abstraction; in reality, it is a sheer impossibility to have an instance of emptiness without appearance. Alternatively, to only appear without being empty would mean that the appearance truly exists. Yet this too is simply a conceptual construction, impossible in reality, because everything that appears is empty. In other words, if there is emptiness without appearance, it is simply an idea of absence, an idea divorced from reality. If there is an appearance apart from emptiness, it is simply a thought of something truly established, and nothing in reality is truly established either. In this way, one-sided conceptions of emptiness and appearance are mistaken, and when reality is experienced authentically, emptiness and appearance are an indivisible unity (see translations 6 and 7).

FOURFOLD VALID COGNITION

Another central feature of Mipam's systematic interpretation is a unique, fourfold valid cognition: two that are conventional and two that are ultimate. In general, ultimate valid cognition is the means through which we know the ultimate truth; conventional valid cognition is the means through which we know everything else, that is, the appearances of phenomena. Put another way, ultimate valid cognition investigates the way things are, and conventional valid cognition investigates the way things appear.

The two conventional valid cognitions are those of (1) confined perception and (2) pure vision.[83] Confined perception is the way ordinary experience operates; it is based within a distorted perspective of the world. Nevertheless, it is a perspective that humans share as ordinary beings in samsara, and thus, there is a level of validity to it for as long as this distortion is in place. Confined perception can be valid, such as seeing a rope as a rope and not as a snake; however, it is not valid in relation to pure vision. Confined perception concerns fundamentally distorted modes of being in the world, whereas pure vision is an extraordinary mode of wisdom's experience. Simply put, confined perception is distorted, while pure vision is perception free of distortion.

Mipam's twofold division of conventional valid cognition into confined perception and pure vision plays a major role in his arguments for establishing appearances as divine, which is a central feature of his view of tantra. We can see how his two-tiered conventional valid cognition serves to affirm the validity of a view of divine appearance while not completely undermining the validity of reality from the perspective of ordinary beings. An important part of this twofold distinction is the difference between the way reality appears from a confused perspective and the way that reality appears to a sublime being's vision. Mipam argues that it is extremely closed-minded to think that only ordinary confined perception is the final word on conventional reality.[84] If the experiences of ordinary people were in fact reality, then one would have to accept that sublime beings were delusional.[85] Here we can see how Mipam's arguments use reason within a framework of the authority of tradition, a tradition embodied in the visionary experience of sublime beings. He uses reason not to show the emptiness of reality, as he so often does, but to affirm reality as a pure, divine expression.

We can see that pure vision is a mode of wisdom's experience, and confined perception is the experience of a distorted mind. The former pertains to a heightened awareness of the divine nature of appearance, where appearances are perceived as deities, sounds as mantras, and thoughts as wisdom. Confined perception, on the other hand, pertains to knowledge of the ordinary world, where, for instance, functional particulars are held to be real in contrast to conceptual imputations. Through these two conventional valid cognitions, Mipam is able to maintain that what is the correct relative truth in the context of sutra (that is, the content of confined perception) is the incorrect relative truth in tantra (where the correct relative is the content of pure vision) and thereby support the Nyingma claim that tantra has a higher view. It is important to keep in mind that these two means of knowledge pertain to knowledge of the way things *appear* and thus are conventional valid cognitions, as opposed to the ultimate valid cognitions that pertain to knowledge of the way things *are,* which are ultimate.

Mipam makes a twofold distinction between ultimate valid cognition as well. His two ultimate valid cognitions are those of (1) the categorized ultimate (*rnam grangs pa'i don dam*) and (2) the uncategorized ultimate (*rnam grangs ma yin pa'i don dam*). The categorized ultimate is the conceptual ultimate, emptiness that is a negation, which is known by mind. It is an absence, the lack of any true existence or real essence in any phenomena. In contrast, the uncategorized ultimate is beyond the mind; it is the inconceivable domain of nonconceptual wisdom and cannot be formulated as an affirmation or a negation.[86] The distinction between these two ultimates is a central feature of his interpretation of the Middle Way to which we will return.

We can see how both subdivisions within the two valid cognitions, conventional and ultimate, are based on the fundamental distinction between conceptual mind and nonconceptual wisdom. Inauthentic experience involves the distorted mind—confined perception and the categorized, or conceptual, ultimate. Authentic experience, on the other hand, is wisdom—pure vision and the uncategorized, or nonconceptual, ultimate. Similar to the way his two-truth models function to incorporate conflicting discourses on the nature of the relative and ultimate truths, we can see how his two-tiered presentation of each of the two valid cognitions serves to incorporate competing systems of thought (such as those of Candrakīrti, Dharmakīrti, and tantra) by situating them in a particular context within a single, integrated interpretation. In the next chapter, we will see how he uses different contexts and perspectives to bring together the Yogic Practice School and the Middle Way (see translation 18).

MIPAM'S FOURFOLD VALID COGNITION

Valid Cogni- tion	Type	Domain of Observa- tion	Two-Truth Model	Primary Associations
Conven- tional	confined perception	way things appear	authentic/ inauthentic experience	Sutra (Dharmakīrti)
	pure vision			Tantra (*Secret Essence Tantra*)
Ultimate	uncatego- rized	way things are	appearance/ emptiness	Consequence School (Candrakīrti)
	categorized			Autonomy School

The dotted line represents that while there is a provisional distinction between appearance and emptiness, they are actually a unity.

SIX

Mind-Only and the Middle Way

A DISTINCTIVE FEATURE of Mipam's work is his keen ability to show the compatibility of different systems of thought and diverse representations of truth.

PERSPECTIVES ON TRUTH

An important aspect of Mipam's approach to philosophical systems in general, which he seems to draw from Dharmakīrti, is a perspectival system that has been called "an ascending scale of analysis."[87] With such an approach, different conflicting statements may be taken as true in one context, yet false from another perspective. In other words, statements from a particular perspective can be said to be *provisionally* true within their own particular world of discourse, yet they are superseded by statements from a higher perspective. For instance, in his famous work of the Yogic Practice School, *Commentary on Valid Cognition,* Dharmakīrti often speaks of external objects as if they existed, although he denies their existence in other places in the same text.[88] In doing so, he creates a dichotomy between what is real (external particulars) and unreal (mentally constructed universals) on one level of analysis, yet on another level, he claims that both are equally unreal. This fact has led to a lot of confusion and debate with regard to Dharmakīrti's own position. However, in terms of levels of analysis, as Mipam interprets him, his system becomes quite cogent.

Mipam presents Mind-Only as the highest conventional presentation.[89] That is, he claims that if we engage in a thorough investigation of the way things appear, we wind up with a Mind-Only position. In a note-worthy statement conveying an ascending scale of analysis, he says that what is "renowned in the world" (the prereflexive, unexamined world of common sense) is the outcome of no analysis; slight analysis corresponds with the Sutra School (*Sautrāntika*); and the product of thorough analysis accords with Mind-Only.[90] In the first case, conventional reality is not examined, and what is renowned or accepted as real in the world—pots, pans, chairs—is simply held to be the way things are. We will see how this perspective is important for the Consequence School of the Middle Way, because there is no analysis of conventional reality within its defining discourse (which emphasizes the uncategorized ultimate). In the second case of slight analysis, the nature of conventional reality is analyzed to a certain extent, and one arrives at the view of the Sutra School. That is, one discovers through analysis that only functional particulars qualify as genuine objects of knowledge; conceptual imputations, which are simply constructions of thought and language, do not. Finally, when reality is analyzed more deeply, one comes to the conclusion that appearances are mind, as in the system of Mind-Only, and the notion of objects outside the mind comes to be acknowledged as a mistaken conception. It is important that Mipam depicts all three of these levels of analysis as functioning in terms of conventional, not ultimate, reality. Thus, he can incorporate a Mind-Only presentation of conventional reality (that is, the nature of appearance is mind) within a Middle Way view of the ultimate (that is, the nature of appearance is emptiness). This is key to the way he integrates the two philosophies of Mind-Only and the Middle Way into the Yogic Practice School of the Middle Way.

Another important aspect of Mipam's presentation of Mind-Only is his distinction between the conventional mode of appearance (*tha snyad snang tshul*) and the conventional mode of reality (*tha snyad gnas tshul*). That is, he states that proponents of Mind-Only do not deny that objects appear as if they were external; however, they concede no external reality in the way these objects are really experienced.[91] In other words, the denial of external reality does not mean that this book does not appear to be external to our minds; rather, it is a denial that the book actually has a reality outside the mind's experience of it. Mipam argues that if the distinction between (1) the way things appear (as external objects) and (2) the way things are (appearances are mind) is not made conventionally in the Mind-Only system, then it would absurdly follow that even a mountain would be a mind.[92] Longchenpa made a similar distinction between appearance (*snang ba*) and the appearing object (*snang yul*), stating that while appearance is mind, the appearing object is not the mind. With this distinction, he apparently sought to avoid the consequence that if objects were minds, then mountains would absurdly be able to perceive things, just like a mind.[93]

The system of Mind-Only offers a richly complex and powerful explanation of the world. The dominant role of the mind in constructing the world is a fundamental feature of the view of tantra too. Like all prominent exegetes of philosophical systems in Tibet, however, Mipam rejects the Mind-Only position and identifies himself with the Middle Way. According to Mipam, the problem with Mind-Only as a philosophical school is that it hangs on to a view that the basis of appearances—that is, the nondual, self-illuminating, and self-aware mind—is ultimately real. In the Middle Way, however, nothing is held to be ultimately real.

PERCEPTION AND REFLEXIVE AWARENESS

Before we turn to the Middle Way, we will briefly examine perception in Mind-Only. Since the philosophical school of the Middle Way develops no alternative account of perception other than "what is renowned in the world" or "simply one's own appearance" (*rang snang tsam*), we will touch on some of the key features of how perception is explained in Mind-Only. Through this, we will be able to see some distinctive features of Mipam's depiction of the relationship between Mind-Only and the Middle Way. If you are not interested in the details of Mind-Only theory, feel free to skip the next two sections and go straight to the Middle Way.

An important part of Mind-Only's account of phenomenal experience is that the process of perception takes place through images. Images (*rnam pa*), not external objects, are the content of perception. Images have a twofold quality: (1) an objective aspect (*gzung rnam*), which is what we perceive as objects, and (2) a subjective aspect (*'dzin rnam*), which is the sense of being a perceiving subject. The two sides of perception—objective and subjective—do not exist as essentially separate but are two aspects of what, in essence, is a single mental event. In this way, consciousness directly interacts with itself, not with an external world. This important feature of consciousness means that awareness by nature is reflexive. That is, an intrinsic property of awareness is that as it knows something, it is also self-aware (*rang rig*). For this reason, awareness is not hidden to itself; it knows that it knows without needing to rely on anything else for confirmation. A common example to illustrate this reflexive property is a lamp, which by nature illuminates itself at the same time as it illuminates objects. Likewise, the mind is self-aware at the same time as it knows an object.

For Mipam, reflexive awareness, even without analysis, is simply what is renowned in the world. For instance, when we see blue, we all know that we are seeing blue; we don't need to ask someone else to confirm that we are seeing blue. Additionally, Mipam gives reflexive awareness a foundational role in the analysis of the nature of conventional reality, the way things appear. He argues that, in the end, our ability to make inferences depends on direct perception, and our capacity for direct perception depends on reflexive awareness. Hence, he concludes that reflexive awareness is indispensable when asserting a presentation of valid cognition of confined perception.[94] That is, he says that reflexive awareness is fundamental, with the implication that without it, a rational account of ordinary experience would not even be possible. Nevertheless, the *ultimate* status of reflexive awareness is negated in the context of the Middle Way (just like everything else), as will be explained (see translation 10).

TRADITIONS OF MIND-ONLY

Concerning the status of mental images, there are two main traditions of Mind-Only: those who assert the images to be real and those who do not. The proponents of "real images" (*rnam bden pa*) hold appearances to be truly real, while the proponents of "false images" (*rnam brdzun pa*) hold appearances to be mere illusions.

With respect to the process of perception, Mipam conveys three different positions among the proponents of real images. One of the three approaches maintains that in perception, the subjective aspect is singular, and the objective aspect is also singular. In this way, a singular consciousness perceives a singular sense-datum. According to this school, when looking at a butterfly, for instance, although it seems that all its different colors are seen at once, each distinct color is perceived (in rapid succession) by a series of singular cognitions. A second approach, which we will call "complex perceptual symmetry," holds that there are just as many facets of subjective consciousness as there are facets to perceived objects. For instance, in the perception of a hand, if five aspects of objective content are cognized (such as five fingers), then there are said to be five subjective aspects of cognition too. Lastly, a third approach, called "perceptual nondualism," maintains that there is just one subjective aspect of cognition that perceives a myriad of objective qualities that are not different from it.[95] Here, in the case of looking at a rainbow, for instance, it is held that a singular consciousness sees all the manifold colors at once.

Mipam states that ultimately all three of these approaches are invalidated (by Middle Way reasons) and that only complex perceptual symmetry can be said to be valid conventionally.[96] Thus, the position of perceptual symmetry is the most practical for him in terms of analyzing the way things appear, because it accounts for just as many aspects of subjective cognition as the objective aspects cognized, and this gives us a more refined way to investigate the way things appear. However, he says that in terms of reflexive awareness, there is also a context for asserting that all the myriad appearances are not distinct from the mind, similar to the position taken in perceptual nondualism.[97] That view, which holds that the multiplicity of objective impressions is singular in nature, is closer to the nature of reality.

In contrast to those who view the perceptual content of images as real, the second division of Mind-Only, the proponents of false images, circumvent a rational account of perception because they do not ascribe any real status to appearances other than stating that appearances are illusions. According to their system, all perceived appearances are none other than the unreal projections of a deluded mind.[98] Mipam suggests that this system, by definition, is not really Mind-Only, because the unreal images are held to be separate from the (real) mind. In a noteworthy remark in his commentary on the *Ornament of the Middle Way,* Mipam states,

> The genuine proponents of Mind-Only are the proponents of real images. The proponents of false images are a little closer to the emptiness of reality because they do not accept the reality of external objects as even mind. Thus, the proponents of false images are a bridge to the Middle Way and are therefore higher in the sequence of philosophical systems. However, since their conventional presentation is not grounded in reason, conventionally one should assert along the lines of the proponents of real images.[99]

Thus, even though the proponents of false images are closer to the Middle Way in that they deny the reality of external objects, the position of the proponents of real images (and that of complex perceptual symmetry in particular) is better suited for an analysis of conventional reality, the way things appear.[100]

THE MIDDLE WAY

To organize the richly complex philosophical traditions of Buddhism, scholars in Tibet have delineated four main Buddhist philosophical systems from India. All four systems assert a distinction between appearance and reality in the context of an ordinary being's perception, such that the way things appear is in conflict with the way things are. However, they all make different assertions regarding how things are. The main difference between the schools is thus not the fact that the way things appear is different from the way they are; rather, the difference lies in how they assert the ultimate truth (the way things are). For instance, in the Great Exposition School, although things appear as complex wholes, in actuality, only the elements (*dharmas*)—the basic building blocks—are fundamental components of reality. Likewise, in the Sutra School, while things appear to be extended in time and space (that is, yesterday's table appears to be today's table, and there seems to be something singular occupying space that is both real and a table), in reality, there are only impermanent, inexpressible, and utterly unique particulars. In Mind-Only, while the objects of perception appear to be external, they are not separate from the mind. For the Middle Way, however, the way things appear is as dependently arising phenomena, and the way they are is empty. The Middle Way is unique in that there is no hierarchy between the two truths of appearance and emptiness; that is, the ultimate truth of emptiness is not better than the relative truth of dependently arising appearance. In fact, things are empty because they arise dependently.

TWO TRUTHS IN FOUR PHILOSOPHICAL SYSTEMS

Philosophical School	Relative Truth (Way Things Appear)	Ultimate Truth (Way Things Are)
Great Exposition School	Distorted (e.g., permanent self)	Irreducible elements (*dharmas*)
Sutra School	Distorted (e.g., real universals)	Particulars
Mind-Only	Distorted (e.g., duality)	Nondual Mind
Middle Way	Distorted (e.g., inherent existence) ---------------- Dependent arising	Emptiness

The dotted line represents a context in the Middle Way where the two truths are a hierarchy (authentic/inauthentic experience) and a context where they are not (appearance/emptiness).

It is important to understand that the mere fact that appearances are said to be the mind in Mind-Only and empty in the Middle Way does not stop phenomena from appearing as real and external to the mind for these traditions. Things appear the way they do by force of habit, and they appear that way until the strong habits of mind that distort reality have been overcome. It is an important fact, for the Middle Way tradition in particular, that phenomena do not stop appearing simply because they are empty; rather, being empty is a necessary condition for something to appear in the first place.

According to the Middle Way, the reason why emptiness is necessary for something to appear is because if something were not empty, but were instead real and independent, it would always stay the same. It would be static and frozen in time; no one would age, and there would only be one season all year round. Something autonomous would necessarily have a changeless identity that is independent in itself; it would not depend on anything else—no other cause, constituent, perceiver, or language. An independently real entity could never change, because in doing so, it would shift the character of what it supposedly is and thereby contradict its assumed identity as something truly real and independent.

Nāgārjuna made this case in the second century. One of the ways he did so was through the paradox of identity and change: he argued that if something had an identity, it would never change, because if it did, it would thereby lose that identity and become something else. So nothing with a real identity could change, because in doing so, it would lose its identity, and by definition, real identity must not change. Considering this, we might assume that change is real but not identity, in other words, that there are no real substances, only real processes. Yet without identity, change would be impossible, because any change presupposes the existence of an identity that transforms. For change to really occur, something (with an identity) must change into something else, but since there is no identity to begin with, there can be no real change.

For example, if a heap of sand were to truly exist as real, it would never change. While its change might appear to occur clearly (such as the gradual removal of sand and loss of the heap), this cannot be real change, because such change would entail a real heap losing its identity. But since the heap lacks any real identity (because no clearly defined heap is identifiable when its essence is sought), there is no real change (since no heap was ever *really* there to begin with). The identity of the heap and its apparent change necessarily happen in dependence on something else: causes, constituents, a perceiver, and language. Therefore, for anything to exist, it must rely on something else. This is the reason why emptiness, the dependent nature of things, is a necessary condition for existence. In the philosophy of the Middle Way, all things are empty because nothing can exist without depending on something else.

For Mipam, the main difference between Mind-Only and the Middle Way boils down to the fact that, in the system of Mind-Only, the nondual reflexive awareness is held to be inherently existent.[101] In the Middle Way, nothing exists inherently or independently. Mipam argues that the dispute between Mind-Only and the Middle Way does not concern whether external objects exist or not. Rather, the dispute concerns the status of consciousness—whether it is inherently existent or not.[102] He endorses the Mind-Only account of the nature of *conventional* reality (the way things appear) when appearances are analyzed and states that only the aspect of clinging to the nature of consciousness as inherently existent is to be negated within the system of Mind-Only.[103]

Thus, the main arguments against the Mind-Only School target the claim that the mind is truly real. The crux of the argument, simply stated, is that the nature of mind cannot be found under analysis, so it is empty. Middle Way reasonings negate the true existence of everything, even the mind. Likewise, according to ultimate analysis (that is, analysis into the ultimate nature of things), reflexive awareness, or self-awareness, is untenable—and according to Mipam, so is awareness of something other. Reflexive awareness is not truly real, because it is a contradiction for the mind to really be both a knower and the object known simultaneously.[104] Proponents of the Middle Way argue that a mind cannot really know itself in the same way that a knife cannot cut itself. By demonstrating that nothing exists independently or intrinsically, Middle Way arguments aim to show that the mind is empty, just like everything else.

Yogic Practice School of the Middle Way

As originally mentioned in chapter 2, the Middle Way has two main subdivisions: the Autonomy School and the Consequence School. According to Mipam, the Autonomy School divides the two truths and holds that while nothing ultimately exists, things exist conventionally. They also make a distinction between the ultimate truth that is conceptually known—the "categorized ultimate"—and the ultimate truth that cannot be conceptually known—the "uncategorized ultimate." They *emphasize* the categorized ultimate in their discourse, but like the Middle Way proponents of the Consequence School, they also *realize* the uncategorized ultimate, so in the end, there is no distinction between the views of these two Middle Way schools according to Mipam's presentation.

As is the case with Mind-Only, in the Yogic Practice School of the Middle Way, there is no world outside the sphere of cognition. For Mipam, this school maintains that the *conventional* reality of the world is mind. In terms of the relative, or conventional truth, Mind-Only and the Yogic Practice School of the Middle Way are not necessarily different; it is in the status of the ultimate truth that they part ways. Both traditions accept the ultimate truth as a presence of nonconceptual cognition, but there is an important difference. According to the Yogic Practice School of the Middle Way, in addition to wisdom being the ultimate truth (authentic experience), wisdom is also acknowledged to be empty. Proponents of Mind-Only, in contrast, hold the mind to be intrinsically real. This is the crucial point that distinguishes the Middle Way from Mind-Only.

It is important to keep in mind that, according to Mipam, the main distinction between the Middle Way and Mind-Only is that followers of Mind-Only hold on to a nondual cognition as real. Other than this, there is no significant difference between Mind-Only and the Middle Way in terms of the view, meditation, or conduct. Thus, the main dispute between the followers of Mind-Only and the Middle Way does not concern the status of an external world, whether or not a world exists apart from mind. Rather, the main issue is the status of cognition. Whereas the Mind-Only school regards the mind as truly real, in the Yogic Practice School of the Middle Way, cognition is empty, just like everything else.

We will see how the mind/wisdom distinction is a primary means by which Mipam separates the Middle Way traditions into the Autonomy and Consequence Schools. The distinction between mind and wisdom is also important for the Yogic Practice School, because (conceptual) mind and (nonconceptual) wisdom is how Mipam separates inauthentic experience from authentic experience. And it is through authentic/inauthentic experience that the two truths are distinguished in the Yogic Practice School. This tradition is often denigrated in Tibet as the philosophy of Mind-Only that is lower on the scale of philosophy than the Middle Way. However, the system of the Yogic Practice School has a central place in Mipam's systematic formulation of the Middle Way. Moreover, the Yogic Practice School plays a fundamental role in his presentation of how we experience the world (see translations 8 and 9).

CONSEQUENCE SCHOOL

The Consequence School is generally held by most Buddhist sects in Tibet to represent the highest view of the Middle Way. However, for Mipam, the view of the Consequence School is not higher than that of the Yogic Practice School of the Middle Way in the end; it simply represents a more direct approach to ultimate truth.

Mipam defines the Consequence School as "discourse that emphasizes the uncategorized ultimate free from assertions."[105] The uncategorized ultimate is the nonconceptual ultimate, in contrast to the categorized ultimate, which is a conceptual understanding of the ultimate, a concept or idea of emptiness. The distinction between the categorized (known by mind) and uncategorized ultimate (known by wisdom) is an important point in Mipam's interpretation.

A conceptual understanding of emptiness—as a lack of intrinsic existence in any phenomenon—is the categorized ultimate. It is a negation, an absence, and hence falls within the realm of ideas. The uncategorized ultimate, however, is not a negation. It can be evoked by language but is not directly expressible; it cannot be conceptualized, theorized, or schematized. The uncategorized ultimate is the genuine meaning of emptiness, whereas the categorized ultimate is just a conceptual approximation.

The language representing the uncategorized ultimate is one of radical denial. For instance, negations of reality are not delimited as negations of a phenomenon's *ultimate* status; rather, nothing—even conventional existence—withstands the distinctive mode of analysis of the Consequence School. For Mipam, what distinguishes the Consequence School from the Autonomy School is that the former overcomes the fixation that holds on to two separate truths.[106] All such divisions, between two truths as well as between the categorized and uncategorized, are thought constructs that are not given any substance in the unique discourse that defines the Consequence School, the discourse that emphasizes the uncategorized ultimate beyond thought and expression. Thus in this unique discourse, no distinctions are made between two truths nor are two types of ultimate truth distinguished. Rather, the Consequence School emphasizes the uncategorized ultimate, which is beyond concepts.

It is important to note that the Consequence School is not defined merely by the use of consequences, as the etymology of its name suggests. Rather, what is significant is the *reason* its proponents use consequences as opposed to reformulating arguments as autonomous reasons (whence the Autonomy School gets its name). The rationale for using consequences is that autonomous reasons, taken as representing one's own position, are tied up within distorted presumptions. From the perspective of the Consequence School, reality cannot even be said to be empty, because in terms of the way things really are, anything that is affirmed rests on false presumptions. Consequences expose this and evoke a view that transcends the distorted structures of thought.

For instance, consider the autonomous reason "The table is empty because it is neither singular nor plural." While this statement may help someone overcome the mistaken conception that the table is real, taking this as one's own claim presumes an objective truth—that there is something that is a table on which everyone agrees. It presumes that a table is a given, that it is somehow an intrinsic part of reality and not simply a cultural artifact, a product of conventional discourse. When analyzed in terms of its ultimate status, however, the table is just another conceptual construct. In contrast, "it follows that the table does not have parts because it is singular" is a consequence—an absurd consequence—that merely points out the fault of a view that assumes a table is really a singular entity. We might think that this consequence also presumes there is a table in the real world, just as the case with the autonomous argument. However, proponents of the Consequence School do not claim anything about a table and its parts *from their own perspective* at the time of ascertaining the nature of reality. Rather, an absurd consequence simply functions to unravel *another* party's wrong view by showing that his or her view of a singular table entails the absurd consequence that a table would thus not have parts. The underlying logic behind the consequence—that a truly singular thing must be one and not a collection of many parts—is unstated but implicit to the opponent. The significant reason why it is left unstated is that such explicit assertions, namely, autonomous arguments taken as representing one's own position, involve a subtle degree of realism that is rejected by the radical language of the Consequence School. In other words, this school exposes the grounding of our unwarranted presumptions when we make an objective claim about the nature of reality or appeal to an ultimate point of view.

Since the nature of reality is empty, any expression of this inexpressible reality is bound to be mistaken. What is significant here is that the Consequence School shows this with words, not silence. It is quite remarkable. The distinctive feature of the Consequence School is thus not based simply on a linguistic form. Rather, inspired by a nonconceptual view, it is a way of using language to point beyond concepts. Mipam likens the method of the Consequence School to the manner of ascertaining the empty nature of reality in the Great Perfection.[107] It thus represents a direct, sudden path to the empty nature of reality. Evoking the nonconceptual by enacting it (rather than theorizing it), the Consequence School unravels a subtle misconception of reality and thus serves as a launching pad for the authentic experience of meditative equipoise (see translations 11 and 12).

Yogic Practice School versus Consequence School

Mipam argued strongly for the compatibility of the Yogic Practice School and the Middle Way by saying that if the way things appear is analyzed well, the system of the Yogic Practice School is not only necessary, but it is the best presentation. Unlike the Consequence School, the Yogic Practice School has a particular set of tools in place to analyze how things appear. Thus, it not only provides us with a means to investigate the way the world appears, but it allows us to improve the way we interpret it along those lines. In this light, the Consequence School can be seen as actually "worse" than the Yogic Practice School in terms of setting forth a means to investigate conventional reality.

For Mipam, the Consequence School is not characterized by a particular way of representing conventional reality, the way things appear; rather, its defining feature is its way of presenting the way things are. The Consequence School can be said to be "better" than the Yogic Practice School in the sense that it gives up on conceptual enterprises that are doomed from the start. In the end, it is better for approaching the ultimate but not necessarily the conventional truth.

According to Mipam, the direct path to nonconceptuality in the Consequence School is similar to the way of approaching the empty aspect of reality in the Great Perfection.[108] Since the Consequence School winds up with a similar approach to emptiness as the Great Perfection, we can say that it is better in the sense that it reflects the highest view for Mipam in terms of the empty aspect of reality. However, we need not claim that it is better at theorizing the experiential dimension of clarity (that is, appearance and awareness), which is the strength of the Yogic Practice School.

According to Mipam, the culminating insight of the Consequence School is perfectly compatible with the Yogic Practice School's insight that appearances are mind. While the Consequence School denies any formulation of the ultimate truth of authentic experience, the Yogic Practice School (and the traditions of other-emptiness) represent the content of authentic experience in affirming language. The philosophy of the Consequence School is thus primarily concerned with clearing away false views instead of formulating the experience of wisdom. That is, the Consequence School is primarily involved in deconstructing conceptual constructions, whereas the Yogic Practice School systematically constructs the way we experience the world conceptually in postmeditation and nonconceptually in meditative equipoise. In this way, rather than theorizing the authentic experience of meditative equipoise in *post*meditation (as in the Yogic Practice School), the Consequence School can be seen as evoking authentic experience in *pre*meditation as a springboard to the nonconceptual.

To work with the approach of the Consequence School, one need not (and perhaps never has to) give up analysis right from the start. Rather, the realization of the Consequence School is the result of an analytical process that no longer needs to engage in analysis, even though analysis was necessary on the way. In any case, the compatibility of (1) the systematic, conventional analysis of the way things appear in the Yogic Practice School and (2) the ultimate analysis of the way things are in the Consequence School is a central part of Mipam's presentation of the Middle Way.

Before moving on from this discussion, there is a legend that recounts a debate worth mentioning, as it concerns the relationship between the Yogic Practice School and the Consequence School. In the legend, Candrakīrti took the position of the Middle Way, "the proponents of naturelessness," based on Nāgārjuna, and his opponent took a position of the Yogic Practice School based on Asaṅga. The debate (which reportedly lasted seven years) drew large crowds of people, who came to sing a song about the exchange. The words of the song are particularly poignant:

Alas! Nāgārjuna's scriptures are medicine for some but poison for others.
The texts of Maitreya and Asaṅga are, for all beings, simply nectar![109]

An important message can be drawn from these lyrics. It points to the fact that it is easy to misunderstand the meaning of emptiness in the Middle Way, and when it is misunderstood, the ultimate truth of emptiness tends to become a nihilistic position (poison). The Yogic Practice School, on the other hand, does not share the danger of being misunderstood as nihilism. Rather, it tends to be misunderstood as an extreme of essentialism, a view that the mind is truly real. In this, we may find a clue to why the Yogic Practice School is acclaimed to be "nectar" for all. Even if it is misunderstood, the extreme of essentialism is better than the nihilistic extreme, because an essentialist view (even a non-Buddhist belief in an eternal creator God) preserves an ethical grounding and thereby tends toward virtuous practices. A view of nihilism, however, looses any ethical ground of virtue and thus tends to bring suffering as a result of selfishly motivated, negative actions. Therefore, in a Buddhist perspective, even if the Yogic Practice School's view is misunderstood as an essentialist view (incompatible with emptiness and thus not conducive to liberation), it still leads to happiness (that is temporary).

In any case, we can see how Mipam's interpretation brings together Asaṅga and Nāgārjuna by showing the compatibility of the Yogic Practice School and the Middle Way. Also, by showing the compatibility of the Yogic Practice School of the Middle Way and the Consequence School, he also brings together Dharmakīrti and Candrakīrti. Unity is a central theme throughout his works, and integrating diverse strands of Buddhist thought into a grand synthesis is a distinctive feature of his Nyingma interpretation.

TURNING ON THE GELUK

In shaping what would come to be the orthodox Geluk position, Tsongkhapa created a rift between the views of the Consequence School and the Yogic Practice School through the way he characterized the unique assertions of the Consequence School. He explicitly stated that this school asserts external objects and argued against the existence, even conventionally, of the fundamental claims of the Yogic Practice School: reflexive awareness and the universal ground (Tib. *kun gzhi,* Skt. *ālaya*).[110]

The universal ground consciousness is an important means by which the Yogic Practice School accounts for the continuity of karma and conscious experience without asserting a self. The status of this consciousness and its relationship (if any) to the view of the Middle Way have been topics of dispute in India and Tibet. By completely rejecting fundamental elements of the Yogic Practice School, Tsongkhapa forcefully argued that the Consequence School has a radically different view from the Autonomy School. Mipam, however, emphasized the compatibility of the two schools by making a case that the distinction between them is only a contextual one. Unlike Tsongkhapa, Mipam argued that the Consequence School does not necessarily reject the conventional existence of reflexive awareness and the universal ground consciousness, nor does it necessarily accept them.[111]

Unlike Mipam, who characterized the Consequence School with reference to the (uncategorized) ultimate truth, Tsongkhapa defined this school primarily with reference to the conventional truth. Tsongkhapa argued that to accept phenomena as if they were established by their own characters, even conventionally, is incompatible with the view of the Consequence School. Given that Mipam did not have a problem with claims to conventional validity and reflexive awareness (in terms of the way things appear), according to this Geluk portrayal, he can be seen as a proponent of the Autonomy School.

Had Mipam only supported the position of the Autonomy School, rather than arguing in support of the Consequence School as well, it is likely that he would have been dismissed as a proponent of what was popularly considered to be an inferior view. He also supported an other-emptiness view, but did not identify it as his own as others in the Nyingma tradition did. Rather, he argued for a unique Middle Way view. In doing so, he turned the standard Geluk interpretation on its head by positioning central features of Tsongkhapa's interpretation into what he classified as an Autonomy School interpretation and even a position of other-emptiness, which were both classic targets of Geluk polemics.

Mipam's characterization of the Middle Way, and its compatibility with the Yogic Practice School in particular, can be seen as a direct challenge to the Geluk interpretation of the Middle Way. For instance, he argued throughout his works against the Geluk tradition's representation of the ultimate truth as solely an absence of true existence. In contrast to the mere notion of absence, Mipam presented the genuine ultimate truth as nonconceptual. While provisionally useful, he repeatedly emphasized that the ultimate truth understood as a mere absence is a product of conceptual analysis and is thus still tied to a distorted conceptual structure. In the end, nonexistence is not the ultimate truth; it is simply the conceptual counterpart of the mistaken notion of existence. For Mipam, the conceptual ultimate, which is the emphasis of the Autonomy School, must give way to the nonconceptual ultimate as highlighted in the discourse of the Consequence School.

He directly countered other characteristically Geluk positions as well. For instance, in the Geluk tradition, negations of phenomena are qualified such that their *ultimate* existence is negated, but their *conventional* existence is not. Mipam claimed that to divide the two truths in this way, and thereby emphasize the categorized ultimate, is a characteristic of the Autonomy School, not the Consequence School.[112] He also pinned other-emptiness on a Geluk view by portraying the stereotypically Geluk claim that "phenomena are not empty of themselves but are empty of inherent existence" as a statement of other-emptiness. He argued that leaving phenomena as they are, while negating something else that is other (that is, inherent existence) is an other-emptiness view.[113] By arguing that the Geluk's own tradition asserts the views of the Autonomy School and other-emptiness—the very positions its followers so often vehemently put down—he turned their tradition on itself.

SEVEN

Emptiness and the Nonconceptual

EMPTINESS IS A CENTRAL topic in Mipam's works. His writings at once clarify emptiness and at the same time retain its nonconceptual (indeterminate) meaning as eluding the mind.

ANALYSIS AND EXPERIENTIAL INSIGHT

When we speak of emptiness as a lack of something, one way we can identify what is being negated is to say that it is *inherent existence*. Another way to identify an object of negation is to say that what is negated in relation to emptiness is *duality* (that is, the distorted framework of experience). In the first case, what is negated is an object, like an inherently existing table (a table that is held to be truly real), and the negation takes place between a subject and an object. That is, an object is falsely construed by a subject, and this falsely construed object is negated. Reason takes an object of analysis and, in doing so, presumes a subject-object structure through which analysis necessarily takes place. This is an important step in the direct realization of emptiness, but it is a step that must eventually be overcome.

In the second case of negating duality, there is technically no "object" of negation in the disclosure of ultimate truth, because such an object of analysis presumes a subject-object structure and a phenomenal "object" abstracted from the lived world of experience. Since an analysis of objects presumes a dichotomous structure, this structure must eventually be expunged by another means. This can be done, according to Mipam, in unscripted meditative practice. This latter approach seeks to suspend distorted presumptions to access the fundamental structure of experience, which in Mipam's case is the unity of appearance and emptiness.

For the Yogic Practice School, negating inherent existence can be seen as going too far, particularly if the facticity of authentic experience is negated by a reductive, "object-ifying" analysis. However, for a Middle Way approach, negating duality has not necessarily gone far enough. In the Middle Way, one must negate inherent existence globally, so even an appeal to a nondual experience is subject to its uncompromising critique. The dialectical interplay between these two modes of inquiry steers the middle path for Mipam.

For him, in addition to the mistaken apprehension of inherent existence, duality must also go. His Nyingma tradition does not approach nonduality in the same way as the Geluk tradition does. One reason for this is that Tsongkhapa stresses that the emptiness known through conceptual analysis is the same as the emptiness known by nonconceptual wisdom. Mipam, however, emphasizes that the emptiness known conceptually—as the absence of true existence—is fundamentally different from the nonconceptual experience of emptiness. While meditation on a semblance of the genuine meaning of emptiness can form a bridge between the conceptual and the nonconceptual for Mipam and Tsongkhapa,[114] for Mipam, the cause (the concept of unity) must resemble the effect (genuine unity) and not simply be the conceptual apprehension of a mere absence.

In Mipam's presentation, we can see that inherent existence is clearly an object to be negated by reasoning; when this false conception of inherent existence is negated, we arrive at the ultimate truth in the appearance/emptiness model of two truths. Duality, however, cannot be negated by reason alone; it involves a restructuring, or *de*structuring, of the way the world is experienced. While both the lack of inherent existence and duality are known through a process of study, reflection, and meditation, the lack of inherent existence is derived from analytical meditation (*dpyad sgom*), whereas the lack of duality is rooted in a distinctive form of resting meditation (*'jog sgom*). Analytical meditation involves object-oriented reasoning and analysis. In contrast, resting meditation is a contemplative practice that carries out focused attention on an object or sustained awareness without an object. While meditating on an object (like an image, a sound, or the sensation of one's breath) can lead to peaceful states and stablity of attention, sustaining the open presence of objectless awareness (as in the practice of the Great Perfection) is necessary to overcome duality. Thus, we can see how the complete eradication of the distortions of apprehending inherent existence and duality occurs primarily in distinctive contexts—one in analytical meditation and the other in (postanalytical) resting meditation. These two are distinct yet complementary, because analysis evokes a uniquely meditative insight.

In the beginning, the negation of inherent existence leaves us with an absence—an absence that counteracts the false apprehension of an inherently existing phenomenon like the self. To become a genuine understanding of emptiness, the conception of this absence must eventually give way to the insight of emptiness beyond any notion of absence. In contrast to the process of negating inherent existence, the process of overcoming duality calls for a participatory orientation with and in the lifeworld, a radical shift from ordinary modes of relating to the world. Thus, the way the emptiness (of inherent existence) is known analytically is different from the way the emptiness (of duality) is known experientially. The emptiness of duality is not structured by language and thought the way the absence of inherent existence is. Significantly, to understand the lack of duality calls for a uniquely participatory approach to the nature of reality, a way of being in which duality no longer structures experience and there is no division of two separate truths.

For Mipam, in the negation of duality, we discover an authentic mode of being in which we have always participated and of which we have always been a part. In contrast, realizing the absence of inherent existence involves overcoming an inauthentic mode of being by uncovering distortion. These two ways of being—seeing what is (nondual) and seeing what is not (inherent existence)—reflect two approaches to the ultimate truth in the authentic/inauthentic and appearance/emptiness models of the two truths. These two models, represented in the Yogic Practice School and the Middle Way respectively, are revealed in the contemplative practices inspired by these two traditions.

It is important to understand the difference between the contexts of (1) postmeditation, when two truths are divided, and (2) meditative equipoise, when there is no division. Even though the experience of the ultimate truth is a product of analysis (as authentic experience proceeds from analysis), that experience itself can no longer be adequately framed within the structures of analysis. When the framework for conceptual analysis has dissolved in meditative equipoise (that is, when a dualistic structure of subject and object and the distinction between two separate truths is no longer a working assumption), conceptual analysis is no longer relevant or necessary. Analysis is not even desired in the context of an experiential encounter with authentic experience, because at that time, analysis—a by-product of a distorting conceptual structure—only gets in the way. Yet conceptual analysis need not necessarily conflict with experiential insight, because conceptual analysis in *pre*meditation can induce meditative experience by breaking down conceptual frameworks. Moreover, conceptual analysis in *post*meditation can play an important role too. By representing meditative experience in a systematic (conceptually framed) structure, it permits a distinction to be made between authentic experience and inauthentic modes of being.

In any case, an essential point here is that to fully understand emptiness, or the nature of reality, analysis is not enough for Mipam. To overcome our deeply ingrained habits of conceptual fixation, we must drop conceptual fixation altogether. Of course, this is easier said than done. Old habits are hard to break, and it is not as if we can simply switch off our conceptual minds as we turn off our computers. It requires a more delicate touch than just thinking, "Don't think!" (After all, it is not hard to see that trying not to think only makes things worse; in the same way that confining your daughter to her room only provokes her wish to go elsewhere, trying to forcibly stop thoughts only makes them more active.) So what can we do? At times, analysis can help, of course, and is necessary in the beginning, but conceptual analysis alone can never completely release the grip of conceptual mind. This is a point Mipam stresses consistently. The simple solution, so it appears, is to do nothing—literally. Not doing anything (and this is the hard part) *without* following old habits. In fact, this advice is often given in the context of the meditative practice of the Great Perfection, a theme that comes up throughout Mipam's works.

STEPS TO THE NONCONCEPTUAL

The Great Perfection offers immediate access to recognizing the nature of reality. Except for the exceptionally gifted few, however, most of us lack the good fortune for instantaneous realization and need to rely on a gradual path of study and contemplation. Mipam describes such a progressive approach to the view of the Middle Way in four stages, which have been said to correspond to the famous four lines of the *Heart Sutra:* "Form is emptiness. Emptiness is form. There is no form other than emptiness. There is also no emptiness other than form."[115] Mipam labels the four stages as follows: *empty, unity, freedom from constructs,* and *equality*. We will briefly consider this process.

Mipam describes the first stage, *empty,* as the time in the beginning of analysis, when we come to see that all things lack true existence and that nothing can be found under analysis. This stage involves reasoning into the nature of things, analyzing their mode of existence to see if it is a singular or multiple entity, and so forth. During this stage, emptiness and appearance are known in alternation: phenomena are empty when analyzed and appear when not analyzed.[116]

After understanding that phenomena are empty, we can then move to the next stage, called *unity*. Even while things are found to be empty, or rather, even though nothing is found under analysis, things do not cease to appear. Here, we come to understand that emptiness and appearance are not in conflict, because dependent arising is the meaning of emptiness. Phenomena are empty simply because they do not exist independently. At this stage, we come to understand that being empty does not stop phenomena from appearing; rather, we recognize that being empty is the necessary condition for appearance. So this stage points further to the genuine unity of appearance and emptiness.

In the next stage, *freedom from constructs,* we come to understand that things being empty and things appearing do not have a different meaning. Other than different modes of expression, or different ways of conceiving reality, we now see that there is actually no difference between appearance and emptiness. In this phase, we recognize that an object "being empty"—as a property separate from that appearing object—is only a linguistic or conceptual distinction: there is no such distinction in reality.[117]

We can appreciate what Mipam is getting at here when we consider that the emptiness of an appearance is like the blueness of a blue sky, it is a quality that is only separable by abstraction. We do not find a separate blueness when we look at the sky. Similarly, empty appearance and appearing emptiness are just two ways of saying the same thing. They are not different in reality. We cannot even say that they are the same, because sameness implies two things being the same; so in reality, they are not (even) one!

The final stage in the fourfold process is *equality*. At this stage, all duality dissolves through our becoming accustomed to the freedom from constructs. We come to understand the meaning of equality beyond constructs by familiarizing ourselves with this truth again and again. Through cultivating this awareness without conceptual fabrication, we directly perceive equality where there is no distinction between buddhas and sentient beings, and we come to integrate this insight within experience.

These four stages—empty, unity, freedom from constructs, and equality—counteract respectively the four extremes (the "tetralemma") of existence, nonexistence, both, and neither. The first stage, empty, negates the first extreme of existence. This is the most dominant extreme, because we are habituated to conceive things (our self, our things, the world) as truly real. By seeing these as empty, we come to recognize that they do not really exist the way we conceive them to be.

The second stage, unity, counteracts the second extreme of nonexistence. After negating the extreme of existence, if we hold on to that absence—a mere lack of true existence—we are still in the grips of conceptual constructs, because this absence is wholly dependent on its binary counterpart of true existence. If existence were truly something to be negated, its negation as nonexistent would be real too. However, since nothing has ever been truly existent, nonexistence cannot be real either. This is the reason why even the negation of existence cannot be affirmed. As is the case with the death of a man who was never born, without existence, nonexistence cannot be real either.

The third stage, freedom from constructs, counteracts the third and supposedly more subtle extreme of both existence and nonexistence. We might think that since reality is neither truly existent nor truly nonexistent, then perhaps it is both. However, to both truly exist and truly not exist is a contradiction. Being and nonbeing, real and unreal, are mutually exclusive; we can only speak meaningfully of one or the other. Of course, we could say that things ultimately do not exist, while conventionally they do, but this is introducing a dichotomy of two truths. Here, we are talking about one truth, how things really are, as the ultimate or true nature of things. In the way things are, nothing is both existent and nonexistent.

The fourth and last stage, equality, counteracts what is said to be the most subtle of the four extremes, that of neither existence nor nonexistence. Since things do not really *both* exist and not exist, we might think they *neither* exist nor not exist. However, this is still bound up within the premises of our conceptual categories. This stage takes us a step further, in a similar way as the move from the first stage to the second (because things do not really exist does not mean they must really be nonexistent either): just because things do not *both* exist and not exist does not mean that they must necessarily *neither* exist nor not exist. This may sound like a contradiction, but it need not be so. The dichotomy of existence and nonexistence, the law of noncontradiction, and the excluded middle are products of thought. They form the framework of our conceptual constructions. Yet even if consistent thought and language must follow these laws, our experience doesn't need to because it is not necessarily confined to our conceptual structures. By first recognizing this experience beyond concepts and becoming accustomed to it, we come to directly experience equality. To know equality is to experience the one taste of all things, where there is no separate self or other in samsara or nirvana.

Through these four stages, Mipam charts a process through which conceptual analysis is used to transcend concepts. The stages have a certain progression, and he says we cannot skip any stage without a proper understanding of the stages that precede it.[118] Consequently, a thorough analysis is essential to this process. Even so, while careful analysis is necessary in the preliminary stages, concepts must eventually be overcome in the end. At some point, the conceptual structure needs to break down for a nonconceptual experience to take place, but the problem is: this cannot be done by concepts alone. For Mipam, the process is something like rubbing two sticks together: we need the sticks in the beginning to make the fire, but in the end, the friction from the sticks of concepts results in the nonconceptual fire of wisdom that consumes those sticks.[119]

In this way, Mipam creates a bridge from a conceptual meaning to a nonconceptual one. What comes about through this kind of conceptual analysis is a semblance (*rjes mthun*) of the meaning of the nonconceptual, an approximation that is supposed to give way to a genuine, nonconceptual realization. This semblance of the nonconceptual is the place where Mipam pivots between a determinate, analytical certainty and an unbounded dimension of experiential insight. Indeed, the role of cultivating a semblance, or an approximation, as a means to understand the genuine plays a major part in the way he depicts the process of coming to understand the view (as the unity of appearance and emptiness), as well as the way he presents meditation (as the process of taking nonconceptual wisdom as the path).[120] One could argue that his appeal to a semblance of the genuine meaning makes his analytical process less rigorous, in that it attempts the impossible (conceptualizing the nonconceptual) and thus sullies a crisp, analytical representation of emptiness. Or one might have the opposite view: that the process of conceptual analysis disrupts the beauty and simplicity of a pure, experiential insight. Yet one might also see how wedding these two approaches—the conceptual cultivation of a semblance of nonconceptuality and the direct experience of it—is an effective means to bring forth genuine insight. Indeed, this fusion is an important part of Mipam's presentation of the view and meditation, and it is a central means by which he brings together sutra and tantra and integrates analytical reason with experiential insight (see translation 4).

Two Meanings of Emptiness

An important part of Mipam's representation of the ultimate truth is a distinction he makes between two meanings of emptiness. This distinction is between (1) emptiness as a clearly determined negation, which is the lack of true existence, and (2) emptiness as nonconceptual, which is not determined in any way as an object of language or thought. We have seen this same distinction in the categorized and uncategorized ulti-mates and also in the discussion of the emptiness that is known when two truths are divided in postmeditation and the emptiness that is known in meditative experience without any divisions. The distinction can also be identified as the difference between the emptiness that is a (conceptual) negation and the emptiness that is a (nonconceptual) unity. The latter is beyond the realm of words and thought; it is not an affirmation nor even a negation. It is the nonconceptual unity that must be known experien-tially. In fact, Mipam explicitly states that it must include the element of awareness.[121]

The meaning of nonconceptual emptiness cannot be directly stated, but it can be shown. It can be approached in analysis based on a concep-tual semblance of its meaning, as we saw earlier in the stages of Middle Way analysis. Similarly, nonconceptual wisdom can be approached in meditation by the mind assuming a semblance of wisdom in unstructured meditation, in just letting be. Unlike the emptiness that is a mere absence, relating to the nonconceptual meaning of emptiness calls for a uniquely experiential, participatory approach.

Conceptually, we can get a better sense of the key distinction be-tween these two meanings of emptiness when we consider the difference between the following two statements: (1) a negative statement of "The two truths are not the same"; and (2) an affirming statement of "The two truths are different." The latter is not necessarily an implication of the for-mer because an affirmation need not be implied by a negation, although it is when we play by certain rules of language and thought. Such rules, however, are not a part of the way reality or language must be; rather, they are tied to a particular thought construction and way of relating to lan-guage.

In the case of a more mundane example, when we consider the state-ment "The cheesecake was not good," we can see that it does not neces-sarily entail that the cheesecake was bad. Maybe the cheesecake tasted neither good nor bad but was so-so, in which case, there is room for a third alternative to be affirmed. Perhaps there was no cheesecake at all, so when asked, "Was the cheesecake good?" the answer to the question could be no, but the answer does not affirm that it was bad either. When there is no cheesecake, or no self, the denial of its qualities of goodness, badness, existence, and so on is not true either. This relates to an important point concerning the distinction between two meanings of emptiness: as an absence and as a nonconceptual unity.

To understand this distinction better, it helps to be aware of two forms of negation used in Buddhist philosophy: an implicative negation (*ma yin dgag*) and a non-implicative negation (*med dgag*). An implicative negation implies something else as a connotation of its explicit negation, like in the classic example "The fat Devadatta does not eat during the day." The implication, of course, is that the fat man eats at night. In contrast, a non-implicative negation implies no such affirmation. For instance, "One should not drink poison," is a non-implicative negation. There is not the same force of implication here; nothing else need be implied in this statement other than negation. Thus, the connotative force of an implicative negation is affirmation; whereas the connotative force of a non-implicative negation is denial. The important feature of the latter is that, other than negation, nothing is assumed or implied by the negation.

Reflected in the difference between these two negations (non-implicative and implicative), we can see two main traditions to which Mipam was responding. In the Geluk tradition, emptiness, as the ultimate truth, is necessarily a non-implicative negation. That is, emptiness simply means the lack of true existence and nothing more. Also, all phenomena share this quality of lacking true existence. The lack of true existence is even a quality of emptiness itself! Hence, there is "the emptiness of emptiness," because even emptiness is not to be concretized as a real entity. In contrast, for the Jonang tradition, ultimate emptiness is represented as an implicative negation. When all relative phenomena are negated, the ultimate ground of reality remains. The ultimate ground is not negated because it is the suchness[122] of all phenomena. Thus, for the Jonang tradition, the existence of this ground of true reality is implied by the negation of all aspects of distortion.

Whereas the Geluk tradition maintains that (conventionally existent) phenomena are the bases for the quality of emptiness, Mipam does not hold that emptiness is *only* a quality of phenomena. It is a quality in the context of analyzing the way things are when two truths are distinguished, but that is not its genuine meaning, because a quality is just another conceptual construct; its genuine meaning is nonconceptual. The Jonang tradition maintains that the ultimate truth is the "other-empty" ground, or basis of all phenomena, but Mipam does not accept that the ultimate truth is somewhere else, disconnected from the relative truth, or that emptiness implies a separate empty ground. Rather, he says the ultimate truth is simply the empty nature of all phenomena, and in reality, the ultimate truth is right here and not somewhere else, because there is no real distinction between phenomena and emptiness—they are a unity.

To understand Mipam's portrayal of emptiness, it is critical to recognize the difference between a conceptually and linguistically bound negation and a negation that evokes what transcends all thought and language. Some of Mipam's commentators have described this difference by making a distinction between two types of non-implicative negation: (1) a non-implicative negation that is free from one extreme, that of existence, and (2) a non-implicative negation that is free from all extremes.[123] The latter more fully represents the meaning of emptiness, which is not solely an absence of true existence but is free from all conceptual extremes (existence, nonexistence, both, and neither). Others have shown this distinction to be between two types of freedom from constructs: (1) a freedom from constructs that is a non-implicative negation and (2) a *genuine* freedom from constructs that is beyond all constructs of negation, affirmation, and so on.[124] The latter shows the radical nature of the uncategorized ultimate, which is not even a non-implicative negation.

One of the questions Mipam asks in his *Beacon of Certainty* is "How is emptiness understood in the Nyingma tradition, as an implicative negation or a non-implicative negation?" There is much debate among Tibetan scholars on this point and even debate about where Mipam comes down on this issue. He is clear when he affirms that emptiness indicated by a negation should be understood as only a non-implicative negation.[125] It would seem, then, that the case is closed. However, a negative *statement* indicating emptiness is within the realm of language and thought. What about emptiness as it is *experienced* in meditation? Is that an implicative or a non-implicative negation? Again, we have recourse to Mipam's own words: he says that in the perspective of wisdom, the view is neither an implicative negation nor a non-implicative negation.[126]

Here we are left with a puzzle. Since the view in meditative equipoise is beyond affirmation and negation, it is also beyond both implicative and non-implicative negations and any other linguistic of conceptual formulation. Yet isn't it the case that this experience, which is beyond words, must be implied or evoked by language? If not, how could it ever be communicated? Indeed, isn't the experience of emptiness, not its conceptual semblance that is a negation, the real import of a statement about emptiness? The relationship between emptiness known experientially versus analytically, and how emptiness should best be represented, are important factors in this debate. These factors play into the debates between the Yogic Practice School and the Consequence School, and between the proponents of other-emptiness and self-emptiness in Tibet.

FREEDOM FROM EXTREMES

Buddhist traditions portray the manner in which the Middle Way is free from extremes in several different ways. The emphasis on unity in Mipam's presentation of the Middle Way notably contrasts with other Tibetan traditions. For instance, in the Geluk tradition, emptiness—and only emptiness—is the ultimate truth. Therefore, Geluk followers argue that the genuine ultimate truth is always emptiness, and appearance is always the relative truth. In their tradition, to undermine the reality of ordinary appearances, like tables and chairs, is to stray to the extreme of nihilism. Yet to say that the genuine ultimate truth is anything other than emptiness (that is, that the ultimate truth is anything other than a *lack* of true existence) is to stray to the extreme of eternalism, or essentialism. The Middle Way according to this tradition is between these two extremes. Thus, we can see how the Geluk tradition defines the Middle Way differently than Mipam does.

We can also contrast Mipam's representation of unity with the Middle Way of other-emptiness in the Jonang tradition. In this tradition, to affirm that the ordinary objects of relative truth exist in reality—such as tables and chairs that exist merely in ignorant, dualistic perspectives—is to fall into the extreme of eternalism. On the other hand, to say that the ultimate truth does not exist and is devoid of its own essence is to stray to the other extreme of nihilism. Avoiding these two extremes is the Middle Way in the Jonang tradition. Its followers claim to avoid eternalism by maintaining that relative phenomena do not exist in reality and claim to avoid nihilism by affirming that the ultimate truth really exists.

The Geluk tradition's Middle Way describes the two truths by emphasizing how they are experienced from the perspective of an ordinary sentient being. The Jonang tradition, on the other hand, describes the two truths by emphasizing how they are experienced from the perspective of a buddha. In contrast to these two influential traditions, Mipam asserts the Middle Way as unity. In unity, there is no duality, so the duality of sentient beings and buddhas has also dissolved. Even though we may know the two truths one at a time (emptiness or appearance) in ordinary perception, they are actually indivisible. The unity of appearance and emptiness is the content of authentic experience, when the duality of two truths—a separate emptiness and a separate appearance—has fallen away.

In Mipam's presentation of the Middle Way as unity, to claim that anything stands up to ultimate analysis is to fall to the extreme of eternalism. Wisdom, or even a divine mandala, cannot be found when its true nature is sought by analysis. Thus, he holds that there is no true essence in anything. According to Mipam, the position that nothing ultimately exists is the claim of self-emptiness, a claim to which he aligns himself.[127] With this claim, he avoids the extreme of eternalism. On the other hand, to deny the reality of what does exist conventionally—like saying that tables and chairs do not exist in ordinary perspectives or that wisdom and divine mandalas do not exist in the perspectives of sublime beings (Tib. 'phags pa, Skt. ārya)—is to fall to the extreme of nihilism. By asserting that these exist conventionally, he avoids this extreme.[128]

An important commentator on Mipam's works, Bötrül (1898–1959), regards Mipam's position as "self-emptiness" as opposed to the Geluk claim of "emptiness of true existence" and the Jonang claim of "other-emptiness." He makes this distinction based on different ways of identifying the object of negation, stating that both the Geluk and Jonang traditions negate something other, whereas the emptiness in Mipam's tradition, in which all phenomena are empty of themselves, is self-emptiness.[129]

Buddhist Tradition	What Emptiness Negates	What Is Empty of What	Type of Negation Used to Indicate Emptiness	Referent of "Empty"
Jonang	unreal phenomena	true reality is empty of unreal phenomena	implicative negation	substrate
Geluk	inherent existence	phenomena are empty of inherent existence	non-implicative negation	quality
Mipam's Nyingma	categorized: inherent existence	categorized: phenomena are empty of inherent existence	non-implicative negation	categorized: quality
	uncategorized: conceptual constructs	uncategorized: reality is empty of conceptual constructs		uncategorized: none/unity

Mipam's categorized ultimate is the emptiness of the Geluk tradition and his uncategorized ultimate can suggest the Jonang tradition's emptiness, yet he is unique in his integration of these traditions, and in his emphasis on unity.

As we can see, Mipam's presentation shares some features with that of the Geluk tradition, because he sets out the Middle Way between the extremes of existence and nonexistence by denying that anything ultimately exists on one hand, while not denying what exists conventionally on the other. His presentation is distinct from the Geluk's in that he asserts the conventional existence of a divine world (in his valid cognition of pure vision) and asserts an ultimate that is not simply an absence of true existence (in his uncategorized ultimate truth beyond all extremes). In Mipam's terms, the two truths in the Geluk tradition are limited merely to the narrow spectrum of ordinary consciousness: the conventional valid cognition of confined perception and the ultimate valid cognition that concerns the categorized ultimate. With his uncategorized ultimate and pure vision, Mipam opens the two truths to the perspective of wisdom.

ULTIMATE AND CONVENTIONAL TRUTH

We have seen the way Mipam portrays the Autonomy School of the Middle Way as asserting that phenomena exist conventionally but not ultimately. He states that proponents of this school hold on to the two truths as separate, and pins this position on a Geluk interpretation.

He does so in an elaborate discussion of a characteristically Geluk claim that "a pot is not empty of pot; it is empty of inherent existence." This statement illustrates how the Geluk tradition seeks to avoid overextending the object of negation; that is, its followers do not want the negation of true existence to also deny the (conventional) existence of phenomena like pots. In this tradition, the object of negation is not phenomena but, rather, true or inherent existence. In other words, a target of the deconstructive reasoning of the Middle Way is not a pot, but the *inherent existence* of a pot. As a result, Geluk followers argue that to negate the existence of a pot conventionally is to negate too much, which is an extreme view of nihilism.

Mipam agrees that, in terms of the conventional (the way things appear), to negate the existence of conventionally existent phenomena like pots is negating too much. When the two truths have been divided, to deny the existence of a conventional truth (such as a pot) because of its ultimate emptiness is to misidentify the domain of ultimate analysis, which investigates the way things are, not the way things appear. Therefore, he agrees that negating the ultimate existence of an object is not to deny its existence conventionally (that is, the fact that it undeniably appears). However, Mipam holds that two truths are only separated provisionally, and he emphasizes how in reality there is no distinction between them. That is, in reality what is empty appears, and what appears is empty. All distinctions, including the distinction between the two truths, are products of the conceptual mind, not reality. Therefore, the existence of a pot (not held within a division of two truths as a conventionally existent phenomenon) is subject to negation for Mipam. In other words, the pot itself is an object of negation by ultimate analysis and not just its inherent existence. Indeed, for Mipam, this kind of radical negation is the domain of the Consequence School's distinctive analysis that accords with nonconceptual meditative equipoise, where no distinctions between two separate truths are made and no concepts lay claim to reality.

In terms of the conventional—that is, in terms of the way things appear when the two truths are divided—we can see how Mipam's position is similar to the claim that a pot is not empty of pot.[130] Nevertheless, in his *Beacon of Certainty,* he argues that it is not appropriate to talk of "a pot not empty of pot" in terms of the conventional, because conventionally speaking, pots are for holding things like water, and there is no reason to say "pot" twice for such a purpose![131] Moreover, when emptiness comes into the conversation, with "a pot not empty of pot," the conversation conflates conventional talk with ultimate talk. Conventional analysis involves an investigation into the way things appear, not the way they ultimately are, so there is no need to talk of a pot being empty or not in conventional analysis (unless the pot is said to be empty of something like water and not itself). In this way, he argues against the way the Geluk tradition brings ultimate talk of emptiness into the domain of conventional analysis.

In terms of the meaning of emptiness as well, Mipam critiques the misleading statement "A pot is not empty of pot; it is empty of inherent existence." He does so by distinguishing the proper way to understand the negation of a pot's inherent existence from a mistaken understanding that takes the pot and its lack of inherent existence as two separate entities. He says a phenomenon's emptiness of inherent existence should be understood precisely as that phenomenon's emptiness of its own essence (such as the pot's emptiness of pot). Thus, the emptiness of a pot is none other than the pot's emptiness of itself, not the pot's emptiness of something separate like "inherent existence." His critique of the earlier statement about the status of a pot (being not empty of pot, but of inherent existence), however, is more of a critique of the *manner* in which it is stated, not necessarily the *content* of the statement when understood correctly. That is, like Tsongkhapa, for Mipam as well (when the two truths are divided), stating that a phenomenon is empty does not annul its *conventional* existence but rather negates its *ultimate* existence as truly real. Therefore, it would be perfectly appropriate for him to say, in the context of dividing the two truths in the discourse of the Autonomy School, that a pot is not empty of pot (conventionally), but it is empty of inherent (or ultimate) existence.

Moreover, Mipam shows how the same principle that does not annul the pot in terms of the conventional also applies to the ultimate in the tradition of other-emptiness. Characteristically turning the tables on a Geluk interpretation, he argues that if the ultimate truth were empty of itself, even conventionally speaking, it would be tantamount to saying that a pot is empty of itself in terms of the conventional as well. Therefore, to negate the conventional existence of the ultimate truth is an overextension of the object of negation and hence an extreme of nihilism. He argues that the ultimate truth in a tradition of other-emptiness (that is, ultimate truth not empty of itself) does not need to be negated conventionally either.[132]

According to Mipam, the proponents of other-emptiness portray the two truths as authentic/inauthentic experience.[133] Simply, the ultimate of authentic experience is "empty" of mistaken modes of being. However, he says that authentic experience is called "ultimate" from a perspective that investigates how things appear, not from one that investigates how things are.[134] Therefore, in contrast to the Jonang tradition's Middle Way of other-emptiness, Mipam's presentation of the Middle Way depicts the authentic experience of wisdom to exist conventionally and not ultimately. Thus, similar to the Geluk tradition, we can see how he claims here that to exist is to exist conventionally.

For Mipam, wisdom cannot be said to exist ultimately, because nothing ultimately exists.[135] Nothing, not even wisdom, is found when its true nature is analyzed. Therefore, the ultimate truth is only emptiness when approached analytically. However, when wisdom is approached experientially in meditative equipoise, we can say that wisdom, as the undistorted encounter with reality, exists as the ultimate truth of authentic experience. Even what appears as the conventional truth of pure vision, given that it is the content of authentic experience, can be said to be the ultimate truth. We can see how Mipam blurs the distinction between the two truths or, rather, how the distinction between two separate truths dissolves in his portrayal of authentic experience. Nevertheless, he is careful not to impute an ultimate status to anything, so even though wisdom is the ultimate truth for Mipam, nothing ultimately exists. Thus, in his presentation, wisdom can be said to be the ultimate truth when representing how the two truths (of appearance and emptiness) are not divided in the experiential presence of unity (in authentic experience) but wisdom is not ultimate when the appearance/emptiness model is analyzed in terms of two separate truths.

SELF- AND OTHER-EMPTINESS

There is a lot of debate among traditional Tibetan and academic scholars about where Mipam stands on his interpretation of ultimate truth: is he, in the end, a proponent of the Yogic Practice School or the Consequence School? Does his position entail a position of other-emptiness or self-emptiness? Does he insist on emptiness as a non-implicative negation, or does he in the end advocate emptiness as an implicative negation? As mentioned earlier, Mipam does clearly say that a statement of emptiness as a lack of true existence should be understood to be a non-implicative negation, not an implicative negation, because the latter simply involves another entity conceptualized in the mind.[136] However, how emptiness is experienced is a different story: the nonconceptual experience of emptiness need not be evoked exclusively by a negation; given that it is nonconceptual, there is no reason why it could not be evoked by an affirmation as well.

We can see that in discussing the meaning of emptiness in Mipam's work, an important distinction should be made between perspectives, or contexts, of discourse relating to emptiness and the experience of it. In the context of meditative equipoise directly experiencing emptiness, there are no concepts. Buddhists do not debate this fact. Nevertheless, when this experience is theorized in postmeditation, we come across different accounts of the experience and disagreements as to how emptiness should best be represented or evoked. In the context of theorizing authentic experience, we have the problem of how best to conceptualize the nonconceptual and express the inexpressible. This issue is at the heart of the self-emptiness versus other-emptiness debate.

Depending on how self-emptiness and other-emptiness are defined, Mipam can be called a proponent of both (or neither). We've already seen how he aligns himself as a proponent of self-emptiness by not asserting that anything ultimately exists. When we consider the way he depicts the ultimate truth of authentic experience, we could say that the *non-* in his portrayal of the nonconceptual is an implicative negation because the word *nonconceptual* implies that there must still be some sort of experience happening, otherwise that experience would be hollow and lifeless, which he denies. Alternatively, we could say that the *non-* in *nonconceptual* is better understood as a non-implicative negation, because its true meaning involves no word or thought and so is best reflected as an utter negation of thought that implies nothing. Mipam's words also suggest this. Taking one or the other of these stances based on Mipam's works, many contemporary scholars, Western Buddhists, and Tibetan academics alike disagree as to how to interpret his view.

We can see how, depending on the purpose at hand and the intended context, a case can be made for Mipam's portrayal of the nonconceptual to be represented by an implicative negation or a non-implicative negation. Yet we should also recognize that, according to him, neither implicative nor non-implicative negations represent emptiness in the perspective of wisdom beyond concepts (after all, it is inexpressible).[137] Insisting that the content of nonconceptual experience be determined undermines the possibility of that experience occurring. Nevertheless, we can also see how each of the two types of negation can play a role in overcoming a conceptual tendency toward reification: a non-implicative negation can function to overcome the tendency to pin the nonconceptual down as some sort of idea, while an implicative negation can function to overcome the tendency to hold on to it as a simple absence by inviting us to open up to its experiential presence. Even so, for Mipam, neither form of negation can adequately represent the nonconceptual unity that can only be known in one's individual experience. As soon as the nonconceptual is determined by thought and language, it will necessarily not adequately reflect that experience because of being a mere conceptualization of it.

EIGHT

Immanent Wisdom

WE HAVE SEEN how emptiness and unity are predominant themes in Mipam's works. Another major theme is buddha-nature, which is one more way he expresses unity, the genuine meaning of emptiness.

BUDDHA-NATURE

According to Mipam, the meaning of buddha-nature is the unity of emptiness and appearance. Buddha-nature also embodies the unconditioned qualities of a buddha (such as wisdom, love, and power), which according to Mipam are essentially present when one is a sentient being. He states that "buddha-nature" refers to the existence of wisdom as the innate nature of the minds of all sentient beings, because when this innate nature of mind is realized, one becomes a buddha.[138] Although one's innate qualities may not be manifest, since the qualities of a buddha are unconditioned, they necessarily cannot arise anew or they would be impermanent and conditioned. The fact that they *seem* to arise anew is only from the perspective of obscuration, like the sun appearing to arise anew when the clouds disperse. In reality, the sun has been shining all along, and it was only obscured from the limited perspective of the observer.

The fact that the unconditioned qualities of a buddha intrinsically exist as the ground of being is an important feature of the Nyingma view. Since wisdom is unconditioned, it cannot be produced by anything, and for this reason, wisdom must be present from the primordial beginning as the true nature, the buddha-nature, of all sentient beings. We might think that if we already have these qualities, then what is the point of doing anything to become a buddha? The point is that even though these qualities exist when we are sentient beings, they are obscured due to defilements, and we are not actual buddhas until these unconditioned qualities are manifest.

In his *Trilogy of Innate Mind,* Mipam argues extensively that wisdom is not conditioned and, further, that wisdom is not just a subtle form of the conditioned mind.[139] According to Mipam, wisdom does not arise from mind but is the nature of mind, in the same way that emptiness does not arise from entities but is the nature of all things.[140] Thus, even though wisdom, like emptiness, is there from the beginning, it does not follow that everyone realizes it, because obscurations prevent us from seeing reality as it is.

Buddha-nature is often represented through metaphors, and Mipam also turns to them to show the way buddha-nature exists in the world. He says that the primordial qualities of wisdom are an intrinsic property of reality, like a knife having the ability to cut, a mirror to reflect, and a gemstone to shine; yet when the knife is in a sheath, the mirror in a box, and the gemstone muddy, the qualities are not evident. While such qualities appear to be newly developed when their obscurations are removed, the qualities are not newly arisen; they have been there all along.[141] Although the qualities of wisdom are primordially present, when not manifest, there is only what is known as "natural purity." When the qualities become manifest at the time of a buddha, there is the twofold purity: (1) natural purity (*rang bzhin rnam dag*) and (2) purity that is free from the adventitious defilements (*glo bur bral dag*), when all obscurations have been removed.[142]

As with the two purities, there are two types of effects: a ripened effect (*rnam smin 'bras*) and a freed effect (*bral 'bras*). Self-existing wisdom is unconditioned, so rather than developing as a newly produced effect, it is actualized as a freed effect when it becomes manifest. In other words, it has been there from the beginning and becomes manifest when the conditions that obscure it are removed. A ripened effect is like a seed becoming a flower; the flower is a new production. Even though the process of becoming a buddha seems to be this sort of transformation, this is only the way it appears, not how it really is. Mipam explains that there only appears to be a new development of a Truth Body (Tib. *chos sku*, Skt. *dharmakāya*);[143] in the way things are in reality, all phenomena are primordially buddha in the essence of the Truth Body, which is the nature of all phenomena.[144]

Buddha-nature is a topic through which Mipam affirms the unity of the two truths—emptiness and appearance. He equates the genuine meaning of emptiness (unity) with buddha-nature. In this light, his position on buddha-nature seems to share a characteristic of a Geluk view. The predominant Geluk tradition, stemming from one of Tsongkhapa's disciples, asserts that buddha-nature is emptiness, that is, the mind's lack of true existence.[145] However, what the Geluk tradition means by emptiness (a lack of inherent nature) is different from what Mipam means by emptiness (unity).

Like Mipam, the mainstream Sakya tradition that follows Gorampa asserts buddha-nature as a unity.[146] However, there is an important difference in the way this tradition represents the wisdom of a buddha to be a new production from the way Mipam depicts it as being there from the beginning. Also, Mipam distinguishes his view of buddha-nature from the unity of clarity, or mind (*sems*), and emptiness, and emphasizes that buddha-nature is the unity of wisdom (*ye shes*) and emptiness. Making an important consciousness/wisdom distinction, he does not accept that buddha-nature is the unity of an impermanent mind (or consciousness) and emptiness.

Given that Mipam asserts the innate presence of the qualities of a buddha when one is a sentient being and that he affirms that these qualities are unconditioned, his view shares significant features with the Jonang tradition. In general, what have come to be the mainstream Sakya and Geluk traditions do not accept the qualities of the buddha to be present from the beginning in this way. They interpret statements in sutras that affirm that the buddha's qualities exist when one is a sentient being to have a basis in another intention (*dgongs gzhi*)[147]; that is, they interpret the real import of these statements to be emptiness. Mipam is more closely aligned with the Jonang tradition in his interpretation of these scriptures because he affirms that the qualities of a buddha are present from the beginning. Unlike the Jonang tradition, however, Mipam does not portray bsuddha-nature to be truly real and not empty of its own essence. By asserting that it is empty in this way too, he represents his view of buddha-nature in a way that is different from that of the Jonang tradition.

By representing buddha-nature as a unity of emptiness and appearance, Mipam synthesizes the middle and last wheels of Dharma. The topic of buddha-nature also functions as a common ground of sutra and tantra. Yet we can also see a distinction in the way that Mipam frames the way buddha-nature is represented in sutra and tantra. According to the "causal vehicle" of sutra, buddha-nature is depicted as the cause of a future effect. In the "resultant vehicle" of tantra, however, the qualities of a buddha are said to be spontaneously present from the beginning, without the notion of temporal causality.[148] Within the path of sutra as well, the middle wheel tends to emphasize the path to becoming a buddha as a process of transformation, in which wisdom is produced anew by a cause. In contrast, in the last wheel, the path to becoming a buddha is depicted as a process of uncovering the wisdom that is already there.[149]

For Mipam, tantra is distinguished by a view that at once marks a definite departure from sutra yet also sustains a fundamental continuity with it. This view can be seen as a natural outgrowth of sutra traditions, as an extension of the view. Before we examine some of the important features of Mipam's presentation of the distinctive view of tantra, we will look briefly at how he lays out the paths to actualize buddha-nature and become a buddha (see translations 14 through 16).

Paths to Enlightenment

What follows is a short explanation of the way Mipam presents the structure of the Buddhist path to awakening. According to him, we can only go so far in the Lesser Vehicle, realizing the lack of a personal self based on its path, but without the Great Vehicle, we will not come to fully realize the lack of self (that is, emptiness) with respect to all phenomena. In other words, those in the Lesser Vehicle realize only part of emptiness (the lack of a personal self) but do not realize the entire scope of emptiness. They hang on to an ultimate foundation of reality (the fundamental elements of reality, or *dharmas*), whereas there is actually no such foundation. Therefore, according to Mipam, one cannot become a buddha based solely on the Lesser Vehicle path; becoming a buddha is the result of the Great Vehicle. Nevertheless, realizing the lack of a personal self is enough to free us from samsara, because in doing so, we relinquish the obscurations of the afflictive emotions.

The afflictive emotions can be included within the "three poisons" of attachment, aversion, and delusion. These afflictive obscurations function to prevent liberation, and they are tied in with the apprehension of a personal self. Based on the notion of such a self, we become attached (to me and mine) and averse (to what is other). This notion of self keeps the wheel of samsara rolling, because it perpetuates the distorted framework through which we selfishly act out attachment and aversion, thus sowing the seeds of suffering. Afflictive obscurations have two aspects: a gross, imputed aspect and a more subtle, innate aspect. According to Mipam, the imputed aspects are relinquished on the first "ground" (Tib. *sa*, Skt. *bhūmi*) when you directly perceive the suchness of reality. This experiential realization is called "the path of seeing."

The imputed aspects of the afflictive obscurations are learned and not inborn like the innate aspects. Imputed aspects involve distortions that are explicitly conceptual, as opposed to the perceptual distortions that comprise the innate aspects. The difference between the imputed and innate aspects can be understood as something like the difference between software and hardware: the innate aspects are embedded more deeply in one's mind-stream and are thus more difficult to eliminate. Imputed ego-clinging refers to imputing qualities to the self that are not there—namely, apprehending the self as a singular, permanent, and independent entity. This is overcome on the first bodhisattva ground in a direct, nonconceptual experience of reality that is the culminating insight of analysis. Nevertheless, the more subtle, innate aspect of ego-clinging hangs on. The innate ego-clinging, as the bare sense of self that is imputed on the basis of the five aggregates, is more difficult to remove. Rather than construing qualities to the self such as singularity or permanence, it is a more subtle feeling of simply "I am" when, for instance, we wake up in the morning. This innate sense of self is a deeply rooted, instinctual habit. It thus involves more than just imputed identity; it is a deeper experiential orientation of distorted subjectivity. Although analysis into the nature of the self paves the way for it to be overcome, it cannot fall away by analysis alone. Rather, it has to be relinquished through cultivating the path of meditation. According to Mipam, there are no innate aspects of the afflictive obscurations left on the eighth ground. However, the afflictive emotions are only one of two types of obscurations, the other being cognitive obscurations.

Cognitive obscurations are nothing less than conceptuality: the threefold conceptualization of agent, object, and action. Conceptuality is tied in to apprehending a self of phenomena, which includes mistaking phenomena as real, objectifying phenomena, and simply perceiving dualistically. Such conceptualization serves to obstruct omniscience. Based on the Great Vehicle, these cognitive obscurations can be completely relinquished; thereby, the result of the Great Vehicle path culminates in not merely escaping samsara, as in the Lesser Vehicle, but in becoming an omniscient buddha.

According to Mipam, up to the seventh ground, the realization (of the twofold selflessness) and abandonment (of the twofold obscurations) are the same in the Great and Lesser Vehicles. As with the Great Vehicle, he maintains that accomplishing the path of the Lesser Vehicle entails the realization of the selflessness of phenomena, to see that phenomena are empty. Those who accomplish the Lesser Vehicle path also realize the selflessness of phenomena, because their realization of emptiness with respect to a person is one instance of realizing the emptiness of phenomena. The final realization of the Lesser Vehicle path, however, is incomplete. Mipam compares it to taking a small gulp of the water of the ocean: we can say that those who realize emptiness in the Lesser Vehicle have drunk the water of the ocean, just not all of it.[150] The final realization of the bodhisattva's path in the Great Vehicle, however, is the full realization of emptiness, like drinking the entire ocean.

Nevertheless, for Mipam, a bodhisattva's realization does not surpass the final realization of the Lesser Vehicle until the seventh bodhisattva ground. Even while surpassing it there, however, the path to becoming a buddha is not yet complete. There is still a subtle remnant of obscuration

GROUNDS AND PATHS

Stage	Path		What is Relinquished	Quality of Knowledge	Metaphor
Ordinary Being	path of accumulation		gross delusion by study and reflection	intellectual understanding	description of moon
	path of joining	warmth / peak	subtle delusion by meditation on a semblance		drawing of moon
		forbearance / supreme quality		experience	reflection of moon
Bodhisattva Ground 1	path of seeing		imputed afflictive & cognitive obscurations	nonconceptual (direct) realization	actual moon (crescent)
Bodhisattva Grounds 2–7	path of meditation		innate afflictive & cognitive obscurations	increasing familiarity with realization...	waxing moon
Bodhisattva Grounds 8–10			innate cognitive obscurations		
Buddha	path of no more learning		complete abandonment	complete realization	full moon

A contour map of the path from an ordinary being to a buddha.

that has not been overcome, even after all ego-clinging to a personal self has been left far behind. While the gross cognitive obscurations, along with all of the afflictive obscurations, have been relinquished on the first seven bodhisattva grounds, the habits of dualistic perception, the last of the cognitive obscurations, have still not worn off—like the scent left in an empty perfume bottle. When these subtle cognitive obscurations are overcome through effortless meditation on the last three bodhisattva grounds ("the pure grounds"), all obscurations are completely relinquished. When this happens, you are a buddha.[151]

The table on page 125 summarizes how Mipam outlines the path to enlightenment. He highlights different aspects in his presentation of the path in tantra. For Mipam, the difference between the views of sutra and tantra pertains mainly to the level of ordinary beings (the paths of accumulation and joining), and once the path of seeing (the first bodhisattva ground) is reached, the difference is not so pronounced. Also, unlike other major Buddhist traditions in Tibet, you can become a buddha without relying on the *path* of tantra (although you must understand the meaning contained therein).[152] In his integration of sutra and tantra, we can yet again see the predominant theme of unity in Mipam's works.

Within the Great Vehicle in general, there are two vehicles: the sutra vehicle and the vehicle of tantra, which is also known as the *Vajrayāna*. The sutra vehicle is also called the causal vehicle, distinct from the resultant vehicle of tantra. In contrast to the descriptive schema of the philosophical systems (*grub mtha'*), vehicles (*theg pa*) include more of a participatory element, highlighting the experiential dimension. Mipam describes the word *vehicle* as "something you ride; when you remain in it, it takes you to your desired effect."[153] Moreover, the metaphor of a vehicle reveals the role of this schema as more of a practical means for traversing the path of realization, as opposed to a philosophical system that functions more to describe and represent reality. In this light, the causal vehicle of sutra and the resultant vehicle of tantra should not necessarily be conflated with different sets of texts (sutras or tantras) but understood to include a participatory, experiential element.

In the context of laying out the structure of the path within tantra,

Mipam emphasizes the experience of wisdom. He describes the time when ordinary beings (those who have not reached the bodhisattva grounds), mainly understand the meaning of tantra through intellectual study and reflection as "the path of accumulation." When the meaning is experienced mainly through meditation on a conceptual semblance of reality, this is called "the path of joining." When what is referred to as "metaphoric wisdom" occurs in our mind (in an experience analogous to actual wisdom), this is a sign of the actual wisdom fire (of the direct perception of reality) on the path of seeing, so it is called "warmth" within the path of joining.[154] Of the four stages within the path of joining, during the first two stages of "warmth" and "peak," the metaphoric wisdom occurs in our mind like seeing a drawing of the moon. At the two higher stages, "forbearance" and "supreme quality," the metaphoric wisdom is no longer merely intellectually understood (*go*); it is experienced (*myong*), like seeing the reflection of the moon in water. When the actual wisdom is directly realized (*rtogs*), we have entered the path of seeing and have reached the first bodhisattva ground (which is like seeing the actual moon in the sky).

Moreover, Mipam explains that when an ordinary being meditates on the nature of reality, it is done by consciousness and not by wisdom. Like seeing a drawing of the moon, that experience of consciousness is a semblance of wisdom,[155] whereas directly experiencing the presence of actual wisdom is like seeing the actual moon. Furthermore, he says that when the unborn reality of mind is realized in accordance with the meaning of the nature of mind pointed out within the Great Perfection,[156] then we experience the metaphoric wisdom. As mentioned earlier, he likens this experience to seeing a reflection of the moon in water. He says that those who meditate on the Great Perfection and the Great Seal[157] realize this experientially through direct perception, not just analytically, and thus many people call this "the path of seeing in tantra." However, while this is a direct realization of the nature of reality, he states that it is not the genuine path of seeing, because the path of seeing (the first bodhisattva ground) needs to have twelve hundred qualities to be genuine. The path of seeing is experiencing actual wisdom, which is likened to seeing the actual moon in the sky.[158] After the initial direct perception of the nature of reality (which at first is like seeing only a sliver on the first day of a waxing moon), it becomes clearer and clearer through the path of meditation. When we eventually become buddhas, it is like seeing the full moon.[159] In this way, he presents the path to becoming a buddha according to tantra.

TANTRA

In Nyingma presentations of philosophical systems, the view does not culminate with the Consequence School of the Middle Way but ascends through the tantras. Another character of the Nyingma tradition is to present internal distinctions within the views of different tantras. In the same way that a hierarchy of four philosophical systems in sutra (Great Exposition School, Sutra School, Mind-Only, and the Middle Way) is represented in an ascending scale, with each level transcending the limitations of the previous one, the hierarchy of views extends through the tantras. Thus, tantra is treated as the next paradigm that resolves the shortcomings of the preceding level (Consequence School) while incorporating its insight. In this way, tantra marks a distinct philosophical horizon for the Nyingma tradition.

In Mipam's works, the hierarchy of views in the four philosophical systems appears to be based on an internal principle of emptiness as ineffability—the higher the view, the more increasingly ineffable reality is acknowledged to be. In this way, he presents the philosophical systems of the causal vehicle of sutra as a hierarchy based on the empty quality of reality—the higher the view, the more comprehensive the representation of emptiness. The four philosophical systems thus primarily reflect an analytical approach. The increasingly immanent *purity* of reality, however, seems to be the internal logic guiding the hierarchy of views within the resultant vehicle of tantra. As such, tantra's hierarchy is oriented more toward an experiential dimension rather than an analytical one. In the context of the four or six classes of tantras,[160] we can see how the hierarchy shifts from the principle of increasing transcendence (emptiness)—as it is in sutra—to the principle of immanence. That is, the higher the view, the more wisdom becomes an immanent reality. Mipam generally distinguishes the hierarchy of all the Buddhist teachings—in both the philosophical systems of sutra in the causal vehicle and the classes of tantra in the resultant vehicle—based on a hierarchy of gradual to sudden. That is, the higher the view, the more sudden the process of realization.

In his depiction of a hierarchy of ascending views, Mipam sets forth a fivefold division of vehicles drawn from the *Secret Essence Tantra*. He describes these five vehicles in a summary that highlights the significant features of each philosophy: (1) *the correct philosophy of the world,* which is the belief in karma, understanding that effects are not disjoined from actions; (2) *the philosophy of the vehicle of characteristics,* which includes Auditors, proponents of Mind-Only, and proponents of the Middle Way, who are distinguished based on the degree to which they have realized the view of selflessness; (3) *the philosophy of the three outer tantras,* which involves methods for quickly becoming liberated from the stains of karma by relying on the techniques of deity and mantra; (4) *the philosophy of the general unexcelled yoga,* which regards suffering as enlightenment and afflictive emotions themselves as the great liberating wisdom; and (5) *the philosophy of consummation,* which is the Great Perfection, wherein all phenomena of samsara and nirvana are acknowledged to be spontaneously present as great purity and equality from the beginning; here, one is primordially free from the stains of ordinary karma, without relying on the efforts of the path.[161] With this scheme, we can see how, in addition to the ascending scale of the fourfold philosophical systems from the causal vehicle of sutra, the views continue to ascend into the tantras. Also, we can see how the hierarchy of vehicles in the tantras is based on the principal of divine reality becoming more of an immanent presence.

Mipam also distinguishes the views of different paths based on the way wisdom manifests. He outlines three ways for wisdom to arise according to three approaches in (1) the causal vehicle of sutra; (2) the outer tantras (Action Tantra, Performance Tantra, and Yoga Tantra); and (3) the inner tantras (*Mahāyoga, Anuyoga,* and *Atiyoga*). The first way of the causal vehicle is called "wisdom arising from behind." Here, the way wisdom arises is compared to letting dirty water settle; in time (three incalculable aeons), wisdom will arise in the future after progressively clearing the impurities of afflicted thoughts. The way of the outer tantras is called "wisdom arising in front." Here, wisdom arises through the profound methods of the interdependence of oneself, the deity, and the ritual substances, having invited the wisdom deities to appear before oneself and performing worship. The method for generating wisdom in the outer tantras is faster than in the causal vehicle of sutra; the result can be attained in a less distant future (such as after seven or sixteen lifetimes). The way of the inner tantras is called "wisdom arising from within." Here, the nature of all phenomena is recognized as the nature of wisdom; buddha is not sought somewhere else or in another time but is recognized as the immediate wisdom inherently residing within one's own mind.[162]

According to Mipam, the inner tantras do not make a qualitative difference between oneself and the deity that is accomplished, as opposed to the view of outer tantras where the two are set apart.[163] As the culmination of his view, the inner tantras play an important part in his presentation. Within the inner tantras, the view also ascends, culminating in the Great Perfection at the summit.[164] When the three inner tantras are added to the three outer tantras and the three classical vehicles (Auditor, Self-Realized One, and Bodhisattva), there are nine vehicles. This nine-vehicle presentation, condensed here into five, is how the Nyingma tradition

ULTIMATE TRUTH IN FOUR PHILOSOPHICAL SCHOOLS

Philosophical School	Ultimate Truth
Great Exposition School	Irreducible elements (*dharmas*)
Sutra School	Particulars
Mind-Only	Nondual mind
Middle Way	Emptiness

The ultimate truth becomes progressively more empty in the four philosophical schools, as indicated by the shading.

commonly lays out the range of Buddhist paths. Mipam asserts that the first eight of these nine vehicles take the *mind* as the path; then within the ninth vehicle, which takes *wisdom* as the path, one becomes a buddha through realizing the meaning of self-existing awareness of the Great Perfection.[165] Here again we see the important place of the mind/wisdom distinction in his works.

BUDDHIST VEHICLES

Three Approaches	Nine Vehicles	How Wisdom Arises	Potential Time Until Becoming Buddha
Sutra Vehicle / Causal Vehicle	Auditor	wisdom arises from behind	n/a
	Self-Realized One		
	Bodhisattva		three incalculable aeons
Outer Tantras	Action Tantra	wisdom arises in front	sixteen lifetimes
	Performance Tantra		seven lifetimes
	Yoga Tantra		three lifetimes
Inner Tantras (Highest Yoga Tantra)	Mahāyoga	wisdom arises from within	one lifetime
	Anuyoga		
	Atiyoga (Great Perfection)		immediate

The reality of a buddha becomes progressively more immanent in tantra, as indicated by the shading.

It is important to see that Mipam does not portray Nyingma tantra as just a unique ritual system; he also emphasizes a special view. Tsongkhapa, in contrast, made the distinction between sutra and tantra by pointing to tantra's deity yoga. Thus, Tsongkhapa argued that the distinction between sutra and tantra is not a difference in view, but simply a difference in method: tantra uses the method of ritual identification of the meditator and the deity. Mipam, however, argued that there is not only a distinct method, there is also a distinct *view* within tantra—namely, the indivisibility of purity (divine presence) and equality (emptiness), which we will see in this chapter. This view is put into play in how one identifies with the divine in the practice of deity yoga. Therefore, in presenting the distinction between sutra and tantra, there is a significant difference in emphasis, with Tsongkhapa focusing on method and Mipam highlighting the distinction in view (see translations 27 and 29).

TWO IN ONE

According to Mipam, the unique view of tantra is the view of great purity and equality of all that appears and exists.[166] Purity and equality, like appearance and emptiness, are indivisible.[167] Mipam describes the view of great purity as seeing beings and the world as divine. In sutra, appearances are seen to be illusions; in tantra, however, appearances are also seen as divine.

Mipam supports the view of divine appearance with reasoning. He argues that people with undefiled perception see reality as it is, while people infected by defilements perceive a distorted reality. This is readily evident in the fact that a sober person sees one moon, while someone who has drunk too much whiskey sees two. Mipam makes a case that even though the way things appear is not necessarily pure, phenomena do not always appear the way they are.[168] Due to delusion (being intoxicated with afflictions), people experience what does not accord with reality, like someone seeing two moons or seeing a rope as a snake. Recognizing the way different people have varied perceptions of things, we can be open to the idea that the world can be experienced in a way other than the one we presently experience and how appearances may actually be pure and divine. Mipam argues that it is not only a fact that different people experience appearances in various ways, but that through training on the path, we can perceive without distortion and see all phenomena as pure.[169]

His arguments to establish purity reflect his arguments for emptiness. For instance, he says that the same reasons that are set forth to show that reality is not empty actually support the case for emptiness. That is, someone might believe that since things have causes and effects, then they are not empty; but actually, their causal relationships—the fact that all things dependently arise—supports the case that they are empty. In the same way, the reasons one may put forth to support that reality is not pure (such as because there are appearances of impurity) are turned around to support the case for their status as pure (for example, they appear as impure due to deluded perception). Mipam argues that since reality does not appear the way it really is due to delusion, one must cultivate the path to actualize it, just as one must with emptiness.[170]

Mipam insists that without the certainty of the ultimate, meditating on the relative as divine is just an aspiration; it is not the view.[171] He argues that meditating on deities while thinking that the nature of samsara is impure is like putting perfume on a vomit bucket. He adds that it is an arrogant contradiction to meditate on the world and beings as pure while thinking they are impure. This will not bring about transformation, just as washing coal will not make it white. Such a path is a mere reflection of the actual one.[172] He concludes that it is only the Nyingma tradition that uniquely establishes the nature of all appearances to be divine through valid cognition, and he attributes this to the works of Rongzom.[173]

Mipam, along with other Nyingma exegetes, enlists reason in tantra to establish what is "extremely hidden" (*shin tu lkog gyur*), or what is typically portrayed as the exclusive domain of scriptural authority.[174] Yet he explicitly states that the view cannot be realized without reliance on scripture and quintessential instructions.[175] Mipam's use of reason in tantra demonstrates a characteristically Nyingma portrayal of tantra as an extension (or rather, the center) of the philosophical systems of sutra. While he often uses reason in the Middle Way to *negate,* even to overturn the legitimacy of a (purely) rational enterprise, he uses reason in tantra to *affirm* the divine.

Mipam refers to his view of the purity of appearances as "the view of phenomena" (*chos can lta ba'i lta ba*). Additionally, he describes "the view of suchness" (*chos nyid lta ba'i lta ba*) with reference to the ultimate truth. Suchness is the innate nature of reality, the "great equality" that is the equal nature of all things in samsara and nirvana. Thus, there is no difference between the views of sutra and tantra in terms of their objective suchness. However, he claims there is a difference between them in terms of subjectivity, the participatory element *within* suchness.[176] We might think that the subjective wisdom arises anew when the objective side of suchness, which is unchanging, is realized. However, even though in the way it appears, wisdom may be experienced as a new occurrence, in the way things are, wisdom and the expanse of phenomena (Tib. *chos kyi dbyings*, Skt. *dharmadhātu*) are indivisible. Thus, there is no duality in reality: the cognitive quality of wisdom is actually inseparable from the objective expanse of phenomena.

From the side of appearance, great purity is established (the view of phenomena), and from the side of emptiness, great equality is established (the view of suchness).[177] Mipam describes a third view, that of "reflexive awareness" as what establishes the indivisibility of the former two. This is the superior truth[178] of the indivisibility of purity and equality. All that appears as pure is equally empty, and everything that is empty dawns as pure appearance—purity and equality are indivisible. This single indivisible sphere, this unity, is what sublime beings experience through reflexive awareness.[179] Like the other views, this has to be realized individually, within one's own experience. Thus, Mipam describes a threefold view (phenomena, suchness, reflexive awareness) that operates throughout Buddhism, in sutra and in tantra. With this threefold scheme, he develops the distinctive theme of unity in the Nyingma tradition.

Mipam presents the unity of purity and equality in tantra in a way that mirrors the unity of appearance and emptiness in sutra. We've seen how he integrates emptiness from the middle wheel and appearance from the Buddha-Nature Sutras of the last wheel by stating that both are the definitive meaning. A similar integration can be seen in his interpretation of the view of tantra. Moreover, we also find this unity of emptiness and appearance in the Great Perfection, where the corresponding qualities of primordial purity (*ka dag*) and spontaneous presence (*lhun grub*), or empty essence (*ngo bo stong pa*) and natural clarity (*rang bzhin gsal ba*), are predominant themes.[180] Once again, we see the theme of unity that characterizes Mipam's interpretation across his Buddhist works (see translations 17 and 26).

Conclusion

IT IS COMMONLY CLAIMED that Mipam fits his position to the subject he is discussing, such that his works on the Yogic Practice School take on this position, his works on the Consequence School follow their tradition, his works on other-emptiness support an other-emptiness position, and so on. While this is true to an extent, it is not the case that his writings on these different subjects are unrelated and contradict each other. Rather, they fit together within a complex, integrated whole. For instance, he did not write a commentary on a Yogic Practice School's text in a way that conflicts with what he says in a commentary on a text associated with the Consequence School. Nor do we need to say that he wrote a text on other-emptiness simply to defend some other tradition's position or in a way that conflicts with his own presentation of the Consequence School in other texts. Rather, we can see that he frames each of his Buddhist works within an all-encompassing, structural whole where the interpretation of each Buddhist tradition and its associated view have a legitimate place. He does this by contextualizing seemingly incompatible views in a way that gives each view a valid place within a specific context and from a particular perspective for which it can be held true. This feature of integration and unity is central to his vision of the Nyingma tradition.

Mipam illuminates the view of the Great Perfection throughout all his works on sutra and tantra. In doing so, he weaves various texts and points of view into a beautifully integrated whole. It is as if his Buddhist writings come together to form a single, multifaceted gem. Just as the various facets of a gem reflect light differently but are parts of a larger whole, each of Mipam's works reflects the light of truth from a distinct perspective. While his lucid and systematic texts address a variety of subjects across the purview of Buddhist scriptures, the view of the Great Perfection is the culmination of his system and thus structures the whole that he presents. Each philosophical tradition, including the Yogic Practice School and the Consequence School, has a vital role to play in his all-inclusive system.

Someone might find the fact that he brings together diverse strands of thought in this way to be a shortcoming, not a positive quality, of his works. One might think that by taking on a synthetic approach, he must necessarily smooth over interesting tensions, ignore essential points, and even water down important issues at stake in Buddhist debates, such as those between the Consequence School and the Yogic Practice School. There is much to be said about the way dialectical tensions and rigorous polemical exchange sustain the vitality of intellectual traditions. Indeed, Buddhists in India were not at all inhibited in their critiques of other Indian Buddhist traditions. Tibet, on the other hand, has been a different story. Buddhist writings from India tend to be treated as sacrosanct in Tibet, and Tibetan scholars have a tendency to make historically spurious links between authors and traditions to preserve the coherency of a unified Indian Buddhist tradition.

Despite the problems of such an approach to the Buddhist textual traditions from India, a unified vision is not without its value. Although critical acumen is vital for perceiving the differences among views, an ability to appreciate the value of a plurality of viewpoints and integrate them so they are mutually supportive can also enrich one's own tradition (which in Mipam's case is the Great Perfection). Along with a critical component of open-minded analysis and debate, another important factor that sustains the vitality of traditions is the ability to assimilate the past with the present and organize diversity into a comprehensive and meaningful whole. Mipam's writings do this, as do the works of Dölpopa, Tsongkhapa, and Gorampa. What distinguishes Mipam's view is that he was able to bring the widest range of doctrines—including the Yogic Practice School, the Consequence School, the middle and last wheels of sutra, and tantra—into his grand, unifying synthesis. For better or worse, the earlier scholars did not make these connections to the extent that Mipam did. One reason for this may be the fact that he lived much later than the other prominent systematizers of the major Tibetan Buddhist sects, and so he had the advantage of a panoramic view of the long history of Buddhist scholarship. Also, he may have been in a good position to bring such a broad range of doctrines together because, unlike the other predominant sects in Tibet, his Nyingma tradition had not been as concerned with commentarial works on the discourses of sutra, such as the Middle Way and valid cognition. Consequently, the boundaries of a strictly delimited Nyingma view on these subjects were not sharply drawn, and this gave his creative genius room to maneuver.

For whatever reasons, Mipam is easily one of the most influential, if not *the* most influential, scholar in Tibet within the last five hundred years. While it is not possible to capture the extent of his contribution in a few pages, I have tried to give a sense of his approach to Buddhist philosophy and practice by highlighting some important themes in his writings. In the following section, we will look at how Mipam treats the issues we have already discussed in translated excerpts from his texts.

PART THREE

Select Translations

1 *Emptiness and Analysis*

For Mipam, emptiness does not simply mean a lack of true existence, although that is one of its meanings. Since the lack of true existence is still tied into the fabricated duality of existence and nonexistence, it cannot be the genuine meaning of emptiness, which is nonconceptual. Even so, using concepts and analysis to move toward an understanding of emptiness remains an essential part of the process of realizing its meaning. While emptiness must be known experientially, beyond all ideas, Mipam emphasizes the role that concepts can play to transcend concepts and evoke experiential insight. In an important way, analysis clears the way for wisdom to shine forth. In the passage that follows, we can see how he attributes a vital role to analysis and how it is a prerequisite for overcoming the habits of misconceiving reality. Emptiness, as both a product of analysis and an inconceivable reality, has a predominant role throughout Mipam's works.

Only at the start, if a lack of true existence is not taught, there will be no method to eradicate the beginningless habit of mistakenly apprehending entities; and if merely that [lack of true existence] is taught as the ultimate, some narrow-minded people will think, "A mere absence—the elimination of the object of negation—is the abiding reality!" This grasping at emptiness will become an incorrigible view. Further, there are two ways to grasp: grasping at emptiness as an entity and grasping at emptiness as a nonentity.

One may think, "It is not suitable to grasp at any extreme!" and throw away the certainty induced by reasoned investigation, which is the source of the nectar of profound emptiness, the antidote for all diseases within existence. Thinking, "It is not suitable to engage the mind at all!" is entering into the thick darkness of oblivion, where it is difficult to view, see, conceive, or experience this profound truth.

—*Words That Delight Guru Mañjughoṣa*, 88

2   *Conceiving the Inconceivable*

The following selection shows how Mipam balances a conceptual representation of the ultimate with its nonconceptual meaning. While Buddhist texts commonly describe the ultimate as inexpressible, they still do so with words. This is the paradox of describing the indescribable. Mipam clarifies this muddy philosophical problem by showing how this paradox need not involve a contradiction that must be resolved with a one-sided solution. He argues that those who claim that all meaning is confined to language and say there is no way to express anything beyond words are close-minded. Yet he also contends with those who claim that words are utterly pointless and can serve no function in leading us to an understanding of the inconceivable ultimate truth. In contrast to these two extreme positions, he formulates an alternative by showing how words and thoughts can disclose the nonconceptual, albeit in an indirect way. That is, even though words are nothing more than words, like a finger pointing to the moon, they can guide us to what is beyond them.

Through scripture and reasoning, you can realize what is free from conceptual constructs. For example, when someone points at the moon with a finger, you can see the moon, yet the moon and finger need not be alike. Likewise, through the path of scripture and reasoning, you can realize what is ineffable and free from conceptual constructs. Yet it is impossible for words of scripture and intellectual reasoning, as they are, to be beyond conceptual constructs. This is the reason why in the sutras and great treatises, the meaning of suchness free from conceptual constructs is explained in two ways: (1) it is said to unexemplifiable, indemonstrable, and not the domain of language or mind; and (2) it is said to be determined by means of examples, arguments, scripture, and reasoning.

Without knowing how to explain the way that these distinctive viewpoints are without contradiction, people who have partial intelligence maintain only one side of the intended meaning and throw out the other by necessity. In this way, if they assert that there is definitely no other profound meaning beyond what can solely be determined by language and the intellect, then they must claim that whatever is knowable is exclusively the domain of confined perception. Thus, the Buddha would not know the suchness beyond the domain of all logic. . . . Or they claim that the ultimate is inconceivable and that its essence is beyond the domain of language and thought, such that there are no words or thoughts through which one could ever come to understand it. In this case, it would not be suitable to be known by anyone; the claim is similar to the assertion of an inconceivable Creator—there is no valid cognition to establish it. Also, there would be no point to the sutras, tantras, and treatises that settle upon the ultimate. Hence, the intelligence of one with partial vision is like an eye of a needle; it is unable to enjoy the bliss of the great ocean of the profound texts difficult to fathom, those of the Victorious Ones and the great bodhisattva chariots.

—*LIGHT OF THE SUN*, 276–78

3   *Unity and Buddha-Nature*

In the following passage, Mipam demonstrates his keen ability to synthesize various strands of Buddhist thought through his interpretation of buddha-nature. He claims that the emptiness taught in the middle wheel of Dharma and the qualities of a buddha taught in the last wheel of Dharma are both the definitive meaning. Distinguishing the definitive meaning from the provisional meaning is an important way in which Buddhist commentators convey a unified interpretation of the different teachings in scriptures that sometimes have contradictory literal meanings. The definitive meaning is the true meaning, the ultimate truth, in contrast to what is simply taught for a provisional purpose, as a temporary means to understand the deeper import of the ultimate truth.

Mipam holds that buddha-nature is the definitive meaning that is taught in the middle wheel as well as the last wheel of Dharma. He claims that the meaning of buddha-nature is taught from the aspect of its emptiness in the middle wheel and from the aspect of the presence of its qualities in the last wheel. This synthetic interpretation is an important means by which he integrates the vast tradition of activity, associated with Asaṅga and the last wheel, with the tradition of the profound view, associated with Nāgārjuna and the middle wheel. His integration responds to a long history of dispute in India and Tibet as to the real meaning of the Buddha's intent and how to harmonize the teachings of emptiness with the teachings on the positive qualities of buddha-nature. He also states that understanding buddha-nature in this way is an important part of understanding the Vajrayāna.

Even though the reasoning that analyzes the ultimate establishes the emptiness of all phenomena, it does not negate the qualities of [buddha-]nature, because although the sublime qualities exist, they are also claimed to be essentially empty. Therefore, the meaning demonstrated by the middle wheel that all the phenomena (of thorough affliction and complete purification) are taught to be empty is established as such because buddha-nature is also the nature of emptiness. However, since this teaching of [buddha-]nature—characterized as neither conjoined with nor separable from the appearances of the empty-natured exalted body (Tib. *sku*, Skt. *kāya*) and wisdom—is the viewpoint of the definitive meaning sutras from the last wheel, then by this fact alone it is superior to the middle wheel. Although the meaning of the last wheel is praised in the sutras and commentaries, [this does] not [refer to] everything in the last wheel, but is spoken in this way concerning the definitive meaning position of demonstrating the [buddha-]nature. This can be clearly ascertained as such through other sutras like those that teach the basic element of heritage through the metaphor of cleansing a jewel. Therefore, the emptiness taught in the middle wheel, along with the exalted body and wisdom taught in the last wheel, should be integrated as a unity of emptiness and appearance. Without dividing or excluding the subject matters of the definitive meaning found in the middle and last wheels, we should consider both to be the definitive meaning just as the omniscient Longchen Rapjam asserted.

By maintaining both of these [wheels] to be the definitive meaning, there is no contradiction that one [wheel] must be held as the provisional meaning. Not only that, but with both wheels integrated, we come to the key point of the quintessential instructions of the Vajrayāna, where buddha-nature as such is taken to be the meaning of the causal continuum.[181] Therefore, you should know how the teachings of the Buddha converge on this single essential point and that this consummate meaning is the single viewpoint of the sublime beings like Nāgārjuna and Asaṅga.

—*Lion's Roar: Exposition of Buddha-Nature,* 585–86

4 Steps to the Middle Way

This selection shows Mipam's explanation of "the four stages of the dawning of the Middle Way." It is taken from his overview of Longchenpa's commentary on the *Secret Essence Tantra,* and nearly the same words can also be found in his commentary on the *Ornament of the Middle Way.* This illustrates the importance of this Middle Way view in the contexts of both sutra and tantra. Through a fourfold scheme, he outlines a process for those who progressively engage in the meaning of nonconceptuality through the stages of *empty, unity, freedom from constructs,* and *equality.* Beginning with the object of negation, true existence, each of the stages probes deeper into the meaning of emptiness and the Middle Way. The process culminates with equality, free from all concepts and dualities, which is beyond all distinctions between sentient beings and buddhas, nirvana and samsara.

When beginners properly investigate using the reasons that establish emptiness—such as [the reason of] being neither singular nor plural— through contemplating the meaning of the nonestablishment of a pot and so forth, they [mistakenly] think that the abiding reality is nonestablishment itself because, although existing when not analyzed, nothing is found upon investigation. Therefore, through alternating appearance and emptiness, the *empty* quality dawns.

At that time, by contemplating that the nonexistence of phenomena also is just a mere imputation not actually established, or by contemplating the manner in which things appear while empty from the beginning, one generates the distinctive certainty that while empty, they appear and while appearing, are empty, like [a reflection of] the moon in water. When the absence of intrinsic nature and dependent arising dawn without contradiction, one has "the understanding of *unity*."

At that time, certainty is generated in the manner that both—the lack of inherent nature and dependent arising—although different in being expressed by two phrases, are indivisible without the slightest difference in essence. Thereby, the thought that apprehends appearance as the basis of negation, which is affixed to an object of negation that is eliminated, naturally deconstructs. And then dawn the qualities of a *freedom from constructs,* such as the ability to remain naturally free from negation and affirmation, adding and removing.

Through becoming familiar with such a freedom of constructs again and again, all aspects of dualistic phenomena, in which one sets apart particular objects and their distinctive suchness, are purified. Through bringing forth an exceptional certainty in the nature of all phenomena as *equality,* one reaches completion.

—*Overview: Essential Nature of Luminous Clarity,* 461–62

5 *No-Self*

The doctrine of no-self is a distinctively Buddhist teaching, yet the meaning of no-self is easily misunderstood. Mipam clarifies this meaning in the following excerpt. He shows that the self is a product of false imagination, of ignorance, and that it does not exist other than as an object of a deluded mind. Liberation is the result of realizing the lack of a real self. Since the self has never existed, it is not something to be annihilated by the realization that it does not exist. Rather, realizing that it does not exist is simply seeing the truth as it is and putting an end to a misconception.

Why is it that all sentient beings think that there is a self? The self is not conceived of because it exists. In fact, although it does not exist, there is merely a conception that it exists because of an erroneous mind that is deluded and mistaken about its existence. This is similar to perceiving a rope to be a snake or like seeing a young lady [as real] in a dream.

It might be thought that if there is a self, then it is reasonable to be bound to samsara by afflictions and to become liberated when cutting through that bondage. However, if there were no self, who then becomes liberated? Therefore, it would be unreasonable to strive to liberate the self!

It is not the case that one strives to liberate an existent self. For instance, if you are frightened when mistaking a rope for a snake, you will feel relieved when you see that there is no snake. Similarly, by conceiving of a self where there is no self, you accumulate afflictions and karma and thereby continuously experience suffering in samsara. When realizing the lack of self through authentic insight, karma and afflictions will cease to be and you will be liberated. Therefore, what is called "liberation" is merely the cessation of a mistake in your mind-stream or the cessation of your deluded mind. There is no liberation of an existent self. If there were a self, then ego-clinging could never be turned away, and if this ego-clinging is not relinquished, then karma and afflictions do not cease. Thus, due to being attached to the self, you continuously enter samsara.

—*A Feast on the Nectar of the Supreme Vehicle*, 102–3

6 *Unmistaken Emptiness*

In the following passage, Mipam emphasizes the radical nature of emptiness. Since its genuine meaning is beyond concepts, it cannot be understood merely by words or ideas. He shows two ways to understand emptiness: (1) through a careful process of analysis that undermines mistaken concepts or (2) through receiving the key points of quintessential instructions and meditating accordingly. Without one of these two prerequisites, the meaning of emptiness will not be understood properly. Through this, he argues that even though other traditions may speak of "emptiness," "nonduality," "pure awareness," and other such terms, these are mere empty words if the key points of the nature of emptiness and the nature of mind are not understood.

Although traditions may claim to be free from extremes, in the end since they constantly depend upon a conceptual reference for a Self, or Brahma, and so forth, how could this manner be the Middle Way?... The Great Perfection is the culmination of extreme profundity, so it is difficult to realize. Most who cultivate idiot meditation—those who do not fully eliminate superimpositions[182] regarding the abiding reality through study and contemplation, or who lack the key points of the quintessential instructions—wind up [making a] similar [mistake]. Without gaining certainty in primordial purity, a mere impassioned thought of a ground that is neither existent nor nonexistent will bring you nowhere. If you hold on to such a ground, which is empty of both existence and nonexistence, as separate and established by its own essence, whether it is called the inconceivable Self, Brahma, Viṣṇu, Īśvara, wisdom, etc., it is merely a different name for a similar [mistaken] meaning. The abiding reality that is free from the four extremes[183]—the luminous clarity of the Great Perfection which is realized reflexively—is not at all like that. Therefore, it is important to rely on the authentic path and teacher.

Although [we share] mere words such as "illusory," "nonentity," and "freedom from constructs," it does not help if you do not know through a firm conclusion, with certainty induced by reason, how Buddhist emptiness is superior to the limited emptiness of non-Buddhists. If you do know, you understand that what the Buddha taught has not been experienced in the slightest by those [non-Buddhists] such as Viṣṇu, and you know that the traditions of "Awareness" and "the Middle Way" they describe are mere words. Although the words may be similar, Buddhists and non-Buddhists cannot be separated by words; the difference, which is like the earth and space, is in the profound essential point.

—*WORDS THAT DELIGHT GURU MAÑJUGHOṢA*, 470–72

7 Meditation on Emptiness

In the following verses, Mipam relates an essential point concerning the meaning of emptiness and the practice of meditation. He conveys an important distinction between the correct and mistaken view and practice. For instance, the meaning of "nothing at all" is not limited to simply the absence of form. A point he frequently emphasizes is that emptiness is not simply nonexistence, because nonexistence is a concept tied to its binary counterpart—existence. Emptiness understood as merely a void is also a mistaken view. In contrast, the meaning of "nothing at all" in the Middle Way is a lack of true nature or essence, and its genuine meaning is emptiness beyond concepts.

Like the meaning of emptiness, the meaning of nonconceptuality—without apprehending anything—plays a crucial role in relating to the meaning of emptiness in meditation practice. This too can be done correctly or incorrectly. For instance, cultivating nonconceptuality does not simply mean being without thought; there is a great difference between someone who sustains awareness of nonconceptual wisdom and someone who is in deep sleep. The difference is in the quality of *clarity,* which is a vital element in genuine meditation practice. Another way that nonconceptuality can be misunderstood is to think that the *idea* of nonconceptuality is nonconceptuality. This mistake is typically associated with Hvashang, an advocate of a Chinese tradition of sudden enlightenment. Hvashang is commonly depicted as the one who misunderstood the meaning of nonconceptuality and the way to cultivate it, hence the phrase "resting blankly." In Tibetan historical works, he is the one who lost the famous debate to Kamalaśīla, who represented India, at Tibet's first monastery (Samyé). Hvashang lost the debate because of his mistaken view of the sudden path to enlightenment as a path that rejects any and all analyses.

At the time of sustaining the actual view
Some people say, "Do not apprehend anything."
The meaning of "Do not apprehend anything"
Is twofold: good understanding and misconception.

The first is free from the constructs of the four extremes:
In the presence of a sublime being's wisdom
Since nothing at all remains
Apprehending naturally subsides—
Like seeing an open, clear sky.

The second is oblivion, the tradition of Hvashang:
By resting blankly, neglecting analysis
With no clarity-aspect of special insight [Tib. *lhag mthong,* Skt.
    vipaśyanā],
One remains like a common stone at the bottom of the ocean.

For example, take the statement "nothing at all":
For a proponent of the Middle Way seeing absence
And one who aspires to an absence that is a lack of form,
Although in mere words these are the same,
The meanings are as different as the earth and space.

—BEACON OF CERTAINTY, 13

8   *Mind-Only and the Middle Way*

In the following selection, Mipam shows the compatibility of Mind-
Only and the Middle Way. He states that the Middle Way tradition
realizes an inexpressible awareness free from all duality, just like Mind-
Only. The distinction between the traditions is not that the Middle
Way rejects this awareness, but that the Mind-Only School fails to
regard this awareness as empty. The Middle Way tradition, knowing
the luminous and clear nature of mind to be in unity with its empty essence, completely realizes the empty nature of this cognition.

When the appearance of perceived objects is established as not having an
essence separate from the perceiving subject, the appearance of the perceiving subject is also established as nonexistent. If [one wonders] why,

it is because the perceiving subject is established in dependence upon the perceived object; it is never established on its own. In this way, proponents of Mind-Only realize the lack of all duality—the awareness free from subject and object, naturally luminous and clear, inexpressible and nondistinct from the nature of the thoroughly established nature liberated from the twofold self. If they must realize it, then there is no need to mention that the proponents of the Middle Way realize this as well. . . .

It is merely the slight philosophical assertion that posits the essence of ineffable cognition as truly established that remains to be negated. Authentic proponents of the Middle Way assert the unity of the primordially pure luminous clarity of one's mind and the emptiness of that nondual cognition. Therefore, other than the distinction of whether this slight fixation is eliminated or not, the Middle Way and Mind-Only are mostly the same in terms of the practices of meditative equipoise and postmeditation.

—Light of Wisdom: Commentary on Distinguishing Phenomena and Suchness, 626–27

9 Mind-Only and the Middle Way II

The following selection comes from Mipam's commentary on the *Ornament of the Great Vehicles Sutras,* a text he classifies as Mind-Only but says can also be understood as compatible with the Middle Way. In this excerpt, Mipam goes into some depth clarifying the relationship between Mind-Only and the Middle Way. He shows how the two chariot traditions are compatible yet how some misguided proponents of Mind-Only claim that the mind is truly real, which is why Mind-Only is sometimes refuted by the Middle Way. He also clearly states that it is not necessary for a follower of the Middle Way to claim the system of Mind-Only also; the Middle Way can stand without it. Nevertheless, he shows that sutras and tantras state that phenomena are nothing other than mind and that samsara and nirvana arise from the mind. With these words, he reveals an affinity for the claims of the Mind-Only tradition. Moreover, in terms of practice, he claims that the Yogic Practice School of the Middle Way is profound; it is the "subtle, inner Middle Way," which he says is also the way that Candrakīrti practiced. Thus, he brings together the Yogic Practice School of the Middle Way and the Consequence School.

According to the Middle Way, all phenomena that appear through the force of dependent origination are not nonexistent conventionally, yet are not existent ultimately. They are also not both existent and nonexistent because ultimate nonexistence is the suchness of all conventionally existent phenomena. These two are not different from each other in reality, for the two are none other than a mere nominal division—similar to a fire's heat or the sweetness of molasses. So could we say that reality is a third category that is neither ultimately nonexistent nor relatively existent? No, because there is no valid cognition that can establish a third category that is neither of the two—a phenomenon or its suchness, emptiness—and such a third category is also not feasible as the nature, or suchness, of conventional phenomena.

Therefore, free from all four extremes of existence, nonexistence, both, and neither, reality is free from all constructs. It is held as the indivisible two truths, in which the phenomenon and its suchness are inseparable, and it is to be realized by individual reflexive awareness. This suchness, free from constructs, is always equality free from origination and cessation, decrease and increase. Therefore, it does not have even the slightest dualistic attribute, such as being pure or impure, and so on.

Moreover, this tradition of Mind-Only asserts that all phenomena are nothing other than mere mental perceptions, and that the ground of appearances substantially exists as the mere clear and aware consciousness that is the dependent nature. If one follows this assertion to its final conclusion, then that consciousness is asserted to be substantially existent simply as the cause of the appearances of all conventional phenomena. And if this consciousness is not held to have an ultimate substantial existence that is truly established, then it does not at all conflict with the tradition of the Middle Way. But if this consciousness is asserted as ultimately, truly established, then it contradicts the tradition of the Middle Way. Indeed, it appears that whether or not there is conflict with the Middle Way comes down to the analysis of merely this difference.

The corpus of the doctrines of Maitreya and the scriptures of the great chariot, Asaṅga, both teach with a single intent that a person on the ground of motivated conduct[184] first understands all phenomena to be merely mind, and then experiences that the mind has nothing to perceive. Then, at the time of the supreme quality on the path of joining,[185] one realizes that since the perceived does not exist, neither does the perceiver. Right after this, the truth of suchness, which is free from dualistic fixation, is directly realized. This is said to be the attainment of the first ground.

The system of Mind-Only also accepts that the cause of all dualistic appearances that manifest as places, objects, and bodies is the universal ground consciousness, which substantially exists conventionally. Yet since it [the universal ground consciousness] is not established as a duality while manifesting in various ways, it is said to be like an illusion and so on. Therefore, it is certainly reasonable that this tradition realizes that the nondual consciousness is not a truly established entity and that it lacks attributes. Consequently, one should understand that the consummate viewpoint of the chariots of Mind-Only and the Middle Way are in harmony.

If this is so, then one may wonder why it is the case that the masters of the Middle Way refute the philosophy of Mind-Only. Some blatantly proud proponents of Mind-Only philosophy assert that external objects do not exist in Mind-Only, but that the mind exists substantially—similar to the way a rope is empty of a snake but is not empty of the rope itself. They have not understood that this assertion is in terms of the conventional. Therefore, this philosophy that fixates upon the ultimate, true establishment of a nondual consciousness is refuted. However, they are not refuting the viewpoint of noble Asaṅga, who clearly realized the proper path of Mind-Only that was set forth by the Buddha. There is nothing unreasonable in speaking in this way, because some learned ones from the Land of Snow assert that Auditors who see the truth also realize the twofold selflessness and are not different from proponents of the Middle Way. If this is the case, then it is needless to mention that they realize the intended meaning of the Middle Way of the great chariot Asaṅga, because he is a sublime being.

In general, it is sufficient for Middle Way proponents to determine that all phenomena that arise in dependent relation are unborn; it is not indispensable for them to accept a Mind-Only philosophy. . . . The sutras of definitive meaning and the tantras of profound mantra state that there are no phenomena other than the mind and that the root of both samsara and nirvana comes down to the mind. Through the force of the mind, the phenomena of samsara and nirvana manifest; if there were no mind, they would cease to be. Through the force of mind, the deluded factors of samsara come into being when the afflictions form karma. Also, the mind cultivates the insight that realizes selflessness and compassion, thereby accomplishing the path of the Great Vehicle. Due to this, with the transformations of the eight collections along with the universal ground,[186] one becomes a buddha with the nature of the five wisdoms. Even Auditors, by means of the mind that realizes the absence of a personal self, achieve a nirvana that does not perpetuate existence. Therefore, all Buddhists must necessarily agree that the root of complete purification depends on the mind. Additionally, if you determine that the mind is without a nature, you will fully realize the path of the Great Vehicle without much difficulty. This is a key point explained in the *Manifest Enlightenment of Vairocana.*

The Master Bhavya, widely renowned as a great scholar in India, stated as follows in his *Precious Lamp of the Middle Way,* which condenses all the key points of the Middle Way: "The Yogic Practice School of the Middle Way is the subtle, inner Middle Way, and the Middle Way that asserts external objects is the gross, outer Middle Way." It is also clearly said that at the time of practice, the Yogic Practice School of the Middle Way is more profound, so even Candrakīrti practiced in this way. If one understands the self-luminous, nondual consciousness, which the proponents of Mind-Only assert, to be a consummate, dualistic consciousness—merely a consciousness inexpressible in terms of what is the perceived and perceiver, truly established and not empty of its essence—then this is what is to be negated. However, if one understands that this cognition has a nature that is primordially without origination and is the self-luminous wisdom free from perceiver and perceived and directly experienced by self-awareness, then it is what is to be affirmed. This is necessarily asserted in both tantra and the Middle Way.

If there were no wisdom of individual reflexive awareness, or no luminous and clear mind, then it would be unreasonable for there to be a mind that realizes the truth of suchness on the path of training. Also, at the time of a nirvana without any remainder [on the path of] no more learning, buddhas would not have omniscient wisdom; [their nirvana] would be no different from the nirvana of the Lesser Vehicle, which is similar to the extinction of a flame. So how then could one assert that the exalted bodies, wisdoms, and activities of a buddha are inexhaustible?

Therefore, although it appears as if the chariots of Mind-Only and the Middle Way have different presentations in elaborating the traditions of the profound and vast Dharma, their consummate viewpoint accords in the single expanse of wisdom. If one understands this integral point, one sees with excellence. In brief, reality—the abiding reality of all phenomena—is in no way partial to appearance or to emptiness; it is a unity that is known through individual reflexive awareness. If you realize that it remains unchanged throughout the ground, path, and fruition, then you will be free from the abyss of wrong views that cleave to extremes.

—*A Feast on the Nectar of the Supreme Vehicle*, 96–101

10   *Reflexive Awareness*

In this passage, Mipam argues that the Consequence School does not negate the conventional existence of reflexive awareness. His position directly contrasts with that of Tsongkhapa, who stated that the Consequence School does not accept reflexive awareness even conventionally. Tsongkhapa's characterization soon became the orthodox Geluk view. In contrast, Mipam states here that while the Consequence School negates the *ultimate* existence of reflexive awareness and the universal ground, their *conventional* existence is neither refuted nor affirmed. He adds that reflexive awareness and the universal ground are indispensable in an analysis of the conventional truth. Mipam's arguments are taken from his commentary on the ninth chapter of the *Way of the Bodhisattva*. His commentary drew a lot of criticism from proponents of the Geluk school. Yet these criticisms and Mipam's responses to the objections have initiated a lively dialogue, which continues to this day, on the nature of the Middle Way and its relationship with the Yogic Practice School.

The negation of reflexive awareness is a negation of its ultimate existence, not a negation of the way of designating reflexive awareness conventionally as that which is simply the opposite of matter. If reflexive awareness were refuted conventionally, one would have to accept that one's own mind is hidden to oneself. It would then absurdly follow that there would be no difference in the way that one cognizes one's own mind and the mind of another. Also, there would be no reason to affirm the existence of a mind in one's own mind-stream. And in the end, the conventions of an awareness of objects as well would be disrupted. Refutations like these were spoken by the lord of reason, Dharmakīrti. One should know that all the negations of reflexive awareness are negations of its ultimate existence (like the reasons that negate the aggregates and so forth); they are not negating its conventional existence such that it does not exist at all.

It has been said, "In this [Consequence School] tradition, reflexive awareness and the universal ground are not accepted even conventionally." However, in this [Consequence School], the refutation is only in terms of the ultimate; conventionally, these are neither negated nor affirmed. Regarding this, some people claim, "If you are a proponent of the Middle Way, you should not accept the universal ground; the universal ground is the tradition of the proponents of consciousness [i.e., Mind-Only]." However, they have not considered well. If the universal ground is not held to be truly real, how does one detract from the Middle Way by asserting it to exist conventionally? That which is unacceptable to assert conventionally, like a permanent universal, is that which is invalidated by a valid cognition that analyzes the conventional. Otherwise, if everything that is refuted by ultimate reasoning were not accepted [even conventionally], then one would have to accept that the aggregates, constituents, and sense-fields did not exist at all. Therefore, in the texts of the Consequence School, the universal ground is refuted as ultimately existent, but it is not refuted conventionally. Moreover, a presentation of it [conventionally existing] is not affirmed either.

It likewise is the case with the assertion of reflexive awareness, for which some people say, "Reflexive awareness is asserted due to the influence of habituation to the predispositions of logic. It should not be accepted." This is nonsense. Although reflexive awareness and the universal ground are certainly not needed to ascertain the ultimate, they are indispensable for investigating a conventional presentation. Moreover, if something is established by a valid cognition analyzing the conventional, there is no reason to refute it, saying, "It does not exist conventionally." If someone contends, "What do you mean there is no reason to refute it? Have you not seen all that is said in the texts by Candrakīrti, Śāntideva, and others?" These reasons [that negate the ultimate status of reflexive awareness] also apply equally to the awareness of objects.

—COMMENTARY ON THE WISDOM CHAPTER, 30–31

11 Consequence and Autonomy

In the following passage, Mipam gives a very simple and direct answer to a very complicated and thorny issue: the distinction between the Consequence and Autonomy schools of the Middle Way. He defines the Consequence School as a form of discourse, a way of speaking, that emphasizes what accords with the uncategorized ultimate as it is known in meditative equipoise. Thus, no assertions are made in the distinctive discourse of the Consequence School.

In contrast, Mipam defines the Autonomy School as a discourse that accords with the conceptual ultimate that is known in postmeditation. Thus, formulating the ultimate truth conceptually, as a negation, is a characteristic of the Autonomy School. He points out that the root of the distinction is the two schools' respective emphasis on the uncategorized or categorized ultimate. The other areas where they are dissimilar, such as whether they have assertions or use autonomous arguments to ascertain the ultimate, are merely offshoots of this root distinction.

The defining character of the Autonomy School is discourse that emphasizes the categorized ultimate with assertions. The defining character of the Consequence School is discourse that emphasizes the uncategorized ultimate free from all assertions. In the context of positing the defining characters for these two, positing a distinction such as whether or not [phenomena] are established by their own characters conventionally, the ways of formulating evidence, and so on, are merely ancillary divisions subsumed within the defining characters above. Also, due to this [emphasis on the categorized or uncategorized] itself, which was just explained, is also the key point of:

- whether or not there are assertions
- whether or not there is acceptance of establishment by own character conventionally
- the way of formulating evidence establishing the lack of intrinsic nature as a consequence or an autonomous argument
- whether or not the qualifier "ultimately" is applied to the object of negation.

—*Words That Delight Guru Mañjughoṣa*, 99

12   *Consequence and Autonomy II*

In this excerpt, Mipam demonstrates another central feature of the distinction between the Autonomy and Consequence schools. The Autonomy School emphasizes a perspective where the two truths are distinct, whereas the Consequence School overcomes this subtle fixation on two separate truths. Thus, the Consequence School directly represents the unity of the two truths according to the way reality is experienced nonconceptually within meditative equipoise. Due to this emphasis on the nonconceptual, proponents of the Consequence School are said to be free from assertions. Nevertheless, this does not mean they must always be mute on all matters. When not settling on the ultimate nature of things, they can still make assertions about the Buddhist path, such as claiming that evil actions lead to suffering and so forth.

Due to conceiving the two truths as separate and making claims for each of them, the Autonomy School also has assertions. They accept that while nothing exists ultimately, things exist relatively. In this way, one should know that the Consequence School's unique object of negation is the aspect of apprehending the two truths as distinct, because if the Autonomy School were free from this object of negation, which is conceiving the two truths as distinct, then other than that view, there would not be the slightest thing to develop within even the Consequence School, etc. Being beyond all assertions and free from conceptual constructs of the four extremes, reason has a hard time ever finding any other conceptual construct to cut through. Therefore, as long as there is a [conceptual] mode of apprehension and the two truths are not one taste, the conceptual domain of thought has not been transcended. Thus, one will not have achieved the nonconceptual wisdom that is the genuine transcendent insight free from the thirty-two superimpositions.[187]

From the start, the Consequence School ascertains the nonconceptual unity of appearance and emptiness. Its reasoning refutes the aspect of holding on to the thought, "while not truly existing, merely in terms of the relative, they exist by way of their own characteristics"; thereby, the conception of difference, as if each of the two truths had its own place, collapses. The two truths become integrated as one taste, and thus all modes of apprehension that conceive existence, nonexistence, and so on fall away.

Therefore, in this [Consequence School] tradition, one does not need to use qualifiers that separate two truths, like "truly established" or "ultimate," for the four extremes. The conceived objects of the four extremes are negated, so the subjective mind is free from all observations and assertions. In accord with a sublime being's wisdom of meditative equipoise, one settles upon great emptiness, the consummate abiding reality. Nevertheless, in postmeditation, it is perfectly reasonable to still posit all phenomena of the path and fruition without hindrance, in accord with how they are observed by the valid cognitions of the two truths. This explanation, distinguishing the Consequence School as neither exclusively with assertions nor without them, is a unique claim of the omniscient Longchen Rapjam.

—*Words That Delight Guru Mañjughoṣa*, 97

13 *Two Truths*

Throughout his works, Mipam emphasizes the unity of the two truths—the inseparability of appearance and emptiness. He also states that this unity is the meaning of buddha-nature, the central topic of the eighteenth chapter of Longchenpa's *Wish-Fulfilling Treasury*, the text on which Mipam comments here. In the following selection, Mipam lays out two models of the two truths. In one model, the two truths are emptiness and appearance; the empty nature of any appearance is the ultimate truth, and that appearance itself (whether of samsara or nirvana) is the relative truth. This model is based on ultimate analysis, an analysis into the true nature of things. The second model presents the two truths of authentic/inauthentic experience, in which authentic experience (appearance in accord with reality) is the ultimate truth, and inauthentic experience (appearance in discord with reality) is the relative truth. This latter model is set forth by conventional analysis, an analysis of the way things appear. Mipam highlights the meaning of unity within both of these models.

What is the nature of this reality that is given the name "indivisible truth?" It is also called "the primordial wisdom of luminous clarity" or "buddha-nature." The name "luminous clarity" illustrates both being free from darkness and having luminosity; it is a name for being unblemished by obscurations and having the cognitive quality of wisdom. Therefore, it is also called "the wisdom that is free from obscurations." This shows the side of awareness, the cognitive quality. Moreover, primordially, from beginningless time, it does not abide in any extreme. Thus, it is complete pacification that has the identity, or nature, of abiding without conceptual constructs. This shows the empty aspect.

An example for these two, awareness and emptiness, is (1) luminosity, the essential nature of the sun, (2) and space free from obscurations. The cognitive quality is spontaneously present and its nature is unconditioned. This expanse, which is the unity of awareness and emptiness, is naturally pure without depending on anything such as effort on the path. Moreover, untouched by the faults of either the conditioned samsara or the one-sided peace of the unconditioned, it is great purity. This nature abides from the beginning. In essence, it cannot be divided into appearance or emptiness that are separate from one another; there is neither a real nirvana to achieve nor a real samsara to eliminate. Therefore, there are no faults to send away or good qualities to bring forth.

Thus, no relative words or thoughts apply to this; relative constructs are cut off. All evaluation by words and thoughts, such as samsara and nirvana, appearance and emptiness, faults and qualities, do not stand up to analysis. Therefore, they are relative; all their maneuvers are completely pacified. Consequently, this reality is beyond the domain of the categories "this is relative" and "this is ultimate." Thus, it is not presented by a philosophical mind fixated upon two truths and making designations such as "what appears to arise is the relative" and "what remains unborn is ultimate." It is beyond this. All constructs, like holding on to existence and nonexistence, are completely pacified. For this reason, in the abiding reality—due to the essential point of indivisibility—there is no division into two separate truths such that things are established in terms of the relative but not established ultimately.

To conclude, in the expanse of phenomena, there is no dual nature of appearance and emptiness, and no twofold division. Therefore, by a mere expression of language—through words—it is also said that the relative truth and ultimate truth are "indivisible." Although the expanse is like this, separate categories are made merely in terms of the conventional, based on the way things appear. In this way, all phenomena included within samsara—all that is comprised by distorted perceptions and all that appears through the power of dualistic thought—are not real when analyzed. They are fluctuating and impermanent; therefore, these deceptive phenomena are the relative truth. And all phenomena comprised by great nirvana—which is difficult to realize and thus profound, free from constructs, and which is the luminous clarity of wisdom's knowing, relinquished from all suffering—are beyond material and momentary phenomena. Therefore, they are free from the misery of change. Having the nature of immutability, they are the ultimate truth.

In this way of positing the relative and ultimate truths—presenting the way things appear and the way things are by positing them as the appearing aspect and the empty aspect—both samsara and nirvana are alike and equal. And here, there is a way of positing appearance in accord with reality [that is, authentic experience] as ultimate, and appearance in discord with reality [that is, inauthentic experience] as relative. These two great ways occur often, even in sutras, so they should not be conflated. This latter way of presenting is to posit the two truths through conventional valid cognition, which distinguishes the authentic and inauthentic. One should know this from this [*Wish-Fulfilling Treasury*] text as well, "To divide by the conventional manner of the two truths . . ."[188] It is important to distinguish these; nirvana does not withstand analysis, it is not established as truly real.

Furthermore, within the domain of dualistic experience, these various appearances of the relative, which have a fluctuating, unstable nature, are like an illusion, a water-moon, an apparition, or a reflection. When analyzed, they do not have a nature that is established in the slightest. Yet, while nonexistent, they appear. When whatever appears is thoroughly examined by the reasoning of ultimate analysis, not even the slightest thing, no gross basis or subtle root, is established. It is empty like space. Also, phenomena being established by way of their own characters does not withstand the scrutiny of analysis. Yet when not analyzed or examined— when let be just as they are—they appear with the nature of various forms. For example, they are like an illusory horse or elephant that appears while not existing.

You may wonder, "Why do they appear even while not existing?" From beginningless time, they arise through habituation to predispositions, the dependent arising of what has a distorted nature. For example, it is like elephants and so on appearing to the eyes of someone who has eaten *dhatura*.[189] These distorted appearances are naturally empty of a self of phenomena, and they lack a personal self. As this is the mode of being, or abiding reality, of appearances, this empty aspect is said to be "ultimate," and its appearing aspect is said to be "relative." In this way, from the very time it appears, it is not established as arising, abiding, and so on. Consequently, the phenomenon and its nature (or abiding reality) are appearance and emptiness, which remain without coming together or parting. Therefore, this is the identity of the indivisible truth.

—COMMENTARY ON THE WORDS OF THE EIGHTEENTH CHAPTER [OF THE WISH-FULFILLING TREASURY], 566–70

14 Unconditioned Buddha-Nature

The following excerpt reveals central features of Mipam's view of buddha-nature. He argues that since everyone has the potential to become a buddha, and since a buddha's wisdom is unconditioned, then it follows that presently the wisdom of a buddha abides in sentient beings. This wisdom is what is meant by "buddha-nature," which is also called "the basic element" and "naturally abiding heritage." For Mipam, buddha-nature is the unchanging wisdom that is the way things are in reality. He claims that because a buddha's wisdom is unchanging, it follows that it is not newly produced when one becomes a buddha. Also, because it never changes, there can be no essential difference between this wisdom at the time of the cause, when one is a sentient being, and at the time of the effect, when one is a buddha. Here he makes an important distinction between the way things appear, in which there is a difference between buddhas and sentient beings, qualitatively and temporally, and the way things are in reality, in which there is no difference.

Through evaluating by means of merely an awareness based on ordinary confined perception, one may think, "Unconditioned wisdom is impossible because there is no common locus[190] of a cognition and a permanent entity."

This is nonsense, because even though partial cognitions that cognize objects are necessarily impermanent, the wisdom that is the one taste of the knower and known, "the one with the space-*vajra* pervading space," is not like that [impermanent cognition]. This is because in the state of unchanging luminous clarity, which is the self-radiance (*rang gdang*) of the unconditioned, all the phenomena of nirvana and samsara are incorporated;

hence, reasoning that examines the consummate [reality] establishes that there is primordially no arising or ceasing in the essence of this. Therefore, wisdom such as this is "the great unconditioned," which does not abide in either extreme of being conditioned or unconditioned; it is not at all like a mere nonentity. Since entities and nonentities are phenomena and are dependent arisings, or dependent imputations, when authentically analyzed they are hollow, fake, lies, and deceptions; buddha-nature is the great unconditioned, the suchness of all phenomena that are entities or nonentities, which is authentically nondeceptive. As is said in the *Root Verses of the Middle Way:*

Nature is uncontrived,
And does not depend on another.[191]

And,

Entities and nonentities are conditioned;
Nirvana is unconditioned.[192]

In this way, if the wisdom of the consummate Truth Body is established—by scriptures of definitive meaning sutras and by reasoning examining the consummate [reality]—to be the nature of the immutable ultimate truth, completely pervading nirvana and samsara, equality, and unconditioned, then the cause, which is able to actualize that [Truth Body] at one time, is presently the nature of the Wisdom Truth Body[193] abiding in the manner of suchness without decrease or increase. Although it may or may not be actualized in the mode of appearance (whether it is free or not free from adventitious defilements), there is not even the slightest qualitative or temporal difference in the mode of reality, because it is the intrinsic nature of the immutable unconditioned. In the *Sublime Continuum,*

As it was before so it is later—
The immutable suchness.[194]

And,

The luminous clarity that is the nature of mind
Is immutable like space.
It is undisturbed by adventitious defilements
Such as attachments that arise from the imagination of the unreal.[195]

All the phenomena of samsara are changing and unstable. While there appear to be transformations within the state of the suchness of all this, it should be known, as was frequently taught, that the purity of mind, the buddha-nature, is without change like space. In this way, the unconditioned expanse of luminous clarity is naturally pure and untainted by delusion; within the self-radiance of the basic nature of the nondeluded, the qualities of fruition, such as the powers, abide without separation—like the sun and light rays. Furthermore, in the *Sublime Continuum,*

The basic element is empty of those adventitious [phenomena] that
    have the character of separability
But not empty of the unexcelled qualities that have the character of
    inseparability.[196]

All of the faults of samsara arise from the deluded mind which apprehends a personal self or a self of phenomena. Since this deluded mind also is adventitious like clouds in the sky, from the beginning neither mixing nor polluting the luminous clarity of the primordial basic nature, these faults are separate from the basic element and suitable to be removed. Therefore, the essence of the basic element is empty of these faults; it is untainted. Without depending on the polluting delusion, the basic element is luminous and clear by its own nature; self-existing wisdom permeates the thusness[197] of all phenomena. It is not empty of that which it is inseparable from, the basic element of consummate qualities, because in its essence, this is the basic nature from which it is inseparable—like the sun and its rays of light.

In this way, the naturally abiding heritage is established as the unconditioned essence of the Truth Body, which is primordially endowed with qualities. Due to the potential to be a buddha, the Wisdom Truth Body, without decrease or increase, necessarily resides in the mind-streams of all sentient beings, because in training on the path, the potential to be a buddha is established by the power of fact. Also, since the Truth Body at the time of being a buddha is unconditioned—it is not possible for it to be a conditioned phenomenon that is newly formed by causes and conditions—it is established that "it presently resides as the essence of the buddha."

Regarding this, some people think, "If it presently resides as the essence of the buddha, why does that omniscient wisdom not dispel the obscurations of these sentient beings?" Or fixating upon the range of meanings of the common vehicle, they think, "Since the buddha is the effect and sentient beings are the cause, the effect being present in the cause is invalidated by reason, using such reasoning as the eating of food would [absurdly entail] the eating of excrement."

For you who have been guided by merely a limited understanding of the common scriptures and have not trained in the meaning of the extremely profound, definitive meaning sutras, it is no wonder that such qualms have arisen! These [objections of yours], however, are not the case. Why? Although the suchness that is luminous and clear wisdom is present in everything without distinction, when adventitious delusion arises in one's mind, the basis of designation of samsara is only this deluded mind together with its object; due to this delusion, one's suchness is not known as it is. For example, when sleeping, due to the power of mental consciousness alone, unrestricted appearances arise such as the body, objects, and eye-consciousness, and so forth. At that time, although the subject and object are observed and apprehended separately, the mental consciousness itself is not able to know its own mode of being, in which the perceived [object] and the perceiving [subject] are not established as different; even though it is not known, there is nothing other than this mode of being. Likewise, all phenomena abide as emptiness; even so, merely being like this does not entail that everyone realizes this, because there is the possibility of delusion—appearances that do not accord with reality.

Therefore, since mind and the wisdom of the essential nature are [respectively] phenomenon and suchness, sentient beings and the Buddha are taught in terms of the mode of appearance and the mode of reality. Thus, using the reason that the effect is present in the cause to invalidate this position is simply not understanding it. In this way, this reasoning is that the evidence of a clear manifestation of the Truth Body at the time of the fruition establishes that the heritage, primordially endowed with qualities, is present at the time of the cause because there is no temporal causality in the mode of reality; nevertheless, in dependence upon the mode of appearance, it is necessarily posited as cause and effect.

—LION'S ROAR: EXPOSITION ON BUDDHA-NATURE, 575–79

15   *Appearance and Reality*

The distinction between appearance and reality plays a major role in Mipam's presentation of the two truths and buddha-nature. In the following passage, he illustrates this distinction in terms of the relationship between buddhas and sentient beings by showing how assertions about the nature of buddhas and sentient beings must be contextualized. That is, statements cannot be taken as objectively true or false outside of any context or perspective. Truth claims must take into account a perspective, in this case, whether it is a statement about the way things appear or the way things are.

In the way things appear, sentient beings are confused, wander in samsara, and suffer, whereas buddhas are held to be enlightened and beyond suffering. However, from the perspective of ultimate truth, this is not the way things are: there are no distinctions between sentient beings and buddhas in this perspective. The buddha is the nature of suchness, the empty and aware ground of being, and such is the nature of sentient beings as well. This is how things are. The difference between buddhas and sentient beings is that buddhas are free from distortions and realize this nature, whereas sentient beings do not. Yet this difference pertains only to the way things (mistakenly) appear, not the way they are.

Someone may ask, "Is the naturally pure ground, the suchness of luminous clarity, the buddha?"

It is the naturally pure buddha. In terms of the natural abiding reality, it is primordially pure with spontaneously present qualities—there is nothing to generate. Since it is unconditioned, it is also called "the buddha." In terms of the mode of appearance, an individual whose mind-stream is endowed with that ground itself, having upheld the conditions of the path and taken the place of liberation through making [that ground] the ground of liberation, is called a "buddha endowed with the two purities."

One may say, "Well, does the buddha have obscurations?"

Not in the mode of reality; however, in the mode of appearance, impure suchness is called "with obscurations." Consequently, assertions are made in terms of either [the modes of] appearance or reality; in the case of one of the modes, the other is not acceptable. If it is the buddha, then since obscurations have been relinquished, there is nothing to relinquish and it is not necessary to make efforts on the path. If it is not the buddha, then the purity from the beginning, the spontaneously present qualities, and the Buddha (not present in the ground) would have to be newly arisen and conditioned.

Since the claims are made having distinguished [the modes of appearance and reality], we do not state one-sidedly that it is the buddha or it is not the buddha, nor that it is pure or impure. Although we do not make claims one-sidedly, conventionally there is no contradiction because it is in terms of one of the individual two truths. Although we do not make one-sided claims, we also do not assert a third alternative that is neither pure nor impure.

It is extremely easy to understand a mere lack of true existence through reasoned analysis. It is difficult to understand unity. Even if unity is understood, it is difficult to understand emptiness with [all supreme] aspects present like [images in] a divination mirror. If this is understood, then suchness is understood, and further, appearance, clarity, bliss, awareness, and the consummate unconditioned are understood. If this is not understood, there is no method to understand the unchanging, coemergent [wisdom]. Hence, what is necessary to understand is unconditioned luminous clarity; the unconditioned that is a mere void does not help. If luminous clarity is understood, then the various aspects of appearance also will be understood as unconditioned reflections of emptiness. If that is understood, since all phenomena are empty while luminous and clear, it is inexpressible. Both samsara and nirvana, which dawn as all the aspects of the self-radiance of luminous clarity, become known as merely reflections of emptiness—appearances of the nonexistent. In this way, one accomplishes the *vajra*-body of great bliss, the buddha that enjoys the equality of the timeless three times within the inconceivable expanse of suchness, free from the eight constructed extremes.[198]

—INTELLIGENT PRESENCE: PART II OF THE TRILOGY OF INNATE
MIND, 526–28

16 *From the Two Wheels of Sutra to Tantra*

The following excerpt shows the process of how sentient beings become buddhas, according to the middle wheel of sutra, the last wheel of sutra, and tantra. Mipam depicts the different ways this process is represented in the three discourses as a hierarchy. According to the middle wheel, which is at the lower end of the spectrum here, it is necessary to accomplish wisdom anew from a cause. In the last wheel, although wisdom is not held to be produced anew, it is still present as a potential that must also be actualized through a cause. In tantra, the summit of the views, the buddha is *always already* present. As such, the buddha is not established anew by a cause nor is buddha sought out somewhere else; rather, the buddha is made manifest through the direct methods of tantra, which take the result as the path.

In the middle wheel of sutra, all phenomena are ascertained as a mere unity of the emptiness that is a lack of intrinsic nature and dependently arising appearance. However, it does not teach the presence of the exalted body and wisdom—the self-appearance (*rang snang*) of self-existing luminous clarity, which is not produced by the causes of karma and afflictive emotions. Therefore, [in the middle wheel of sutra,] the exalted body and wisdom must be accomplished anew by a cause; the accumulations of great compassion are asserted because the sole realization of emptiness, or suchness, cannot [accomplish] them.

In the last wheel [of sutra], since the suchness of mind, which is the expanse of phenomena, is itself taught to be primordially inseparable from the appearance of the exalted body and wisdom, all sentient beings are pervaded by buddha-nature; having this heritage of the Great Vehicle, they are potential buddhas. [Actualizing it,] however, is taught to depend on a cause, which is accomplishing the two accumulations; it is this cause that illuminates that [buddhahood].

In tantra, the mandala of the primordially pure buddha as such naturally abides as spontaneously present; in merely realizing this through the method taken as the path, the buddha as such is made manifest: there is no need to search some other place for a buddha that is newly established through a cause.

—*INTELLIGENT PRESENCE: PART II OF THE TRILOGY OF INNATE MIND*, 490–91

17 *Establishing Appearances as Divine*

In the following excerpt, Mipam responds to a doubt regarding a fundamental element of tantra: the divine nature of the world. In the practice of tantra, one takes on the outlook of all-encompassing purity, seeing the environment as divine and the inhabitants as deities. An important part of this practice is to assume the "divine pride" of identifying with the deity. However, Mipam does not make the tantric distinction simply one of method. Rather, he grounds tantric practice within reason and argues to support the position that there is a distinctive *view* in tantra by defending the divine purity of the world with much the same logic he uses to defend the emptiness of things. To support his argument, he says that just as emptiness is the way things are when the nature of appearances—as it is—is seen correctly, likewise purity is the way things are when they are seen authentically. Even though things may not appear pure to everyone, with training, they can be seen in this way. And even though everyone may not see things as empty, with training, the mind can learn to see the empty nature of things.

Some small-minded people might say, "Meditating on the path of the pure environment and inhabitants is merely a cause for their potential pure appearance, but they are not actually pure. This is so because they appear like this with the nature of [the truths of] suffering and origin."

We also accept that those of us with impure minds and impure eyes perceive impurity as the mode of appearance. Similarly, if everyone had pure appearances, what would there be to dispute about? Although the mode of appearance is like this, the mode of reality is not: we assert it to be naturally pure. Appearances are not necessarily in accord with the mode of reality, because minds polluted by delusion have distorted appearances—like an eye cognition that perceives a snow mountain as blue. Therefore, from the *Root Verses of the Middle Way,*

When disputation is done through emptiness
Whatever is stated to contend [with emptiness]
Does not contend [with emptiness]
Because [a proof of nonemptiness] is similar to what is established
 [i.e., empty].[199]

This should be known as it's stated. For example, when ascertaining that all phenomena are empty, no matter what phenomena are set forth as a means to prove the nonempty—[for example,] the causality of karma, samsara, nirvana—that very means of proof is similar to what is established in the former [i.e., empty]; it also can be proven to lack intrinsic nature. Hence, whatever is put forward as a means to prove the nonempty also works to assist the reasoning that establishes emptiness, like adding kindling to the fire. Therefore, just as nothing is found within the sphere of what can be known that can refute emptiness, here [in tantra] as well, anything whatsoever that is put forward to prove phenomena to be impure, that very means of proof also is itself what is established as pure. Therefore, an argument that is able to refute the reasoning that establishes all phenomena as pure in the mode of reality is not found within the sphere of what can be known.

When disputation is done through great purity
Whatever is stated to contend [with great purity]

Does not contend [with great purity]

Because it [a proof of impurity] is similar to what is established [i.e., pure].

[One may think,] "If sentient beings are buddhas, then it would also follow that buddhas suffer when sentient beings are suffering in hell." Such consequences are not established, because suffering in hell is from the perspective of deluded ones who have not realized the mode of reality; it is merely the mode of appearance. Since they are not buddhas from the perspective of this mode of appearance, there is no fault. Also, suffering, etc., does not exist in the mode of reality. As is stated in the *Extensive Magical Manifestation*,

> Without the intelligence of reflexive awareness that knows authentically,
> Even the buddha-fields are seen as abodes of the lower realms.
> When the meaning of equality in the supreme vehicle is realized as it is,
> The abodes of the lower realms themselves are the abodes of the Unexcelled [Akaniṣṭha] and the Joyous [Tuṣita].

Moreover, there are those who hurl consequences such as, "If all phenomena are the nature of the buddha from the beginning, then it follows that they would appear [that way] to everyone; and so it would not be necessary to train on the path." These [people] have extremely coarse intellects and are worthy of compassion: "If conches are white, then it follows that they must appear that way even to those with faulty eyes! It follows that it is not necessary to strive in the methods of healing faulty eyes!" Such statements are exactly the same.

Therefore, appearances that do not accord with the mode of reality arise from pollutants that come from delusion; hence, in order to remove delusion, one needs to train on the path; even though the nature of all phenomena is emptiness, one needs to tread the path in order to actualize it.

—*OVERVIEW: ESSENTIAL NATURE OF LUMINOUS CLARITY*, 457–59

18 *Fourfold Valid Cognition*

In the following excerpt, Mipam gives an explanation of his two conventional valid cognitions of confined perception and pure vision, which are the means by which he describes how the world appears to an ordinary being (confined perception) and to a sublime being (pure vision). These two perspectives are fundamental to the way he supports the validity of a pure world, as described in the tantras, without undermining the provisional validity of the world of ordinary experience.

The valid cognitions correlate with two tiers of the relative truth—the incorrect and the correct. In terms of confined perception, the perception of grass as red is incorrect while seeing it as green is the correct relative truth. What counts as the correct relative truth in the context of sutra, however, is incorrect in the context of tantra. In tantra, the world, seen as it is, is all-encompassing purity. Therefore, the world is divine in the perceptions of sublime beings during postmeditation, and Mipam calls this the valid cognition of pure vision.

It is of vital importance to know that the relative, the phenomena of whatever there is, is twofold: (1) the mode of appearance from a deluded perspective and (2) the mode of reality of the relative itself. It is extremely close-minded to think that (1) the valid cognition of conventional analysis is exclusively confined, ordinary perception and (2) merely what is perceived by that [confined perception] is the consummate, conventional mode of reality. When investigated well, it is only a coarse intellect that does not even distinguish how it is reasonable to differentiate the white conch-apprehension and the yellow conch-apprehension as valid and invalid cognitions.

If there were no other mode of reality for entities other than the way that they appear to just an ordinary being, then the appearance of a yellow conch to the one who perceives it as yellow also would be true as the mode of reality of the conch. One may think, "But that is a perception that is polluted by a deluding cause. It is not a perception of the mode of reality." Even though these impure appearances, which are polluted by predispositions that have distorted them, are suitable to appear to ordinary beings, their mode of reality is how they appear to those with pure mind-streams free from the pollution of predispositions. It is unsuitable to assert otherwise.

Therefore, to briefly show an extremely profound essential point, there are two thoroughly conventional valid cognitions: (1) the thoroughly conventional valid cognition based upon confined perception and (2) the thoroughly conventional valid cognition based upon pure vision. To briefly express the distinctions between these two, there are four aspects: (1) cause, (2) essence, (3) function, and (4) effect. The cause of the first [conventional valid cognition based upon confined perception] is as follows: it is brought forth through the power of properly investigating its object—a limited phenomenon. Its essence is awareness that is temporarily nondeceptive regarding merely its own object. Its function is to eliminate superimpositions regarding the objects of confined perception. Its effect is engagement, having thoroughly discriminated its object at hand.

The cause of the latter [conventional valid cognition based upon pure vision] is as follows: it is attained subsequent to a proper observation of suchness as it is. Its essence is insight of the vast—subjectivity regarding whatever phenomena there are. Its function is to eliminate superimpositions regarding the domain that is inconceivable to an ordinary mind-stream's confined perception. Its effect is the accomplishment of the wisdom that knows whatever there is.

Examples for these two are [respectively] like a human eye and a divine eye. The domain of confined perception is known by the latter [conventional valid cognition based upon pure vision], but the domain of the latter is not known by confined perception. Therefore, the unique domain of this latter is (1) that which appears such that it conflicts with the objects of ordinary confined perception and (2) that which is an inconceivable domain such as

- an appearance of as many [buddha-]fields as dust motes within the breadth of a single dust mote;
- a show of many aeons' activities in one moment of time;

- showing a display of emanations without wavering from the immutable expanse of phenomena; and
- knowing all objects of knowledge simultaneously with a nonconceptual mind.

What cannot be established [by ordinary confined perception] can be established as extremely reasonable by this valid cognition [of pure vision].

This valid cognition of pure wisdom occurs through the power of the reason of inconceivable suchness; hence, it is extremely powerful, never deceptive, transcendent, pure, unexcelled, and unequaled. Therefore, what can also be established by the path of confined perception—what is taught commonly such as establishing the teacher [Buddha] as valid cognition, etc.—is established by the former [conventional valid cognition of confined perception]. The extraordinary domain of the *Tathāgatas*—what is inconceivable—is established by the latter [conventional valid cognition of pure vision] through the manner of arriving within suchness. In this way, one should be learned in the essential point that the profound meanings—all phenomena are primordially buddha, etc.—are not established only by confined perception, yet are not utterly without a valid means of establishment either.

—*Overview: Essential Nature of Luminous Clarity,* 447–48

19 Practical Advice for Beginners

The following short text is translated in its entirety. Most often, advice "for beginners" seems to be the best advice for everyone, beginner or not. In this text, Mipam counsels us to renounce samsara, remember death, investigate our mind, meditate one-pointedly in solitude, cultivate devotion, and rest in the nature of mind. In the last stanza, he encourages us to gather the accumulations and purify obscurations, spurring us on to practice diligently. What more advice could a Buddhist need?

Alas! All actions of samsara are futile.
They are unreliable, fluctuating like a play of light.
It is uncertain when death will arrive here,
Yet death is an absolute certainty. Without making elaborate plans,

Focus on the practical instructions of your teachers and
Determine what your mind is one-pointedly in a solitary place.
The mind is like a flash of lightning, the wind, a cloud.
It is distorted by myriad concepts, uncontrolled thoughts.

If you investigate well, it has no basis or root;
Like a mirage in space, its essence is empty.
While empty it appears, and while appearing, it is empty.
Rest your mind at ease and remain in the natural state.

If your practice becomes firm, you will see your mind's fundamental nature.
If your devotion to your teacher is great, you will receive the blessings.
If you gather the accumulations and purify obscurations, realization will come forth.
So practice with diligent effort!

—ADVICE FOR BEGINNERS, 186–87

20   Practical Advice for Monastics

In the following text, Mipam gives brusque advice to members of the monastic community. Much of this advice, however, pertains not only to monks and nuns, but to everyone. He reminds his audience of the value of human life, its impermanence, the importance of renunciation, and the law of karma. Understanding these topics is fundamental to Buddhist practice. Although the words he uses are direct, simple, and easy to understand, the meaning cuts to the root of Buddhist practice, which is not so easy to really take to heart.

Simple words—as reminders of the fundamentals of practice—are held dear by Buddhist practitioners because they extract the quintessence of practice. Such instructions have an important place at the heart of the lived and living Buddhist tradition. The text is translated in full.

Having paid homage to my teacher, Mañjughoṣa,[200]
I will say a few sensible words to my close friends:
If I were to speak profound words, they may be understood, but they are
    difficult to practice.
Words are not that hard to understand, are they?

The abundant food you eat turns into a pile of shit.
The body you sustain gives way to old age, sickness, and death.
Doesn't it make sense to take only the food that you need to live
And make this opportunity of a human life meaningful?

A lot of talk spins the wheels of distraction.
The tumult of desire and anger disturbs the mind.
All such prattle is utterly pointless.
Doesn't it make sense to put effort into reciting texts with great purpose?

There is no end to the flow of thoughts;
You fool yourself, like doing business in a dream.
Doesn't it make sense to let go of these meaningless waves of sorrow
And meditate with one-pointed concentration?

Amassing wealth makes you desperate and stingy;
It brings the stress of acquiring, protecting, and losing.
As much as you make, it will certainly be left behind.
Doesn't it make sense to let go of wealth and practice the sacred Dharma?

With a large family, it is difficult to guard your mind and take care of a
    home.
A family brings much misery and pain.

No matter how long you're together, the end is separation.
Doesn't it make sense to let go of samsara and stay in a solitary place?

As much as you indulge in sleep, games, beer, and sex,
The more you'll desire them as time goes by.
The more you avoid them, the less power they have over you.
Doesn't it make sense to maintain a healthy balance?

All the attractions of samsara are futile:
The more you get, the more you crave, satisfaction never found.
Knowing this, those who leave them behind and rest their minds at ease
Have happiness exceeding that of gods and highest kings.

When too distracted by the flavor of the eight worldly concerns,[201]
You become dazed by these demons and stray from the Dharma—
As the flashing drama of this life fades out,
You'll be summoned by unbearable regret.

Death is unstoppable—it is everyone's fate.
The time of death is uncertain—this too is shared by all.
After dying, you helplessly follow the path of your karma.
Isn't now the time when you're in control?

It is impossible not to care for yourself.
Since everyone wants to be happy, the Victorious One taught
The method for achieving this goal.
Alas! Don't just waste your time carelessly!

Monastic discipline is a beautifying ornament that benefits you,
Relying on a spiritual friend is exalted as the root of the path,
And education brings forth your own fulfillment.
When you take up these three, happiness and goodness will flourish.

To seek out this sacred Dharma,
The Supreme Teacher gave up his life many times.

There is nothing more meaningful to learn than this.
Isn't it reasonable to listen well when you study it?

Even if you are not able to pursue the Dharma your entire life
To begin to engage the Victorious One's teaching,
It is reasonable, from time and time, to put some effort
Into a few practices from the path of sutra and tantra.

—A TALK TO MONASTICS, 267–69

21   *Practical Advice on the Path of Illusion*

The following text, translated in its entirety, presents a contemplative practice of seeing the illusory nature of things. Buddhist scriptures remind us that nothing we see, hear, or think is permanent and that everything is empty—no essence can be found in anything when we look for its true nature. While we may feel that we understand this and even claim to acknowledge it as true, we likely still find ourselves falling back into the habit of seeing the world as if it were solid, lasting, and real.

To regard phenomena as illusory loosens the ties of these delusional habits. It frees us from our compulsive reactions of attachment to what we like, aggression toward what we don't like, and the dissatisfaction that results from misguided hopes and fears. The practice Mipam describes here of "bringing illusion onto the path" does not advise us to deny our experiences with cold detachment. For even though all things are empty, like illusions, they appear. Rather, without fixating on the reality of our experiences, we can avoid misconstruing them as something they are not and learn to appreciate them for what they are. When appearances are seen for what they are—as they are—they are self-liberated.

Mindfulness dispels the darkness of samsara, these distorted perceptions.
Mañjuśrī, the illuminating sun, bestow virtue and goodness!

We are faced with bad times, filled with all kinds of misery;
Beings are dishonest, greedy, and hateful.
This is a time full of sadness, any way you look at it.

Wherever you live, it is difficult to find harmonious conditions.
Whatever you do, people are not pleased,
And however you think, virtuous acts do not abound.

What is of sole importance is to tame your mind
Without thinking much about external things:
Apply the essential points of the practice that brings illusion onto the path.

All that you see with your eyes are just like reflections—
Baseless when analyzed and captivating when not.
When thoughts chase after them, you are caught up in attachment;
When let be, they neither harm nor help.

So all that appears as form
Regard as illusion, as a dream.
Without joy in their arrival or sorrow in their passing,
Let them go without judging their help or harm.

Whatever you hear with your ears is like an echo—
Baseless when analyzed and captivating when not.
So all the words you hear with your ears
Regard as illusion, as a dream.

Without joy in pleasant words or sorrow from cruel ones,
Let them go without judging their help or harm.

Whatever comes to mind is like a mirage in space—
Baseless when analyzed and captivating when not.
So whatever thoughts come to mind
Regard as illusion, as a dream.

Without joy in positive thoughts or sorrow from the negative ones,
Let them go without judging their help or harm.

Illustrated in this way, all phenomena that appear and exist, samsara and
   nirvana,
Are unreal like an illusion or a dream.
Help and harm, hope and fear are distortions of our thoughts;
Let be now, thought-free, without accepting or rejecting.

From the time they arise, all these appearances
Seem to be real, solid, and true,
Yet they are momentary and impermanent like lightning or a cloud,
Gradually changing and ceasing in the end.

Outwardly, there is formation, abiding, and disintegration, and the
   seasons of time;
Inwardly, there is old age, youth, increase, decline, joy, suffering, and the
   like;
They fluctuate without certainty—consider this fact well.
Don't hold tightly to their permanence or true reality; see them as
   illusions.

From beginningless time until now
Whatever has appeared as self and other, happiness or sadness is like an
   illusion.
Where has it gone? It does not exist, so it neither helps nor harms right
   now.
Everything that appears in the present and future is like this.

When investigated well, all the various appearances of happiness and
   sorrow—
Whatever appears in samsara and nirvana—
Are just constructions of thought
Without any essence like an illusion or a dream.

By understanding this, you see through the deception of thought—
The source of your pointless suffering.
The hundredfold effort for joy and sorrow, hope and fear, accepting and
   rejecting,
Dissolves like an image drawn on the surface of water—how delightful!

Under the influence of delusion from beginningless time
You'll find it difficult to become adept in just a short time.
As you become accustomed, without forgetting the practice,
These infallible appearances that dependently arise
Appear yet resemble a mirage in space.

As expressions in the expanse of the innate nature of mind,
Various illusory appearances of samsara and nirvana are disclosed.
Not held by thoughts, you find natural liberation as it is.
Within the state of awareness—the abiding reality of the unchanging
   fundamental nature—
The fleeting expressions are vividly self-liberated!

In the yoga of those with eyes of self-existing insight,
The darkness of fear and suffering is extinguished.

Emaho! By the magical display of the *vajra*-illusion,
Which is the blessing of the Youthful Mañjuśrī forever in my heart,
May all fortunate beings through these instructions
See the viewpoint that is self-arisen and self-liberated!

—CONCISE POINTS OF BRINGING ILLUSION ONTO THE PATH:
ADVICE FOR PRACTITIONERS, 274–77

22   Stages to Calm Abiding

This selection presents the stages in the process of meditative concentration that leads to calm abiding. The nine stages, the techniques ap-

plied at each stage, and the five corresponding experiences are common to presentations of the path to cultivate calm abiding. Mipam's presentation is particularly lucid and conveys practical advice to meditators within the structure of these nine stages. He concludes the stages of cultivation by condensing the essential elements of the practice into five points, then four points, then two, then one. Thus, he simplifies the techniques and makes them practicable for those of us who are less gifted meditators.

Generate faith and aspiration through the power of the practical instructions for the methods of setting the mind, [and bring to mind] the faults of not attaining meditative stabilization and the good qualities of attaining it. Relinquish laziness, etc., through strenuous effort. Then settle on the objective of the generation and completion stages for whichever object is observed. This is the first method, [setting].

At that time, even though [the mind], moving like lightning, does not abide for even an instant, with enthusiasm keep trying, training again and again. Through the power of contemplating what you have heard about the meaning of the practical instructions on meditative stabilization, maintain the continuity of abiding on the previous observation as much as you can. This is the second [method, continuous setting].

At the time of the first two methods, even though it is difficult to remain continuously, you should settle in that continuity by means of firm concentration and a tightened mental engagement. When the mind, moving like a shooting star, is distracted elsewhere from the continuity of its previous observation, bring it back on track through mindfulness— like drawing a strong current of water into a conduit. This is the third [method, resetting].

At the time of these first three methods of setting, there is an experience of movement resembling a piece of paper being carried by the wind or a torrent of water rushing down a steep mountain. Therefore, conceptuality is very strong; it is difficult to find an opportunity to abide. Consequently, you should make a strong effort without losing heart, as if building a dam in a powerful current of water. Like a wild horse, this mind is extremely difficult to tame. Tightly bind it with the rope of mindfulness and put it in the corral of relaxed equanimity. It is crucial to guide it with the reins of exertion.

When mindfulness becomes a little more powerful than before, a slight stability commences in the mind, which is abiding to some extent in an unclear way on just the observed object in front of the mind. Through gathering your attention in a single-pointed manner, practice close setting on only that observed object. This is the fourth [method, close setting].

At this time, the mind just circles around its observed object, like birds flying in the air around a carcass. Birds do not leave the carcass and go elsewhere, but when they land on it, they are not able to stay; they all fly back and forth around the carcass. Consequently, it is important to just gain stability in the continuity of mindfulness.

From there, a small degree of natural delight is brought forth in the meditative stabilization. Then, like a bee moving quickly, not staying for long in one place to extract nectar, an aspiration arises to settle. When this happens, you attain some discipline over the intolerable movement of thoughts as they had been before. This is the fifth [method, disciplining].

For both close setting and disciplining, it is a bit more comfortable to settle than in the first circumstances [of setting, continuous setting, and resetting]. Consequently, it is called "the experience of attainment." This is the start of the first arising of meditative stabilization, or the attainment of a little warmth. Nevertheless, this is exemplified by water in a gorge, as many frenzied, subtle thoughts are gathered in a stream of whirling current. As such, the example of water in a gorge shows that it is a little gentler than water rushing down a steep mountain.

At the time of disciplining, there is an incessant movement of thoughts when the mind is directed toward an object, even though the observed object is not lost by the mind. It is like a bee that is put in a jar—it has no power to leave the jar until it is let out, but it does not stay still inside the jar. At that time, it is crucial to abide with attentiveness, without shifting the mind from the state of that observation.

In this way, if agitation and laxity arise when abiding with attention on that [observation], cultivate the intention to eliminate them by means of the proper application of their respective antidotes. Thereby, the various concepts, the obstacles, naturally subside and are pacified. This is the sixth [method, pacifying]. When pacified in this way, settle in that state without moving, free of the faults of agitation and laxity, like water cleared of impurities. Like a person relaxing, abide attentively within a state of equanimity.

Through further developing the slight pacification of conceptuality, the subsidiary afflictive emotions—the domain from which thoughts proliferate—are also thoroughly pacified. Thereby, distraction is abandoned like silted water progressively becoming clear. This is the seventh [method, thorough pacifying].

When the faults of distraction are cast away by both pacifying and thorough pacifying, the experience of meditation is said to be like a river. From a distance, it looks as if a slow-moving river is not moving. However, observed up close, it is constantly in motion. Likewise, although it seems like the mind is abiding, when observed closely, there are a lot of subtle movements. At that time, the essential point is to develop further and further through diligence. From resetting up until here [thorough pacifying], when interrupted by agitation and laxity, it is extremely important to discipline the mind by three means—attentiveness, intention, and equanimity—since you are still in the context of applying mental engagement to the observation.

Through the power of generating diligence, it [remaining on the observation] becomes superior to what it was before: you are still making effort, however, thoughts cannot disrupt it. This abiding one-pointedly on the observation is called "with [stream-lined] application" or "single-pointedness"; it is the eighth [method]. The experience based on this is said to be like an ocean without waves. As the mind abides and you still make effort, this is the context of uninterrupted, applied mental engagement. At this time, it is important to abide in equanimity with regard to the observation.

Through developing further the contexts that involve application, you attain the setting in equipoise, which is naturally engaged and freed of effort. This is the last of the nine mental abidings. This is also called "the single-pointedness of the Desire Realm mind." It is attained through the power of complete familiarity with assimilation of the previous ones. Here begins the experience of completion, unwavering and unshifting like a mountain.

In rendering the mind of the Desire Realm as single-pointed, the directed mind mingles with the observation free of effort. In all activities, it [the mind] naturally abides. When setting naturally without thinking anything at all, appearances cease and there is an experience of the mind mingling with space. When you arise from this, it feels as if your body has suddenly materialized. Also, during postmeditation, the strength of [afflictive emotions], such as attachment and aggression, is weak and intermittent. Various experiences of bliss, clarity, and non-thought arise. For instance, when the experience of clarity is strong, you feel as if you can count the number of subtle particles in [objects] such as pillars. Even sleep seems to be mixed with meditative stabilization, and most dreams appear as pure too.

Also, such meditative stabilization has the character of truth or the character of a gross tranquility, but it must be established as the foundation of a path common to insiders and outsiders [Buddhist and non-Buddhists]. Yet when not embraced with pliancy, it is not even genuine calm abiding—how could it be special insight? Therefore, within bliss, clarity, and nonthought also there are two [alternatives]: (1) meditative experiences of meditative equipoise on thatness and (2) those which are not. Hence, you need to be learned in the essential points of the path and not assume that a slight experience of mental abiding is the high road.

Through familiarization with such a state (the single-pointedness of the Desire Realm mind), mind and body become workable; this is called "pliancy." This mind can be utilized in a virtuous observation for as long as desired; it is under control like a very tame horse. Also, there is bliss due to being completely free from assuming negative states, such as the unpleasantness of being weary, etc. From the power of this [pliancy], a workable energy moves through the body, by which you are free from assuming the negative states of not being able to utilize a heavy body, etc. The spine [straight] like a stack of gold coins, the body light like cotton fiber, and the body as if instantly pervaded by a stream of warm milk—with this character of bliss, there is pliancy of a body that is able to be utilized for any virtue you desire.

For such a pliancy also, there is a succession from first bringing forth the gross [pliancy] and then the subtle. The gross also begins minutely and in the end clearly appears when it is brought to thorough completion. The gross [pliancy] moves the mind and progressively loses its strength. Then a minute pliancy, fine like a shadow, appears in accord with the meditative stabilization of nonmovement. This is called "calm abiding." Through this, no matter what meditation you do, generation or completion stage, it becomes genuine.

This process was a detailed demonstration of how to accomplish meditative stabilization. In short, with enthusiasm for meditative stabilization, place [the mind] on the observation. Generate uninterrupted effort in this and maintain mindfulness continuously. With attentiveness, avoid agitation and laxity. When there are no faults, stay in equanimity. Practice again and again by means of these five: enthusiasm, effort, mindfulness, attentiveness, and equanimity. Thereby, you will naturally be free from distraction and accomplish well an abiding freed of movement. Or you can accomplish this by means of four [practices]: (1) set with enthusiasm, (2) generate effort, (3) guard with attentiveness, and (4) abide in equanimity. Or by means of two: (1) generate enthusiasm and (2) abide in the observation. Or condensed into one: set [the mind] on the observation for as long as you can.

—OVERVIEW: ESSENTIAL NATURE OF LUMINOUS CLARITY, 479–85

23 Stillness, Movement, and Awareness in the Great Seal

In the following untitled text, Mipam presents a concise guide to meditation in the tradition of the Great Seal and the Great Perfection, whose meditative practices have a lot in common. A fundamental part of these traditions is to come to acknowledge that there are no appearances other than what is experienced in mind, yet these appearances—and the mind too—are empty and baseless. Emptiness is not a mere void; it is inseparable from the quality of clarity, or awareness. The uncontrived unity of emptiness and clarity is the nature of mind, the luminous clarity of awareness. This unity of emptiness and awareness constitutes what is called "emptiness endowed with all supreme aspects."

Within this short text, we can see how major elements of Mipam's meditation instructions play into the themes of mind and emptiness in his works on the Yogic Practice School and the Middle Way. His philosophical texts on the view are not divorced from his writings on the applied practice of meditation; they are deeply intertwined. We can see here how the view plays a fundamental role in the practice of meditation.

If you practice simply the threefold stillness, movement, and awareness within the Great Seal, you can come to see the truth of suchness. The essential point of this relies on the existence of buddha-nature, the suchness of mind, and also relies on the power of applying the key points of the quintessential instructions about it. Since the root of all phenomena comes down to the mind, if you seek out the key point of mind and come to know the mind's secret, you will be learned in all phenomena and realize the meaning of selflessness. In this context, we will give up a lot of analysis and follow the quintessential instructions of those with realization.

When you turn within and look at your mind, if it remains without proliferation, it is called "still." If lots of thoughts proliferate, this is called "movement." In either case, the mind that is aware of itself in this way is called "awareness." If you sustain this continuously, you will come to understand the essential point of how various perceptions of joy and sorrow arise from the mind and dissolve into the mind. When this is understood, all appearances are recognized as the mind's self-appearance.

Then, by looking nakedly at the essence of this mind that is still or moving, although there are various appearances, you come to understand that they are empty, lacking any real essence whatsoever. Yet "empty" is not a void emptiness like space. Rather, you come to know emptiness endowed with all supreme aspects, in which the quality of clarity—fully cognizant and fully aware—is unobstructed, while its nature is not at all real. When you realize the essential point of the mind's secret like this, you experience the innate nature of mind, which is luminous and clear by nature, yet undifferentiated into a viewer and an object viewed. This is called "the recognition of awareness." This is also what is pointed out in the Great Seal and the Great Perfection. If you can sustain it, what will happen, in the words of Saraha is that "By looking again and again at the nature of space, which is pure from the beginning, viewing comes to an end." This is the meaning stated in the *Mother [Perfection of Wisdom Sutra]:* "The mind is devoid of mind; the nature of mind is luminous clarity."[202] There is nothing easier than this. It is very important to practice!

—*Stillness, Movement, an Awareness in the Great Seal,*

22–23

24   Method for Sustaining the Nature of Awareness

The following is an instruction on key points of meditation in the tradition of the Great Perfection. It is concisely divided into three phases: recognize the nature of awareness, perfect the strength, and attain stability. In the Great Perfection, sustaining the nature of mind is itself a complete path to becoming a buddha, because the nature of mind is the buddha. Recognizing the nature of mind as it is, unclothed by the distortions of thought and contrived effort, is the first step to becoming a buddha. But recognition alone is not enough. One must gain familiarity with sustaining this recognition of the natural state of awareness and overcome the chronic habits of getting caught up in the story lines of conceptual distortion. This is the second step in the process, perfecting the strength. The last step is attaining stability: one stabilizes the recognition of awareness and comes to experience the all-encompassing purity of all that appears and exists. This is the stage of a complete and perfect buddha.

Homage to the glorious primordial protector!

In sustaining the nature of mind, there is a threefold process: (1) recognizing, (2) perfecting the strength, and (3) attaining stability. First, through the quintessential instructions of your teacher, scrutinize your mind until you nakedly see the very face of awareness free of conceptual discrimination. Having determined what its nature is, it is important to sustain exclusively this nature. It is not enough to simply recognize; you must perfect the strength. Moreover, when you first recognize the nature of awareness and initially rest within it, thoughts will interrupt, making it difficult for awareness to dawn nakedly. Thus, at this time, it is important to prolong this state by resting again and again in uncontrived awareness, letting thoughts be without suppressing or pursuing them. By gaining familiarity in this way, the waves of thought become less strong, and the nature of awareness will be sustained more lucidly. When this happens, stay with this in meditative equipoise as long as you can, and in postmeditation, rely on the mindfulness of recalling the nature of awareness.

Becoming accustomed to this, you will come to perfect the strength of awareness. When thoughts first arise, you do not need to rely on another remedy to obstruct them; left alone, in a while they are self-liberated, just like a knotted snake unravels itself. By becoming further accustomed, the arising of thoughts causes a slight disturbance, but immediately dissipates on its own, like a picture drawn on the surface of water. By becoming further accustomed to this state, the arising of thoughts has no negative effect whatsoever. Without hope or fear of thoughts arising or not, an experience dawns for which they neither help nor harm—like a thief entering an empty house.

By becoming further accustomed to this state, the final perfection of strength is when all thoughts, along with the fluctuating winds of the universal ground, dissolve into the Truth Body in the end. This is awareness seizing its natural state. Just as you cannot find any ordinary stones when you look on an island of gold, all of appearance and existence dawns as the field of the Truth Body. When everything without exception becomes all-encompassing purity, this is the attainment of stability—the hopes and fears for birth and death in samsara or nirvana are completely dismantled.

Without needing to rely on another practical instruction, the process of mastery of thought and awareness during the daylight also corresponds to the night; know that this similarly is the way of embracing luminous clarity during a dream, during light and deep sleep, and so on. Until attaining stability, you should continue free of distraction to persevere like the flow of a river.

—*WISDOM ESSENCE: THE METHOD FOR SUSTAINING THE NATURE OF MIND, 218–20*

25 A Quintessential Instruction on the Vital Point in Three Statements

The following is a complete translation of Mipam's short work presenting an instruction on the practice of the Great Perfection. Here, he draws from the style of meditation teachings based on the last testament of the Indian master Garap Dorjé, which is called "Three Statements That Strike the Vital Point." Garap Dorjé's words were popularized in a famous commentary by Patrul Rinpoché, who was one of Mipam's teachers. Mipam here contributes his own quintessential instruction, in verse, around three statements that similarly articulate the view, meditation, and conduct of the Great Perfection. Reflecting the direct style of quintessential instructions, he highlights the importance of personal experience as opposed to dry intellectual thought.

Homage to Mañjuśrī!

The carefree, ordinary mind
Cannot be shown by words; it must be known by oneself.
When fabrication, artifice, and fixation subside in themselves,
This is called "recognizing the nature of mind."

Without being caught in the tangled knots of thought, and
Without deviating from the innate state,
When deliberate effort and fixation are gone,
This is called "sustaining meditation."

The mind is at ease when
All the manifold waves of thought, like clouds in the sky,
Neither help nor harm.
This is called "liberation in itself."

This quintessential instruction on the vital point in three statements,
Composed by Mipam Namgyel,

Is realized by those with inner experience;
Empty-talking intellectuals just don't get it!

—A QUINTESSENTIAL INSTRUCTION ON THE VITAL POINT IN
THREE STATEMENTS, 134

26 Ground, Path, and Fruition of the Great Perfection

The Great Perfection, or Atiyoga, represents the highest view and practice in the Nyingma tradition and thus can be seen as the guiding principle of Mipam's presentation of Buddhism. Drawing from Longchenpa's *Wish-Fulfilling Treasury,* Mipam presents a concise outline of the main points that characterize the Great Perfection. After first discussing various systems of non-Buddhist thought, his full text presents a broad scope of Buddhist philosophical systems, beginning with the Great Exposition School and proceeding through the Consequence School of the Middle Way all the way up to the Great Perfection. This selection is from the conclusion of the text, the last section of the ground, path, and fruition of the Great Perfection. It thus represents the pinnacle of Buddhist philosophy and practice.

There is also ground, path, and fruition for Atiyoga. The ground is as follows: All phenomena are ascertained as equality—as the self-existing wisdom primordially abiding within the essence of the single sphere itself. Moreover, all phenomena are merely perceptions in your mind; the nature of appearance is not established in any way, it is false. The nature of mind abides from the beginning as the identity of the three exalted bodies: the empty essence is the Truth Body; the natural clarity is the Enjoyment Body;[203] and the all-pervasive compassionate resonance is the Emanation Body.[204] Within the state of this reality that is the indivisibility of primordial purity and spontaneous presence, all phenomena of samsara and nirvana—without accepting or rejecting—are ascertained as the nature of equality, the great mandala of spontaneous presence.

The path is as follows: Having realized the ground in this way, one actualizes the stages of the meaning of suchness as it is through resting without effort—without adding or removing, negating or affirming—within the wisdom of the essential nature that abides within. Moreover, although similar in effortlessly taking self-existing wisdom as the path, one completes the four visions, having overturned the ground of distortion by means of (1) the practice of content-free (*rnam med*) primordial purity, such as the four means of resting freely,[205] and (2) the practice of spontaneous presence with images (*rnam bcas*), such as the three gazes of direct-crossing (*thod rgal*).[206]

The fruition is as follows: Once you have completed abandonment and realization through becoming free from all adventitious defilements, on the ground of the wisdom teacher (*ye shes bla ma*), the essence of the self-aware mind of awakening abides free from increase or decrease—nondual with the pervasive sovereign, the primordial protector, Samantabhadra.[207]

Moreover, within the Great Perfection, there are two [sections] that mainly emphasize the practice of the meaning of primordial purity:

- The Mind Section (*sems sde*), which mainly teaches the view that ascertains the essence of the self-aware mind of awakening, and
- The Expanse Section (*klong sde*), which mainly teaches the meditation of unfabricated meditative equipoise by means of the five expanses of wisdom pervading samsara and nirvana.

Mainly emphasizing the practice of spontaneous presence, there is

- The Quintessential Instructions Section (*man ngag sde*), which captures the essential point of suchness unerringly, without distortion, through ascertaining with the direct perception of the sense faculties the wisdom of luminous clarity abiding within.

Within each of these, there are several presentations concerning the manner of ascertainment in the internal divisions of the path. These should be known elsewhere, from the tantras and the great treasuries of good explanations by the omniscient Longchenpa. In this way, although many divisions are made, in meaning it comes down to the same essential point: effortless engagement through naturally ascertaining the self-existing wisdom itself—abiding as the unity of primordial purity and spontaneous presence—which is free from the mind's obscuring covering.

—CONCISE SUMMARY OF PHILOSOPHIES FROM THE
WISH-FULFILLING TREASURY, 498–500

27   Bringing Afflictions onto the Path

While a common element in the practice of tantra is the use of afflictive emotions, such as desire, on the path to liberation, it is rare that anyone offers a theoretical explanation of just how this works—as Mipam does here. He shows how the five main afflictive emotions—desire, anger, stupidity, pride, and jealousy—in their ordinary forms, are expressions of the mind's nature. Ordinarily, these afflictions arise through the distorted structure of ego-clinging, which brings forth suffering. Yet the source of this manifestation is simply the expressive power of mind, which can manifest as wisdom or affliction, depending on whether or not ego-fixation is present. Therefore, it is not necessary to reject afflictive emotions, as in the path of the Lesser Vehicle, nor transform them with some extrinsic technique. In Highest Yoga Tantra, the afflictive emotions themselves can be taken as the path, because they are known to manifest the energy of wisdom when they are not distorted through the filter of ego-fixation. Thus, without the distorting structure of a mistaken identification of self, the afflictive emotions—as they are—are the expressive power of wisdom, the manifest nature of mind. It is for this reason that each of the afflictions reflects a particular quality of mind's expressive nature and thus correlates with one of the five wisdoms and five buddha families.

Desire is a mind that has the character of aspiring toward an object, taking it in. Due to the mind having such an expression, (1) at the time of the path, there is aspiration toward the supreme qualities of the path and fruition, and (2) at the time of the fruition, there is perception through taking in all phenomena, without turning away. Desire has the identity of discerning wisdom; it is established as Amitābha.

Anger has the character of expelling what is not in harmony. Due to the mind having such an expression, (1) at the time of the path, the discordant factors of the path are not permitted to stay within your mind-stream, and (2) at the time of the fruition, what is dispelled are the defilements of delusion concerning the nature of what is. Anger has the nature of mirror-like wisdom; it is established as Akṣobhya—the destroyer of all demons and obstacles.

Stupidity has the character of turning away from the nature of objects. It has the nature of abiding in equanimity, without concepts about those objects. Due to the mind having such an expression, (1) at the time of the path, you do not hold on to attributes (*mtshan 'dzin*), and (2) at the time of the fruition, you are free of conceptualizing any constructed objects. Stupidity has the identity of the wisdom of the expanse of phenomena; it is established as Vairocana.

Pride has the character of presumed superiority. Due to the mind having such an expression, (1) at the time of the path, you engage wholeheartedly, and you maintain that nothing is superior to the path of tantra; and (2) at the time of the fruition, because you are endowed with all good qualities, there is no sense of impoverishment or hesitation. Pride is the essence of the wisdom of equality, without any pains of imbalance whatsoever; it is established as Ratnasambhava.

Jealousy is a mind that, upon observing self and other, confronts inequality and cannot bear it. Due to the mind having such an expression, (1) at the time of the path, you take up what should be done and turn away from what should not, and (2) at the time of the fruition, you benefit disciples and avoid harming them. Jealousy has the nature of the all-accomplishing wisdom; it is established as Amoghasiddhi.

Like the potency of a medicine or the luster of a jewel, the mind possesses these five self-expressions from the beginning. Consequently, these five create all the workings of samsara when not realized; however, when realized, they create all the activity of a pure nirvana. If the strength of these five expressions is not present—like an arrow shot that has expended its force or a machine with a broken engine—you are not able to fully accomplish your goals, like entering into an Auditor's peace. Therefore, it is impossible for the mind's own expression to cease so that it never arises again. Also, it is not necessary to stop [the mind's own expression] because when it is not polluted by delusion, it arises as the five wisdoms.

—OVERVIEW: ESSENTIAL NATURE OF LUMINOUS CLARITY,
520–22

28   *Mind and Wisdom*

In the following selection, Mipam addresses topics that shed light on significant facets of his view. He discusses the relationship between mind and wisdom and states that they are not the same conventionally, but ultimately they are not different. He also says that, in reality, buddhas are not different from sentient beings; they are merely different in the way they appear. This distinction between appearance and reality is an important element in his description of buddha-nature. It is also a principal means by which he lays out the ground, path, and fruition across his interpretation of sutra, tantra, and the Great Perfection.

The two truths indivisible—the emptiness endowed with all supreme aspects that is the object of individual reflexive awareness—is the consummate expanse of phenomena and the consummate emptiness. When this is realized, verbal expressions make distinctions such that the realized object, which is the expanse of phenomena, is realized by wisdom; however, in reality, [wisdom and the expanse of phenomena] are not the slightest bit different.

The definition of consciousness is that which is clear and aware and has the nature of conceptuality. The definition of wisdom is nonconceptual luminous clarity that has the nature of individual reflexive awareness of the abiding reality. The suchness of consciousness is wisdom.

The definition of the buddha is the consummate wisdom that is completely free of the two obscurations and predispositions. From the aspect of perceiving suchness, that wisdom is called "the wisdom that knows what is." From the aspect of perceiving the entirety of phenomena, it is called "the wisdom that knows whatever there is." Although they are designated by their contradistinctive aspects, in essence, they are not different and nothing other than the sole omniscient wisdom. This is so because it is this wisdom that perceives the consummate reality of the indivisible two truths.

Therefore, phenomena, which are the eight collections of consciousness,[208] and the wisdom that is suchness, which is the nature of those [consciousnesses], are not asserted as either the same or different. As Longchen Rapjam stated in accordance with the words in *Elucidating the Viewpoint* (*Saṃdhinirmocana*),

The character of the conditioned realm and the ultimate
Is a character free from being the same or different;
Thus, those who conceive [them] as the same or different
Have entered into an improper view.[209]

Conventionally, the two are not the same because (1) wisdom, the suchness of mind, is not realized by merely realizing the mind, and (2) [mind and wisdom] are phenomena and suchness. Ultimately, they are not different because, due to the nature of mind being wisdom, (1) when wisdom is realized, the mind is also not observed as different from that [wisdom], and (2) when wisdom is realized, the mind arises as self-liberated. This [presentation] makes an important essential point.

Analyzed in this way, the abiding reality of suchness, which is the luminous clarity itself, pervades buddhas and sentient beings like space. However, in the mode of appearance, the suchness of each particular individual with a continuity of the respective eight collections [of consciousness] appears separate and cut off like the partial appearance of space within a jar. For this reason, although the appearances of the ground, path, and fruition are specifically relevant to that [individual], in reality, other than appearances from the nature of the great all-pervasive suchness, there is nothing at all that is individually established as separate.

For this reason, concerning sentient beings, who are imputed upon the mode of appearance as adventitiously deluded, it is not necessary for all to be liberated upon one becoming liberated; nor is it that if one is deluded, all are deluded. All liberation and delusion are alike, without difference, as they arise from the state of the primordial ground-expanse. Therefore, in terms of the naturally pure, primordial suchness, it is necessary to posit the buddha from the beginning because buddhas arise from realizing the equality of existence and peace.

For this reason, all ascertainments of the profound paths of the causal and resultant vehicles attain the consummate fruition through ascertaining suchness as it is and meditating in harmony with it. Therefore, all the philosophies of the Vajrayāna are in terms of the reasoning of the nature of things. Not only here [in Vajrayāna], but the Middle Way also realizes suchness and meditates on it. However, liberation through meditation under the powerful sway of dualistic phenomena was not taught by the Buddha in either the causal or resultant vehicles.

Although in terms of the ultimate abiding reality, appearance and existence are asserted to be primordially buddha and one should meditate like this, in terms of the conventional way of appearance, insight makes three distinctions: (1) the ground, the heritage which is the potential to be a buddha; (2) the path, which is the occasion of practice; and (3) the fruition, which is the consummation of purity. These [three] are accepted all the way up to the Great Perfection. Even the scriptures of the Great Perfection assert that one becomes a buddha through completing the five paths of break-through and the four visions of direct-crossing;[210] it is never asserted that one becomes a buddha without completing the path in the mode of appearance. Therefore, through differentiating these [modes of appearance and reality], the darkness of ignorance about the topics difficult to realize in either the causal or resultant vehicles will be dispelled, and an irreversible light of certainty will come forth. Consequently, distinguishing these is by all means important.

—*INTELLIGENT PRESENCE: PART II OF THE TRILOGY OF INNATE MIND*, 446–50

29 Sutra and Tantra

While Mipam makes a clear distinction between the paths of sutra and tantra, he does not claim that there is a difference in their results. He says that both paths lead to the state of buddhahood. Also, he shows that the difference between the two paths pertains not only to a particular method of practice, but also to a distinctive philosophical view. Here, he describes the difference in view in terms of three ways that wisdom arises in the causal vehicle of sutra, the outer tantras, and the inner tantras. The path of sutra holds that the wisdom of the buddha is something to be attained in the distant future; therefore, it is said to be that "wisdom arises from behind." In the outer tantras, the wisdom of the buddha is seen as coming from outside oneself. Wisdom is held to be bestowed from *out there*, coming from a deity in front of oneself that is evoked in meditation practice. Thus, it is said to be that "wisdom arises in front." In contrast, within the inner tantras, the nature of mind is the buddha, and wisdom is not sought in some other time or place; thus, "wisdom arises from within." Through the path of this unexcelled tantra, one can become a buddha in a single lifetime.

There are three ways that wisdom arises. The way that wisdom arises in the three causal vehicles of characteristics is said to be "great wisdom arising from behind." In the way that dirty water reflects images after becoming clear, the pollution of afflicted thoughts are progressively cleared by remaining for a long time within the nonconceptual. At the end of the tenth ground, one is said to become an omniscient buddha on the stage of "thorough illumination." This wisdom is held to arise in the future after three incalculable aeons. Thus, it is called "wisdom that arises from behind."

In the three outer tantras, it is said to be "great wisdom arising in front." Through invoking the Buddhas that presently reside in the Unexcelled [Akaniṣṭha] (the three or five families together with their retinues),[211] prostrating and making offerings to them in the space in front, one receives accomplishment. Thus, the deities are seen as bestowing accomplishment. Through practicing with the profound methods of the interdependence of oneself, the deity, and the substances, it is held that the consummate fruition is acheived in seven or sixteen human lifetimes. In attaining the result, these [outer tantra] paths are swifter than the causal vehicle of characteristics; therefore, here it is said that "wisdom arises in front."

The inner tantras, the three vehicles of method, are said to be "wisdom arising from within." No phenomenon whatsoever is beyond the state of the great identity that is self-existing wisdom. Therefore, while abiding within the great bliss that is the nature of mind itself, there is no buddha that need be sought elsewhere, and one can become a manifest buddha in this very life. Thus, it is said that "wisdom arises from within."

In this way, the perfection vehicle states that nonconceptual wisdom is the main element of any path: without conceptualizing any object whatsoever, lacking any mental fixation, and free of all conditioned movements, it is the way of abiding within the profound meaning of transcendent insight. The lower vehicles come to understand the nonconceptual domain, suchness free from constructs, by means of an object-universal (*don spyi*).[212] The scriptures of the causal vehicle claim that, through the force of gathering immeasurable accumulations, this [wisdom] can be actualized—produced anew at some time in the future.

Here in the vehicle of tantra, the thusness of secret mantra—the mandala of mind that is naturally luminous and clear—cannot be affected by any thoughts. It cannot be seen as it is by any effort that involves mentally contrived meditation. The profound quintessential instruction for seeing this is due to the essential point of primordial suchness, the nature in which nothing is added or removed. This method is taught in the scriptures of unexcelled tantra but is not found in the path of sutra. Therefore, the path of tantra is superior.

This self-existing wisdom is presented, from the aspect of the quintessential instruction of the method for progressively or instantaneously engaging it, in the threefold generation (*bskyed*), completion (*rdzogs*), and Great Perfection (*rdzogs chen*). One may think, "Since there are distinctions in the paths, then are there distinctions in the results attained in the causal and resultant vehicles?" There are no distinctions [in the result]. The consummate fruition is simply the wisdom of the buddha, which they equally achieve. Yet tantra is superior in method and insight; therefore, it is the swift path by which the consummate fruition is actualized in this life. This cannot be done by other paths.

—DISCOURSE ON THE EIGHT COMMANDS, 43–46

30 Sword of Intelligence: Method for Meditating on Bodhicitta

Mipam composed two sets of five short texts called the "five swords" and the "five lilies." The next excerpt is one of the swords, and the following selection is one of the lilies. The sword is associated with Mañjuśrī, who wields the blazing sword of wisdom that cuts through deception. In this text, Mipam describes the method of meditating on bodhicitta in the context of tantra and the Great Perfection in particular. Bodhicitta, which literally means the "mind of awakening," is cultivated in different ways according to various sutra and tantra practices. Here, Mipam poetically correlates the syllables in Mañjuśrī's mantra—OM A RA PA TSA NA DHIH—with different elements of the practice. An important point of the practice is the fact that bodhicitta, the unity of wisdom and compassion, dwells within.

Vajra-intelligence knows how things are,
Completes the transcendent perfections, and
Reveals the meaning of the four mudras,[213]
To you, great treasury of knowledge, I pay homage!

All phenomena that appear and resound
Are mere appearances when left as they are, unexamined;
They are the conventional, relative truth.
When analyzed, they are not real;
This abiding reality is the ultimate truth.

When assessed by the two valid cognitions,
The two truths are posited separately.
In the consummate meaning, the two truths are indivisible:
Even while no phenomenon is established from its own side,
Mere appearances are undeniably seen.

This essential unity, free of concepts and extremes,
Abides from the beginning as the nature itself;
At that time [of actualizing it], what intelligent one does not realize this unity
To be merely self-appearance?

The manifold mind, like a dream and an illusion,
Has no nature when analyzed;
All perceptions have the nature of the moon reflected in water.
Know that mind is the unity of clarity and emptiness.

When this is not merely conceptually determined, but
Comes to be understood within self-awareness, then
The wisdom body of all the buddhas—
The essential nature of the Dharma, the innate mind, and
The definitive meaning of the youthful Mañjuśrī—
Is directly seen by nonconceptual awareness.

In the abiding reality, as it is,
Rest the mind naturally without fabrication:
"Look authentically at the authentic;
By seeing what is authentic, you are free."[214]

The four *vajra*-syllables correspond to
The reality of the four natures, the four lamps,[215]
And the four mudras;
They accomplish the four methods of the path.[216]

A is the gateway to unborn phenomena.
The expanse arises from the unborn expanse;
Naturally clear, filled with rainbow light,
The expanse is the lamp of purity.

Ra is the gateway to the immaculate.
The eye of wisdom is unobstructed;

Shining infinite rays of light,
It is the far-reaching water lamp.

Pa is the gateway to the appearing ultimate.
Emptiness and awareness are not two;
Luminously clear, free from constructs,
It is the lamp of self-existing insight.

Tsa is without birth, death, or transference.
The natural luminosity of the assembly of five families;
Present from the beginning
Is the lamp of the empty spheres.

Na is the gateway to the nameless.
All these lamps,
Beyond the qualities of signs and conceptual formulations,
Are decisively known without labeling.

Dhih is the gateway to the presence of intelligence.
The qualities of the three exalted bodies abiding within the
    ground
Manifestly appear at the time of the path;
Therefore, this is supreme among the nine stages of the
    vehicles.

When the consummate fruition is reached,
All phenomena, entities and nonentities,
Dissolve into the expanse of great luminosity,
Pacified without reference.

From the outer radiance, the array of
Great clouds of exalted bodies and wisdoms
Come to pervade constantly and masterfully
While liberating beings, for as long as space endures.

By this virtue may infinite beings
Actualize effortlessly the treasure of bodhicitta
Abiding within themselves, and all together
Become liberated within the three exalted bodies!

—*Sword of Intelligence: Method for Meditating on Bodhicitta*, 491–94

31 *Lily of Wisdom's Presence*

The following text is a translation of one of five short texts known as the five lilies. Here, Mipam again conveys the way that self-existing wisdom abides innately within all beings from the beginning. These verses poetically evoke important themes in the Great Perfection: the natural capacity of wisdom; the primordial Buddha Samantabhadra; the three qualities of the ground of the Great Perfection (empty essence, radiant nature, and unimpeded compassion); and the superiority of the Great Perfection as the direct antidote to ignorance.

The blaze of wisdom-knowledge
Illuminates with great light—
Such brilliant luminosity—
I pay homage to the wisdom-being!

Pure from the beginning,
The nature of mind is luminous clarity.
The exalted body and wisdom are inseparable.
The defilements are adventitious.

The threefold nature of the wisdom that abides within the ground
Is essence, nature, and compassion.
Primordial purity is the deep radiance, free from signs.
Inner radiance abides as the youthful vase-body.

Without partiality or restriction,
The cognitive quality is unceasing, radiant within the expanse.
The self-lucidity of love is unceasing;
Therefore, it is spontaneously present within the ground.

Natural Samantabhadra
Is the expanse of the great equality, the fourth time.
The immutable luminous clarity
Is the partless, omnipresent sovereign,
The sacred self, which is immaterial and immaculate.
The wisdom-body is self-existing;
It always abides as the essential nature of all beings,
But is not known.

Due to distortion, all beings in the three realms
Stray into the impure wheel of delusion.
Even those who are pure—the sublime Auditors, Self-Realized Ones, and
    Bodhisattvas—
Are not able to fully realize
The consummate nature of this
Until they achieve extreme purity.
When the two obscurations and their predispositions are entirely
    eliminated,
The abiding reality of the ground is completely realized.

Therefore, the method for eliminating defilements
Should be cultivated through making effort on the path.
Within this too, there are two ways: the common and the extraordinary.
For the common, one gathers the accumulations for an incalculable
    duration;
The result is sought out somewhere else.
For the extraordinary path of tantra as well,
In the outer yogas, one proceeds through a path
That has a view of accepting and rejecting with regard to the two truths.

For the inner vehicle of method,
Even while there is the great equality of the two truths indivisible,
One traverses all the grounds and paths in sequence.
The extreme yoga of the Great Perfection
Has the quintessential instructions of the supreme secret—
The ground and fruition are the great spontaneous presence.
Through the blessings of a teacher with realization,
Awareness free from conceptual mind is pointed out.

Through the yoga that does not waver in three ways,[217]
One rests in the state of primordially pure awareness.
For enhancement, the path of the great secret looks to
The yogas of the four lamps,
The wheels of luminous clarity, and the three essential points.[218]

Perfecting the strength of the appearances of the path,
All distorted perceptions come to the state of exhaustion,
And in this life, one attains the rainbow body of great transference.

On this path of self-existing wisdom that abides within,
All the lower paths are complete.
Wisdom awareness is incompatible with ignorance,
So it is a strong antidote.

Whatever other path you might train in
Does not directly contradict this [ignorance],
So it is not able to destroy the two obscurations from the root.

Therefore, *vajra*-wisdom is stable,
Having a nature that is
Undivided, uninterrupted, and indestructible.
Thus, no adventitious afflictions
Can affect it.

The fundamental nature of self-existing luminous clarity
Has never been tainted by defilements.
Its nature is purity,
And the adventitious stains can be removed.
Therefore, since it accords with the way things are,
This path has power.
When defilements are dispelled by this path,
The qualities of great, immeasurable compassion
And wisdom manifest.

The potency of its power is inconceivable.
Its enlightened activity is constant and pervasive,
Spontaneously present without effort, it occurs naturally.
Objects of knowledge and unconstructed thusness are indivisible
And integrated with wisdom.

This itself is called the Wisdom Truth Body
Of all the buddhas.
While not wavering from this itself,
For the benefit of disciples, pure and impure,
Various miraculous displays of activity are shown
In Emanation and Enjoyment Bodies.

Moreover, from the basic element of the primordial ground,
Actualized as it is,
Comes the self-appearance of self-existing wisdom,
Which never recedes.

May what is profound, peaceful, and free from constructs—
The great, nonconceptual wisdom—
Be discovered by all sentient beings.
May the secret mind of all the buddhas be accomplished!

—*Lily of Wisdom's Presence*, 479–83

32 Verse of Auspiciousness

It is a Tibetan Buddhist tradition to conclude an activity with an aspiration prayer or a verse of dedication. Following this tradition, we will bring this last section to a close with a translation of a short verse composed by Mipam.

May there be auspiciousness for the welfare of beings and the teachings to greatly flourish,
May there be auspiciousness for our wishes and needs to be spontaneously fullfilled,
May there be auspiciousness for our lives to be long, free of sickness, and full of joy,
May there be auspiciousness for prosperity in the Dharma and in the world!

—*VERSE OF AUSPICIOUSNESS*, 742–43

ACKNOWLEDGMENTS

SEVERAL TEACHERS have helped me to appreciate Mipam, particularly Chökyi Nyima Rinpoché and his late father, Tulku Urgyen. I owe a debt of gratitude to many Buddhist scholars who have shared their vast and profound knowledge of Mipam with me, including Khenpo Yeshé Trinlé, Khenpo Namdröl, Khenpo Sherap Zangpo, Khenpo Jampa Lodrö, Khenpo Sherap Dorjé, Khenpo Pema Sherap, Khenpo Kātyāyana, the late Khenpo Wangchuk Sönam, the late Khenpo Apé, Tulku Nyima Gyeltsen, Khenpo Tsülnam, Tulku Tenzin Gyatso, Khenpo Tsültrim Lodrö, and Khenpo Loden, among others. I wish to show my appreciation to Larry Mermelstein for sending me a copy of a Tibetan biography of Mipam, and to Ann Helm for sharing with me a draft of her then-unpublished English translation of it.

I also wish to thank the following people who gave me valuable feedback on this work: Ryan Conlon, Cortland Dahl, Catherine Dalton, Ani Damchoe, Thomas Doctor, James Gentry, Jeff Gold, Andreas Kilchmann, Arthur McKeown, Frank Quillen, Krim Natirbov, Jann Ronis, Raul Schiappa-Pietra, and Gail Stenstad. I owe a special thanks to the talented editors at Shambhala Publications, whose input greatly improved the quality of this book. Michele Martin in particular worked with me closely on multiple drafts of the manuscript, and she is the one who conceived the idea for the book and its structure, so I owe her an enormous debt of gratitude.

May all the ḍākinīs and Dharma protectors, scholars, practitioners, and scholar-practitioners forgive any of my mistakes, omissions, additions, digressions, and transgressions!

A grant from the Research and Development Committee of East Tennessee State University and a summer stipend from the National Endowment for the Humanities helped me bring this project to completion. May it be virtuous! *Sarva mangalaṃ.*

NOTES

1. Although he has several other names too, I will refer to him simply as Mipam.
2. Künzang Chödrak, *Essential Biography and Catalogue of Works*, in *Mipam's Collected Works* (Dilgo Khyentsé's expanded redaction of *sde dge* edition; Kathmandu, Nepal: Zhechen Monastery, 1987), 8:629; English trans. in John W. Pettit, *Mipham's Beacon of Certainty: Illuminating the View of Dzogchen, the Great Perfection* (Boston: Wisdom Publications, 1999), 24.
3. Ibid.
4. Although there is no evidence that Mipam had a consort, he is said to have taught in traditional Tibetan dress and not monk's robes. Khenpo Tsültrim Lodrö, personal communication, June 2006.
5. Künzang Chödrak, *Essential Biography*, 629; English trans. in Pettit, *Mipham's Beacon of Certainty*, 24.
6. Künzang Chödrak, *Essential Biography*, 628–30; English trans. in Pettit, *Mipham's Beacon of Certainty*, 24.
7. Künzang Chödrak, *Essential Biography*, 633–34; English trans. in Pettit, *Mipham's Beacon of Certainty*, 25.
8. Künzang Chödrak, *Essential Biography*, 634; English trans. in Pettit, *Mipham's Beacon of Certainty*, 25.
9. Künzang Chödrak, *Essential Biography*, 631; English trans. in Pettit, *Mipham's Beacon of Certainty*, 24.
10. Künzang Chödrak, *Essential Biography*, 642–44; English trans. in Pettit, *Mipham's Beacon of Certainty*, 29–30.
11. Künzang Chödrak, *Essential Biography*, 641; English trans. in Pettit, *Mipham's Beacon of Certainty*, 29.
12. Künzang Chödrak, *Essential Biography*, 635; English trans. in Pettit, *Mipham's Beacon of Certainty*, 26.
13. Ibid.
14. Künzang Chödrak, *Essential Biography*, 636–37; English trans. in Pettit, *Mipham's Beacon of Certainty*, 26–27.
15. The "Sarma tiger" refers to the Geluk scholar, Pari Rapsel (*dpa' ris blo bzang rab gsal*, 1840–1910). Kuchuk, *Opening the Eye of Clear Intelligence: A History of the Transmission of the Middle Way View in Tibet* (Beijing: China's Tibetan Studies Press, 2004), 374.

16. Künzang Chödrak, *Essential Biography*, 644–45; English trans. in Pettit, *Mipham's Beacon of Certainty*, 30–31.

17. For ease of reading, I will use *tantra* both to translate the texts and to refer to the path of mantra, or Vajrayāna.

18. Künzang Chödrak, *Essential Biography*, 645–46; English trans. in Pettit, *Mipham's Beacon of Certainty*, 31.

19. Mipam, *Beacon of Certainty*, in *nges shes sgron med rtsa 'grel* (Sichuan, China: Nationalities Press, 1997), 19; English trans. in Pettit, *Mipham's Beacon of Certainty*, 209.

20. Sherap Gyatso, *A Short Biography of Gendün Chöpel* (Chengdu, China: Nationalities Press, 1988), 19–20.

21. Künzang Chödrak, *Essential Biography*, 650; English trans. in Pettit, *Mipham's Beacon of Certainty*, 33.

22. Künzang Chödrak, *Essential Biography*, 641; English trans. in Pettit, *Mipham's Beacon of Certainty*, 29.

23. Künzang Chödrak, *Essential Biography*, 661; English trans. in Pettit, *Mipham's Beacon of Certainty*, 38.

24. Mipam, *Words That Delight Guru Mañjughoṣa: Commentary on the* Ornament of the Middle Way, in *dbu ma rgyan rtsa 'grel* (Sichuan, China: Nationalities Press, 1990), 446; English trans. in Thomas Doctor, *Speech of Delight*, 621. The six ornaments are Nāgārjuna and Āryadeva (the two ornaments of the Middle Way), Vasubandhu and Asaṅga (the two ornaments of Abhidharma), and Dignāga and Dharmakīrti (the two ornaments of valid cognition).

25. The four "Mind-Only Sutras" are the *Descent into Lanka Sutra* (*Laṅkāvatārasūtra*), the *Elucidating the Viewpoint Sutra* (*Saṃdhinirmocanasūtra*), the *Flower Garland Sutra* (*Avataṃsakasūtra*), and the *Densely Arrayed* (*Gaṇḍavyūha*).

26. Mipam, *Words That Delight Guru Mañjughoṣa*, 112; English trans. in Doctor, *Speech of Delight*, 137.

27. The Collection of Reasonings comprises six texts by Nāgārjuna: *Root Verses of the Middle Way, Precious Garland, Dispelling Objections, Seventy Verses on Emptiness, Sixty Verses of Reasoning*, and *Finely Woven*.

28. The Collection of Advice refers to a group of Nāgārjuna's texts that includes his *Letter to a Friend (Suhṛllekha)*.

29. The Collection of Praises refers to a group of Nāgārjuna's texts that includes his *Praise to the Expanse of Phenomena (Dharmadhātustotra)*.

30. The five treatises of Maitreya are the *Ornament of Clear Realization* (Tib. *mngon rtogs rgyan*, Skt. *Abhisamayālaṃkāra*), the *Ornament of the Great Vehicle Sutras* (Tib. *mdo sde rgyan*, Skt. *Mahāyānasūtrālaṃkāra*), *Distinguishing Phenomena and Suchness* (Tib. *chos chos nyid rnam 'byed*, Skt. *Dharmadharmatāvibhāga*), *Distinguishing the Middle and the Extremes* (*dbus mtha' rnam 'byed*, Skt. *Madhyāntavibhāga*), and the *Sublime Continuum* (Tib. *rgyud bla ma*, Skt. *Uttaratantra*).

31. Another alternative, known as "dual-aspect monism," holds that all phenomena have a mental and a physical component, an interior and an exterior dimension.

32. See Mipam, *Words That Delight Guru Mañjughoṣa*, 458–59; English trans. in Doctor, *Speech of Delight* 639.

33. Künzang Chödrak, *Essential Biography*, 8:639–40; English trans. in Pettit, *Mipham's Beacon of Certainty*, 28.

34. There is some ambiguity in Tibetan portrayals of what constitutes a particular (that is, the things that are causally efficacious *ultimately* in the Sutra School): extended objects of common sense (such as a pen) or irreducible particles. For a discussion of this issue, see John Dunne, *Foundations of Dharmakīrti's Philosophy* (Boston, MA: Wisdom Publications, 2004), 69–79.

35. Mipam, *Words That Delight Guru Mañjughoṣa,* 83; English trans. in Doctor, *Speech of Delight,* 95.

36. See, for instance, Chandrakirti, *Introduction to the Middle Way: Chandrakirti's* Madhyamakavatara *with Commentary by Jamgön Mipham* (Boston, MA: Shambhala Publications, 2002), VI:76, 92.

37. A problem with both of these naive stereotypes is the narrowly delimited sense of Buddhist "practice" that is presumed and thus the mistaken assumption of what constitutes a Buddhist "practitioner."

38. Rongzom, *Secret Essence Commentary,* in *Rongzom's Collected Works* (Sichuan, China: Nationalities Press, 1999), 1:56.

39. Künzang Chödrak, *Essential Biography,* 8:629; English trans. in Pettit, *Mipham's Beacon of Certainty,* 38.

40. Khenpo Künpel (1870/2–1943). See Tulku Thondup, *Masters of Meditation and Miracles* (Boston, MA: Shambhala Publications, 1996), 272–73.

41. Achim Bayer, "The Life and Works of mKhan-po gZhan-dga' (1871–1927)," (master's thesis, University of Hamburg, 2000), 33, 173–74. For more on Khenpo Zhenga, see David Jackson, *A Saint in Seattle* (Boston, MA: Wisdom Publications, 2003), 27–28; Georges Dreyfus, "Where Do Commentarial Colleges Come From?" *Journal of the International Association of Buddhist Studies* 28, no. 2 (2005): 288–92.

42. For Dilgo Khyentsé's encounter with Mipam, see Ani Jinpa Palmo, trans., *Brilliant Moon: The Autobiography of Dilgo Khyentse* (Boston, MA: Shambhala Publications, 2008), 10–18. Dilgo Khyentsé's statement regarding Khenpo Zhenga is cited in Bayer, "Life and Works," 173–74.

43. Georges Dreyfus, *The Sound of Two Hands Clapping: The Education of a Tibetan Buddhist Monk* (Berkeley, CA: University of California Press, 2003), 148; Anne Klein, *Meeting the Great Bliss Queen: Buddhists, Feminists, and the Art of Self* (Boston, MA: Beacon Press, 1995), 150, 262n2.

44. Tulku Tondrup, *Masters of Meditation,* 244–45.

45. Khenpo Zhenga wrote interlinear commentaries on the "thirteen great scriptures," which include two Vinaya texts, *Vinaya Sutra* and *Individual Liberation Sutra;* two Abhidharma texts, *Treasury of Abhidharma* and *Compendium of Abhidharma;* four texts of the profound view (of the Middle Way), *Root Verses of the Middle Way, Introduction to the Middle Way, Four Hundred Verses,* and the *Way of the Bodhisattva;* and the five treatises of Maitreya, *Ornament of Clear Realization, Ornament of the Great Vehicle Sutras, Distinguishing the Middle and the Extremes, Distinguishing Phenomena and Suchness,* and *Sublime Continuum.* Mipam commented on all of these scriptures with the exception of two: the *Vinaya Sutra* of Guṇaprabha and the *Four Hundred Verses* of Āryadeva.

46. In the colophon of his interlinear commentary on the *Introduction to the Middle Way,* Khenpo Zhenga states that he wrote his commentary "without mixing even a hair of the individual opinions of the Tibetan masters," and in his commentary on the *Sublime Continuum,* that he "did not make anything up himself." See Douglas Duckworth, *Mipam on*

Buddha-Nature: The Ground of the Nyingma Tradition (Albany, NY: SUNY Press, 2008), 196–49.

47. E. Gene Smith, *Among Tibetan Texts* (Boston, MA: Wisdom Publications, 2001), 232–33.

48. Mipam's main teacher, Jamyang Khyentsé Wangpo, began to compile the thirty-two volume *Compendium of Tantras,* which was completed in 1892 by the Sakya scholar, Loter Wangpo (1847–1914). Loter Wangpo also put together the fourteen-volume *Compendium of Methods for Accomplishment,* which is a collection of ritual practice texts (*sādhanas*) from mainly the new schools, or Sarma traditions. He was also instrumental in the preparation of the seventeen-volume *Path and Fruit: Explanations for Trainees,* an important corpus of Sakya texts. See Smith, *Among Tibetan Texts,* 327–779, 328–798–99.

49. Mipam is also credited with writing a catalog for the collected works of Patrul Rinpoché, his direct teacher. Künzang Chödrak, *Essential Biography,* 8:672.

50. The impetus for printing Gorampa's collected works reportedly came from Khenpo Zhenga. One of his students asked him what he could do to promote the Sakya doctrine, which had become feeble. Khenpo Zhenga responded that publishing Gorampa's works would certainly be of benefit. See Bayer, "Life and Works," 33, 45, 251n274; see also David P. Jackson, *A Saint in Seattle,* 58.

51. See Tashi Tsering, "Nag-roṅ mgon-po rnam-gyal: A Nineteenth Century Khams-pa Warrior," in *Soundings of Tibetan Civilization,* ed. Barbara Aziz and Matthew Kapstein (Delhi, India: Manohar Publications, 1985), 196–214.

52. See Elliot Sperling, "The Chinese Venture in K'am, 1904–1911, and the Role of Chao Erh-feng," in *The Tibet Journal* 1, no. 2 (April/June, 1976): 26–27.

53. See Melvyn C. Goldstein, *The Snow Lion and the Dragon: China, Tibet, and the Dalai Lama* (Berkeley, CA: University of California Press, 1997), 22–24.

54. Such texts include his commentaries on the *Introduction to the Middle Way,* the *Root Verses of the Middle Way,* the *Ornament of Clear Realization,* and the *Sublime Continuum.*

55. Mipam, *Words That Delight Guru Mañjughoṣa,* 495; English trans. in Doctor, *Speech of Delight,* 687–89.

56. He wrote *Shedding Light on Thusness* in response to Pari Rapsel's (*dpa' ris blo bzang rab gsal,* 1840–1910) critique and *Light of the Sun* in response to Drakar Tulku (*brag dkar dpal ldan bstan 'dzin snyan grags,* 1866–1928).

57. Among the five treatises of Maitreya, Mipam states that the *Sublime Continuum* and *Ornament of Clear Realization* are Middle Way treatises; the *Ornament of the Great Vehicle Sutras* is a Mind-Only treatise; and *Distinguishing the Middle and the Extremes* and *Distinguishing Phenomena and Suchness* concern the Great Vehicle in general.

58. He wrote a commentary on the *Recollecting the Three Jewels Sutra* (called *Inexhaustible Melody of Auspiciousness*) and also composed interlinear commentaries on the *Individual Liberation Sutra* (called *Steps to Definitive Goodness*) and on the *Condensed Perfection of Wisdom Sutra* (called *Elegant Discourse Introducing the Unmistaken Meaning of the Intended Meaning of the Victorious Ones' Mother*). Additionally, he wrote a text called *Words of Maitreya* that correlates the *Condensed Perfection of Wisdom Sutra* with Maitreya's *Ornament of Clear Realization.*

59. Mipam, *Collected Works,* vol. 8 (*hung*), 131–34.

60. Mipam, *Treasury Illuminating Elegant Discourse: A Clear Explanation of the* Commentary on Valid Cognition, in *Mipam's Collected Works,* vol. 20.

61. Longchenpa, *White Lotus: Autocommentary on the Precious* Wish-Fulfilling Treasury, in *Seven Treasuries*, Tarthang Tulku ed. (Sichuan, China, 1996), 1389–90.

62. The first text of this trilogy, with a commentary by Khetsün Zangpo (1920–2009), has been translated by Jeffrey Hopkins, who intends to translate the whole trilogy. See Jeffrey Hopkins, *Fundamental Mind: The Nyingma View of the Great Completeness* (Ithaca, NY: Snow Lion Publications, 2006).

63. Künzang Chödrak, *Essential Biography and Catalogue of Works*, 8:660; English trans. in Pettit, *Mipham's Beacon of Certainty*, 38.

64. The author is Changkya Rolpé Dorjé (*lcang skya rol pa'i rdo rje*, 1717–1786). See *Mipam's Collected Works*, 4:821–67; English trans. in Karl Brunnhölzl, *Straight from the Heart: Buddhist Pith Instructions* (Ithaca: Snow Lion Publications, 2007), 391–428.

65. This text is mentioned in a catalog of his works but is not included in the Zhechen or Kaḥtok editions of his collected works.

66. Mipam, *Banner Victorious Over All: An Interlinear Commentary on the Treasury of Reasoning*, in *Mipam's Collected Works*, 11:549–752.

67. Mipam, *Supplication Supplement for the Jonang Lineage*, in *Mipam's Collected Works*, 27:279–80.

68. Mipam, *Lamp Illuminating the Miraculous Knots*, in *Mipam's Collected Works*, 16:1–814.

69. Mipam, *Collected Works*, vol. 17 (*e*) and vol. 18 (*waṃ*).

70. Mipam, *Vajra Melodies: An Interlinear Commentary on Saraha's* Treasury of Songs, in *Mipam's Collected Works*, 12:759–95.

71. Mipam, *White Lotus: Background for the* Treasury of Blessings, in *Mipam's Collected Works*, 15:9–1010.

72. Mipam, *White Lotus: An Explanation of the Seven-Line Supplication to Guru Padmasambhava*, in *Mipam's Collected Works*, 19:277–370; English trans. in Jamgön Mipham Rinpoche, *White Lotus: An Explanation of the Seven-Line Prayer to Guru Padmasambhava*, translated by the Padmakara Translation Group (Boston, MA: Shambhala Publications, 2007).

73. Mipam, *Ornament of Rule: A Treatise on Kingship*, in *Mipam's Collected Works*, 1:1–157.

74. Karma Phuntsho, "'Ju Mi pham rNam rgyal rGya mtsho—His Position in the Tibetan Religious Hierarchy and a Synoptic Survey of His Contributions," in *The Pandita and the Siddha: Studies in Honour of E. Gene Smith*, ed. Ramon N. Prats (Dharamshala, India: Amnye Machen Institute, 2007), 7.

75. Mipam, *A Divination Manual That Delights Mañjughoṣa*, in *Mipam's Collected Works*, 5:349–98; English trans. in *MO: Tibetan Divination System*, Jay Goldberg, ed. and trans. (Ithaca, NY: Snow Lion Publications, 1990).

76. Mipam, *Garland of Flowered Jewels: A Short Treatise on Letter Writing*, in *Mipam's Collected Works*, 14:929–40.

77. Karma Phuntsho, "'Ju Mi pham rNam rgyal rGya mtsho," 8–9.

78. Mipam, *Intelligent Presence*, in *Mipam's Collected Works*, 24:446.

79. Mipam, *Words That Delight Guru Mañjughoṣa*, 57; English trans. in Thomas Doctor, *Speech of Delight*, 57–59. See Duckworth, *Mipam on Buddha-Nature*, 6–13.

80. Mipam, *Words That Delight Guru Mañjughoṣa*, 407; English trans. in Doctor, *Speech of Delight*, 561. See Duckworth, *Mipam on Buddha-Nature*, 8.

81. Mipam, *Difficult Points of Scriptures in General*, in *Mipam's Collected Works*, 22:452, 465; Mipam, *Shedding Light on Thusness*, 304. See Duckworth, *Mipam on Buddha-Nature*, 11–13.

82. Mipam, *Difficult Points*, 450. See Duckworth, *Mipam on Buddha-Nature*, 74.

83. Mipam, *Sword of Insight*, in *Mipam's Collected Works*, 4:800. See Duckworth, *Mipam on Buddha-Nature*, 124–29.

84. Mipam, *Overview: Essential Nature of Luminous Clarity*, in *bka' brgyad rnam bshad dang spyi don 'od gsal snying po yang dag grub pa'i tshig 'grel bcas bzhugs* (Sichuan, China: Nationalities Press, 2000), 447; English trans. in *Luminous Essence: A Guide to the Guhyagarbha Tantra*, trans. Dharmachakra Translation Committee (Ithaca, NY: Snow Lion Publications, 2009), 48.

85. Mipam, *Overview: Essential Nature of Luminous Clarity*, 446; English trans. in *Luminous Essence*, 47.

86. Mipam, *Words That Delight Guru Mañjughoṣa*, 366; English trans. in Doctor, 499. See Duckworth, *Mipam on Buddha-Nature*, 28–32.

87. Georges Dreyfus, *Recognizing Reality* (Albany, NY: SUNY Press, 1997), 83–99.

88. See Dreyfus, *Recognizing Reality*, 103–5.

89. Mipam, *Words That Delight Guru Mañjughoṣa*, 50, 85; English trans. in Doctor, *Speech of Delight*, 49, 97–99.

90. See Mipam, *Eliminating Doubts*, in *dbu ma rgyan rtsa 'grel* (Sichuan, China: Nationalities Press, 1990), 558.

91. Mipam, *A Logic Primer*, in *Mipam's Collected Works*, 27:351. See also Mipam, *Eliminating Doubts*, 525–26.

92. See Mipam, *Eliminating Doubts*, 528.

93. See Longchenpa, *White Lotus: Autocommentary on the* Precious Wish-Fulfilling Treasury, in *Seven Treasuries*, 7: 162–65, 1104.

94. Mipam, *Words That Delight Guru Mañjughoṣa*, 208; English trans. in Doctor, *Speech of Delight*, 273.

95. These three subdivisions of the proponents of real images are also known as half-eggists (*sgo nga phyed tshal ba*); equal number of perceived and perceiver (*gzung 'dzin grangs mnyam pa*); and nondual diversity (*sna tshogs gnyis med pa*). See Mipam, *Concise Summary of the Philosophies from the* Wish-Fulfilling Treasury, in *Mipam's Collected Works*, 21:476.

96. Mipam, *Words That Delight Guru Mañjughoṣa*, 200; English trans. in Doctor, *Speech of Delight*, 261.

97. Mipam, *Words That Delight Guru Mañjughoṣa*, 198; English trans. in Doctor, *Speech of Delight*, 259.

98. There are two divisions of the proponents of false images: the "pure [cognition]," and the "impure [cognition]." Proponents of the pure cognition hold that images are still perceived by a buddha. The proponents of the impure cognition, however, maintain that when the defilements of the mind have been removed, there are no appearances, and the nonconceptual experience that remains as mere reflexive awareness is the Truth Body. See Mipam, *Concise Summary*, 478.

99. Mipam, *Words That Delight Guru Mañjughoṣa*, 285; English trans. in Doctor, *Speech of Delight*, 381–83.

100. Thus, in his description of conventional truth according to the Yogic Practice School of the Middle Way, we can say that Mipam follows the Mind-Only tradition of complex perceptual symmetry.

101. See Mipam, *Overview: Essential Nature of Luminous Clarity*, 407; English trans. in *Luminous Essence*, 18.

102. Mipam, *Eliminating Doubts*, 544–45.

103. Mipam, *Words That Delight Guru Mañjughoṣa*, 48; English trans. in Doctor, *Speech of Delight*, 47.

104. There is an important difference between reflexive awareness (*rang rig*) in the context of a sentient being's ordinary perception and the wisdom of individual reflexive awareness (*so so rang rig pa'i ye shes*), which is the wisdom of a buddha. The former is an intrinsic quality of *consciousness*, whereas the latter is *wisdom* realizing its own nature. Although the two should be clearly differentiated, a reflexive property of awareness is common to both.

105. Mipam, *Words That Delight Guru Mañjughoṣa*, 99; English trans. in Doctor, *Speech of Delight*, 117. See Duckworth, *Mipam on Buddha-Nature*, 33.

106. Mipam, *Words That Delight Guru Mañjughoṣa*, 97; English trans. in Doctor, *Speech of Delight*, 115. See Duckworth, *Mipam on Buddha-Nature*, 36.

107. Mipam, *Words That Delight Guru Mañjughoṣa*, 76; English trans. in Doctor, *Speech of Delight*, 85. See Duckworth, *Mipam on Buddha-Nature*, 39.

108. Mipam, *Words That Delight Guru Mañjughoṣa*, 76; English trans. in Doctor, *Speech of Delight*, 85; Mipam, *Beacon of Certainty*, 19; English trans. in Pettit, *Mipham's Beacon of Certainty*, 209. See Duckworth, *Mipam on Buddha-Nature*, 39.

109. Tāranātha, *History of the Dharma in India* (Sichuan, China: Nationalities Press, 1986), 190.

110. Tsongkhapa, *Thoroughly Illuminating the Viewpoint* (Sarnath, India: Central Institute of Higher Tibetan Studies, 1998), 226. See Duckworth, *Mipam on Buddha-Nature*, 235–36–77.

111. Mipam, *Commentary on the Wisdom Chapter of the* Way of the Bodhisattva (Sichuan, China: Nationalities Press, 1993), 30–31.

112. Mipam, *Words That Delight Guru Mañjughoṣa*, 97; English trans. in Doctor, 115.

113. Mipam, *Difficult Points*, 448–49. See Duckworth, *Mipam on Buddha-Nature*, 72.

114. See Mipam, *Light of the Sun*, in *spyod 'jug sher 'grel ke ta ka* (Sichuan, China: Nationalities Press, 1993), 556–57; Tsongkhapa, *The Great Exposition of the Stages of the Path* (Qinghai, China: Nationalities Press, 2000), 789.

115. See Bötrül, *Ornament of Mañjughoṣa's Viewpoint: An Explanation of the Words and Meanings of "Distinguishing the Views and Philosophies: A Lamp of Essential Points,"* in *lta grub shan 'byed gnad kyi sgron me'i rtsa 'grel* (Sichuan, China: Nationalities Press, 1996), 173–74; English trans. in Bötrül, *Distinguishing the Views and Philosophies: Illuminating Emptiness in a Twentieth-Century Tibetan Buddhist Classic*, trans. by Duckworth (Albany, NY: SUNY Press, 2011), 176–78.

116. Mipam, *Overview: Essential Nature of Luminous Clarity*, 461; English trans. in *Luminous Essence*, 57.

117. Mipam, *Overview: Essential Nature of Luminous Clarity*, 461; English trans. in *Luminous Essence*, 57–58.

118. Mipam, *Overview: Essential Nature of Luminous Clarity*, 462; English trans. in *Luminous Essence*, 58.

119. Mipam uses this analogy in *Commentary on the Wisdom Chapter of the* Way of the Bodhisattva, 83.

120. See Mipam, *Light of the Sun*, 557.

121. Mipam, *Precious Vajra Garland*, in *Mipam's Collected Works*, 24:599. See Duckworth, *Mipam on Buddha-Nature*, 91.

122. "Suchness" (Tib. *chos nyid*, Skt. *dharmatā*) is the nature of reality.

123. Khenpo Namdröl (*mkhan po rnam grol*, b. 1953) stated this in an oral commentary on Mipam's *Beacon of Certainty*, recorded on tape (Mysore, India: Ngagyur Nyingma Institute, 1997?).

124. Khenpo Chökhyap (*chos dbyings khyab brdal*, 1920–1997) stated this in an oral commentary (recorded on tape) on *Distinguishing the Views and Philosophies*, a text composed by his teacher, Bötrül (1898–1959).

125. Mipam, *Commentary on the Wisdom Chapter*, 10. See Duckworth, *Mipam on Buddha-Nature*, 87.

126. Mipam, *Beacon of Certainty*, 5, 49; English trans. in Pettit, *Mipham's Beacon of Certainty*, 196, 236. See Duckworth, *Mipam on Buddha-Nature*, 86–87.

127. Mipam, *Difficult Points*, 450. See Duckworth, *Mipam on Buddha-Nature*, 74.

128. See Mipam, *Words That Delight Guru Mañjughoṣa*, 420; English trans. in Doctor, *Speech of Delight*, 579.

129. See Bötrül, *Distinguishing the Views and Philosophies: A Lamp of Essential Points*, in *lta grub shan 'byed gnad kyi sgron me'i rtsa 'grel* (Sichuan, China: Nationalities Press, 1996), 37; English trans. in Bötrül, *Distinguishing the Views and Philosophies*, trans. by Duckworth, 57–58.

130. Mipam, *Immaculate Crystal Rosary: Commentary on the* Introduction to the Middle Way, in *Mipam's Collected Works*, 1:539. See Duckworth, *Mipam on Buddha-Nature*, 76–77.

131. Mipam, *Beacon of Certainty*, 7; English trans. in Pettit, *Mipham's Beacon of Certainty*, 197.

132. Mipam, *Immaculate Crystal Rosary*, 539–40; *Lion's Roar: Affirming Other-Emptiness*, 370, 374; English trans. in Pettit, *Mipham's Beacon of Certainty*, 421, 424. See also Duckworth, *Mipam on Buddha-Nature*, 76–77.

133. Mipam, *Difficult Points*, 450. See Duckworth, *Mipam on Buddha-Nature*, 74–75.

134. Mipam, *Words That Delight Guru Mañjughoṣa*, 56–57; English trans. in Doctor, *Speech of Delight*, 57. See
Duckworth, *Mipam on Buddha-Nature*, 6–7.

135. Mipam, *Difficult Points*, 450. See Duckworth, *Mipam on Buddha-Nature*, 74–75.

136. Mipam, *Commentary on the Wisdom Chapter*, 10. See Duckworth, *Mipam on Buddha-Nature*, 87.

137. Mipam, *Beacon of Certainty*, 5, 49; English trans. in Pettit, *Mipham's Beacon of Certainty*, 196, 236. See Duckworth, *Mipam on Buddha-Nature*, 86–87.

138. Mipam, *Vajra Essence*, in *Mipam's Collected Works*, 24:392–93. See Duckworth, *Mipam on Buddha-Nature*, 100.

139. This is a theme throughout Mipam's works in general and an issue he treats in his *Trilogy of Innate Mind* in particular. See, for instance, Hopkins, *Fundamental Mind*, 99–117.

140. Mipam, *Vajra Essence*, 372. See Duckworth, *Mipam on Buddha-Nature*, 80.

141. Mipam, *Intelligent Presence*, in *Mipam's Collected Works*, 24:536–37. See Duckworth, *Mipam on Buddha-Nature*, 100–101. Mipam responds to the consequence that even a dog would be a buddha by saying that the qualities are present but obscured and thus not actualized—like a knife that can cut but is in a sheath, or like a mirror that can reflect but is in a box. See also Mipam, *Difficult Points*, 454.

142. See Mipam, *Vajra Essence*, 538–39.

143. The Truth Body is the unchanging reality of the buddha's mind.

144. Mipam, *Lion's Roar: Exposition of Buddha-Nature,* in *Mipam's Collected Works,* 4:596; English trans. in Duckworth, *Mipam on Buddha-Nature,* 172.

145. This is asserted by Tsongkhapa's student, Khedrupjé (*mkhas grub rje dge legs dpal bzang,* 1385–1438). For references to this assertion, see Duckworth, *Mipam on Buddha-Nature,* 242n4.

146. See Duckworth, *Mipam on Buddha-Nature,* 98, 244n14.

147. In his commentary on the the *Sublime Continuum,* the Geluk scholar, Gyeltsapjé (1364–1432), says that emptiness is the basis of intention of the buddha-nature taught as a universal ground separate from the six collections of consciousness. See Gyeltsapjé, *Commentary on the* Sublime Continuum, in *Gyeltsapjé's Collected Works* 75a–78b. Sakya Paṇḍita also states that buddha-nature taught in the *Sublime Continuum* has emptiness as its basis of intention. See Sakya Paṇḍita, *Clear Differentiation of the Three Vows,* in *A Clear Differentiation of the Three Codes,* trans. Jared Douglas Rhoton (Albany, NY: SUNY Press, 2002), I.138–39, 285. Tsongkhapa says that emptiness is the basis of intention of the Buddha-nature which was taught in the *Laṅkāvatārasūtra* and in the *Introduction to the Middle Way* (under VI.95). See Tsongkhapa, *Essence of Eloquence,* in *Tsongkhapa's Collected Works* (Lhasa, Tibet: Zhol spar khang, n.d.), 14:92a–95b; see also Tsongkhapa, *Thoroughly Illuminating the Viewpoint* (Sarnath, India: Central Institute of Higher Tibetan Studies, 1998): 325–26. For further discussion of Geluk interpretations of buddha-nature, see David S. Ruegg, *Three Studies in the History of Indian and Tibetan Madhyamaka Philosophy* (Vienna, Austria: Arbeitskreis für Tibetische und Buddhistische Studien, 2000), 75–76n171.

148. Mipam, *Concise Summary of Philosophies from the* Wish-Fulfilling Treasury, in *Mipam's Collected Works,* 21:488. See Duckworth, *Mipam on Buddha-Nature,* 131.

149. According to the path of sutra (in contrast to tantra), among the qualities of a buddha, it is only the Truth Body that is held to be essentially present when one is a sentient being; the Form Bodies (the Emanation Body and the Enjoyment Body) are newly developed. According to tantra, however, both the Truth Body *and* the Form Bodies are essentially present from the beginning. This distinction between sutra and tantra was stated by Khenpo Chökhyap.

150. Mipam, *Words That Delight Guru Mañjughoṣa,* 436; English trans. in Doctor, *Speech of Delight,* 607.

151. Mipam, *Commentary on the Wisdom Chapter of the way of the Bodhisatta,* 55; Mipam, *Words That Delight Guru Mañjughoṣa,* 427, 441, 445; English trans. in Doctor, *Speech of Delight,* 592, 613, 619.

152. Mipam, *Overview: Essential Nature of Luminous Clarity,* 441–42; English trans. in *Luminous Essence,* 43–44. Mipam's statements here also contrast with the Zur tradition of the Nyingma, which insists on the reliance on the path of tantra and explains the *Secret Essence Tantra* according to Mahāyoga rather than the Great Perfection, as Longchenpa and Mipam do.

153. Mipam, *Words That Delight Guru Mañjughoṣa,* 462-3; English trans. in Doctor, *Speech of Delight,* 643.

154. See Mipam, *Overview: Essential Nature of Luminous Clarity,* 424–26; English trans. in *Luminous Essence,* 31–33.

155. Mipam, *Intelligent Presence,* 433.

156. Mipam states that the self-existing wisdom pointed out through the instructions

of the Great Perfection is itself the introduction to the actual coemergent wisdom; the confidence generated is of "equal fortune" with the greater path of accumulation, experiencing it through cultivation is the path of joining, realizing it is the path of seeing, and perfecting its strength is the path of meditation. See Mipam, *Intelligent Presence*, 522.

157. Like the practice of the Great Perfection, the Great Seal (Tib. *phyag chen,* Skt. *mahāmudrā*) involves directly engaging the nature of mind to actualize our ever-present buddha-nature. Mipam states that the practices of some quintessential instructions of the Mind Section of the Great Perfection, the Great Seal, the Great Middle Way, the Path and Fruit (*lam 'bras*), and Pacification (*zhi byed*) are all different words with the same meaning due to equally being a practice in wisdom that transcends conceptual mind. However, he says that the distinguishing feature of the Great Perfection is its profundity and extensiveness within the three sections of Mind, Expanse, and Quintessential Instructions. See Mipam, *Beacon of Certainty*, 24; English trans. in Pettit, 213.

158. Mipam, *Intelligent Presence*, 433–34. See also Mipam, *Precious Vajra Garland,* in *Mipam's Collected Works*, 24:601–2.

159. Mipam, *Intelligent Presence*, 458.

160. The four classes of tantra are Action Tantra, Performance Tantra, Yoga Tantra, and Highest Yoga Tantra. In the Nyingma tradition, there are six: the first three are the same as those in the preceding sentence, but in place of Highest Yoga Tantra, there are the three "inner tantras": Mahāyoga, Anuyoga, and Atiyoga (the Great Perfection).

161. Mipam, *Overview: Essential Nature of Luminous Clarity*, 412; English trans. in *Luminous Essence*, 22.

162. Mipam, *Discourse on the Eight Commands,* in *bka' brgyad rnam bshad dang spyi don 'od gsal snying po yang dag grub pa'i tshig 'grel bcas bzhugs* (Sichuan, China: Nationalities Press, 2000), 40–41.

163. Mipam, *Overview: Essential Nature of Luminous Clarity*, 407; English trans. in *Luminous Essence,* 19.

164. See Mipam, *Overview: Essential Nature of Luminous Clarity*, 410–11; English trans. in *Luminous Essence*, 20–22.

165. Mipam, *Vajra Essence*, 371; English trans. in Hopkins, *Fundamental Mind*, 78.

166. Mipam, *Overview: Essential Nature of Luminous Clarity*, 435; English trans. in *Luminous Essence*, 39.

167. One of Mipam's commentators elaborates on this by delineating three kinds of indivisibility: (1) "partial indivisibility," like a white and black thread spun together; (2) "nominal indivisibility," like the emptiness of the imagined nature in the dependent nature in Mind-Only; and (3) "genuine indivisibility," like fire and heat. He says that the indivisibility of purity and equality is the genuine indivisibility, the last of the three. Bötrül, *Ornament of Mañjughoṣa's Viewpoint*, 212; English translation in Bötrül, *Distinguishing the Views and Philosophies,* trans. by Duckworth, 211–12.

168. See Mipam, *Overview: Essential Nature of Luminous Clarity*, 457; English trans. in *Luminous Essence*, 54–55.

169. Mipam, *Overview: Essential Nature of Luminous Clarity*, 459; English trans. in *Luminous Essence*, 56.

170. Mipam, *Overview: Essential Nature of Luminous Clarity*, 457–59; English trans. in *Luminous Essence*, 54–56.

171. Mipam, *Beacon of Certainty*, 26; English trans. in Pettit, *Mipham's Beacon of Certainty*, 215. See Duckworth, *Mipam on Buddha-Nature*, 130.

172. Mipam, *Beacon of Certainty*, 29; English trans. in Pettit, *Mipham's Beacon of Certainty*, 218.

173. Mipam, *Beacon of Certainty*, 34; English trans. in Pettit, *Mipham's Beacon of Certainty*, 222.

174. In general explanations of valid cognition, what is evident is the domain of direct perception, what is hidden is the domain of inference, and what is extremely hidden is the domain of scripture.

175. Mipam, *Discourse on the Eight Commands*, 43–44. See Duckworth, *Mipam on Buddha-Nature*, 129.

176. Mipam, *Overview: Essential Nature of Luminous Clarity*, 436–37; English trans. in *Luminous Essence*, 41.

177. Mipam, *Overview: Essential Nature of Luminous Clarity*, 463; English trans. in *Luminous Essence*, 59.

178. Mipam uses the term "superior two truths" to describe the "superior relative truth" and the "superior ultimate truth" in the view of the Mahāyoga. See Mipam, *Concise Summary of the Philosophies from the* Wish-Fulfilling Treasury, 497.

179. Mipam, *Overview: Essential Nature of Luminous Clarity*, 437, 463; English trans. in *Luminous Essence*, 40, 59.

180. One of Mipam's students also demonstrates unity as characteristic of Nyingma exegesis. Within the threefold internal division of the Great Perfection—the Mind Section, Space Section, and Quintessential Instructions Section—he states that the Quintessential Instructions Section is superior to the other two sections because in the Mind Section there is a tendency to reify appearances of expression (*rtsal*) and display (*rol pa*), and in the Space Section there is a tendency to stray toward reifying emptiness. Thus, we can see that the Quintessential Instructions Section is superior, because it most effectively integrates appearance and emptiness. Such an indivisibility from sutra to tantra, and within the divisions of the Great Perfection, is a central theme in Mipam's synthesis of Buddhist doctrine. See Yönten Gyatso, *Moonlamp: A Commentary on the Precious Treasury of Qualities* (Bylakuppe, India: Ngagyur Nyingma Institute, n.d.), 3:600.

181. The "causal continuum," or "ground-continuum," is the first of a threefold division that also includes "method-continuum" or "path-continuum," and "result-continuum." For more on this, see Mipam, *Overview: Essential Nature of Luminous Clarity*, 398–404; English trans. in *Luminous Essence*, 12–16.

182. "Superimposition" (*sgro 'dogs*) refers to a misconception of holding what does not exist to exist.

183. The four extremes are those of existence, nonexistence, both existence and nonexistence, and neither existence nor nonexistence. All of these extremes are mistaken conceptions, because they remain tied into a conceptual framework.

184. "The ground of motivated conduct" is to be an ordinary being on the paths of accumulation and joining before reaching the path of seeing, when one becomes a full-fledged bodhisattva.

185. "The supreme quality" is the highest of four stages of the path of joining, which is followed by the path of seeing—the first bodhisattva ground—in which suchness is directly realized.

186. The eight collections of consciousness are: (1–5) the five sense consciousnesses, (6) the mental consciousness, (7) the afflicted mind, and (8) the universal ground consciousness.

187. There are two superimpositions, of existence and nonexistence, for each of the sixteen aspects of the four noble truths.

188. Longchenpa, *Precious Wish-Fulfilling Treasury,* in *Seven Treasuries* (Sichuan, China: 1996), 7:111.

189. A hallucinogenic plant.

190. A common locus (*gzhi mthun*) is when something shares the same basis, as in the case of a golden ring: the gold and the ring have a common locus.

191. Nāgārjuna, *Root Verses of the Middle Way,* XV.2.

192. Nāgārjuna, *Root Verses of the Middle Way,* XXV.13.

193. The Wisdom Truth Body (*ye shes chos sku*) refers to the buddha's omniscient mind.

194. Maitreya, *Sublime Continuum,* I.51.

195. Maitreya, *Sublime Continuum,* I.63.

196. Maitreya, *Sublime Continuum,* I.155.

197. "Thusness" is the unconstructed nature of reality.

198. The eight constructed extremes are arising and ceasing, permanence and annihilation, coming and going, difference and sameness.

199. Nāgārjuna, *Root Verses of the Middle Way,* IV.8.

200. Mañjughoṣa ("gentle melody") is another name for Mañjuśrī, the deity associated with wisdom.

201. The eight worldly concerns are (1–2) gain and loss, (3–4) fame and disgrace, (5–6) praise and slander, and (7–8) pleasure and pain.

202. One version of these famous lines is found in the *Perfection of Wisdom Sutra in Eight-Thousand Lines;* English translation in Edward Conze, *The Perfection of Wisdom in Eight Thousand Lines & Its Verse Summary* (Bolinas, CA: Four Seasons Foundation, 1973), 84.

203. The Enjoyment Body (Tib. *longs sku,* Skt. *saṃbhogakāya*) is the buddha form that appears to pure bodhisattvas.

204. The Emanation Body (Tib. *sprul sku,* Skt. *nirmāṇakāya*) is the form that buddhas take to teach ordinary beings.

205. The four means of resting freely (*cog bzhag bzhi*) are (1) ocean, (2) awareness, (3) appearance, and (4) mountain. For a description of these, see Longchenpa, *Treasure Trove of Scriptural Transmission: Autocommentary on the* Precious Treasury of the Expanse of Phenomena, in *Seven Treasuries* (Sichuan, China, 1996), 3:422–38; English trans. in Longchen Rabjam, *A Treasure Trove of Scriptural Transmission,* trans. Richard Barron (Junction City, CA: Padma Publishing, 2001), 226–35.

206. "Direct-crossing" refers to an esoteric practice of the Great Perfection that uses gazes and postures to directly manifest the embodied presence of wisdom.

207. Samantabhadra is the primordial Buddha, the self-aware nature of reality enlightened from the beginning.

208. See note 186.

209. This is from chapter 3 of the *Elucidating the Viewpoint Sutra;* Tibetan and English editions appear in John Powers, *Wisdom of the Buddha: The Saṃdhinirmocana Mahāyāna Sūtra* (Berkeley, CA: Dharma Publishing, 1995), 48–49. The last verse is rendered here in a slightly different way than the verse in the sutra; Mipam adds the word *view.*

210. The four visions (*snang ba zhi*) are (1) manifestation of suchness (*chos nyid mngon sum*),

(2) increased experience (*nyams snang gong 'phel*), (3) culmination of awareness (*rig pa tshad bab*), and (4) exhaustion into suchness (*chos nyid zad phebs*).

211. The three families are the Tathāgata family (represented by Śākyamuni or Mañjuśrī), the Padma family (represented by Avalokiteśvara), and the Vajra family (represented by Vajrapāṇi). The five families are the Tathāgata family (Vairocana in the center), the Vajra family (Akṣobhya in the East), the Padma family (Amitābha in the West), the Karma family (Amoghasiddhi in the North), and the Ratna family (Ratnasambhava in the South).

212. Understanding by means of an "object-universal" is a technical way to say the understanding is conceptual, so suchness is not known directly but through an abstract representation.

213. A common enumeration of the four mudras is: *mahāmudrā, dharmamudrā, samayamudrā,* and *karmamudrā.* For more on the meaning of these mudras, see Mipam, *Overview: Essential Nature of Luminous Clarity,* 568–76; English trans. in *Luminous Essence,* 138–44.

214. Maitreya, *Sublime Continuum,* I.154.

215. The four lamps (*sgron ma bzhi*) are: (1) the lamp of the far-reaching water [eyes] (*rgyang zhags chu'i sgron ma*), (2) the lamp of the expanse of awareness (*rig pa dbyings kyi sgron ma*), (3) the lamp of the empty spheres (*thig le stong pa'i sgron ma*), and (4) the lamp of self-existing insight (*shes rab rang byung gi sgron ma*).

216. This can be understood as the four means of resting freely (*cog bzhag bzhi*), as stated to me by Khenpo Loden (Spring 2008). See note 205.

217. The threefold unwavering is that of body, speech, and mind, as stated in a personal communication by Khenpo Pema Sherap (*padma shes rab,* b. 1936) (December 2007).

218. The three essential points can be understood as the three statements that strike the vital point: (1) recognize your own nature, (2) decide on one point, and (3) gain confidence in liberation, as stated in a personal communication by Khenpo Pema Sherap (December 2007).

GLOSSARY

Abhidharma (Tib. *chos mngon pa*): One of the three main sections of the Buddhist canon containing philosophy, cosmology, and psychology. An important feature of the philosophical analysis found in these texts is that complex phenomena are explained in terms of their more fundamental constituents, or elements (*dharmas*), that are held to compose reality.

afflictive obscuration (Tib. *nyon sgrib,* Skt. *kleśāvaraṇa*): An emotional outgrowth of ego-clinging, such as attachment or hatred, that functions to prevent liberation.

Asaṅga (Tib. *thogs med;* ca. fourth century): Important systematizer of the Yogic Practice School.

Autonomy School (Tib. *rang rgyud pa,* Skt. *svātantrika*): School of interpretation of the Middle Way that emphasizes the categorized ultimate; divides the two truths; and asserts that while nothing ultimately exists, things exist relatively.

bodhicitta (Tib. *byang chub kyi sems*): Literally, "the mind of awakening"; the wish to become a buddha for the benefit of others.

bodhisattva (Tib. *byang chub sems dpa'*): One who is intent on becoming a buddha for the benefit of others.

buddha (Tib. *sangs rgyas*): The complete absence of obscuration and the complete actualization of wisdom.

buddha-nature (Tib. *bde gshegs snying po,* Skt. *tathāgatagarbha*): The fundamental qualities of a buddha and the genuine meaning of emptiness, which is the unity of awareness and emptiness.

Candrakīrti (Tib. *zla ba grags pa;* ca. 600–650): Author of the *Introduction to the Middle Way* and a pivotal figure who is identified with the Consequence School of interpretation of the Middle Way.

categorized ultimate (Tib. *rnam grangs pa'i don dam,* Skt. *paryāya-paramārtha*): The ultimate truth that is an absence; the negation of true existence.

cognitive obscuration (Tib. *shes sgrib,* Skt. *jñeyāvaraṇa*): A conceptual framework; the working assumption of the threefold conceptualization of agent, object, and action, which serves to prevent the attainment of complete buddhahood.

confined perception (Tib. *tshur mthong*): A limited perspective based within ignorance that is maintained by ordinary beings in the world.

consciousness (Tib. *rnam shes,* Skt. *vijñāna*): As opposed to wisdom (Tib. *ye shes*), the ordinary conceptual mind.

Consequence School (Tib. *thal 'gyur pa*, Skt. *prāsaṅgika*): School of interpretation of the Middle Way that uses language in accordance with the uncategorized ultimate—reality free from constructs as experienced in a sublime being's meditative equipoise. In this school, the two truths are not held as separate when ascertaining the nature of reality.

conventional truth (Tib. *tha snyad bden pa*, Skt. *vyavahārasatya*): The way things appear, as opposed to the ultimate truth, which is the way things are. Often used interchangeably with *relative truth*.

dependent arising (Tib. *rten 'brel*, Skt. *pratitya-samutpāda*): Something that comes to be dependent on, or in relation to, something else.

Dharmakīrti (Tib. *chos kyi grags pa*, ca. 600–660): Author of influential texts on valid cognition who laid out a system of knowledge that distinguishes real particulars—which are perceived nonconceptually in direct perception—from universals—which are unreal, conceptual imputations.

Dölpopa (Tib. *dol po pa shes rab rgyal mtshan*, 1292–1361): Forefather of the Jonang school, renowned for his unapologetic affirmation of other-emptiness.

emptiness (Tib. *stong pa nyid*, Skt. *śūnyatā*): (1) The genuine meaning is the inconceivable nature of reality; (2) the limited, or provisional, meaning is the lack of inherent existence in anything.

first wheel of Dharma: One of three sets of sutras that contain teachings on the four noble truths and emphasize the teachings of impermanence, suffering, and no-self.

Gorampa (Tib. *go rams pa bsod nams seng ge*, 1429–1489): Important scholar of the Sakya school who notably critiqued Tsongkhapa's formulation of the Middle Way.

Great Exposition School (Tib. *bye brag smra ba*, Skt. *vaibhāṣika*): The lowest among the four main philosophical systems in Tibet; this Lesser Vehicle philosophical school holds the view that irreducible material particles and indivisible moments of mind are substantially existent.

Great Perfection (Tib. *rdzogs chen*): A textual and meditative tradition, central to the Nyingma school, that embodies the most direct path to awakening; it is the culmination of all philosophies and paths. The tradition affirms that the fundamental qualities of a buddha are always already present and that no contrived effort is necessary to produce this fundamental reality anew.

Great Vehicle (Tib. *theg pa chen po*, Skt. *mahāyāna*): A path to become buddha that involves bodhicitta, the method of compassion, and the wisdom that thoroughly realizes emptiness.

inherent existence (Tib. *rang bzhin gyis grub pa*, Skt. *svabhāva-siddhi*): Objective, ultimate, or real existence; the quality of something that essentially exists on its own.

last wheel of Dharma: One of three sets of sutras that contain teachings of buddha-nature and the Mind-Only School.

Lesser Vehicle (Tib. *theg dman*, Skt. *hīnayāna*): A path to enlightenment that emphasizes the renunciation of samsara in the quest for personal liberation. This tradition does not accept the Great Vehicle scriptures (i.e., the middle and last wheels of Dharma) as the word of the Buddha.

Longchenpa (Tib. *klong chen rab 'byams*, 1308–1364): Systematizer of the Great Perfection who was Mipam's most important Tibetan influence.

mantra (Tib. *sngags*): *See* tantra.

Middle Way (Tib. *dbu ma*, Skt. *madhyamaka*): The philosophical tradition systematized by Nāgārjuna that avoids the extremes of eternalism and nihilism, disclosing reality free from all extremes.

middle wheel of Dharma: One of three sets of sutra teachings that emphasizes the explicit teaching of emptiness.

mind (Tib. *sems,* Skt. *citta*): As opposed to awareness (Tib. *rig pa*), ordinary conceptual consciousness.

Mind-Only (Tib. *sems tsam,* Skt. *cittamātra*): One of four main philosophical systems that asserts that there is no external world independent of mind and that nondual, self-illuminating, reflexive awareness is ultimately real. Also known as the Yogic Practice School.

Nāgārjuna (Tib. *klu grub,* ca. second century): Important systematizer of the philosophy of the Middle Way who formulated the equality of emptiness and dependent arising.

nirvana (Tib. *mya ngan las 'das pa*): Liberation from suffering.

Nyingma (Tib. *rnying ma*): The "old school" of translations of Buddhist texts into Tibet that traces its heritage to the eighth century, as opposed to the new schools (Sarma) that developed from the eleventh century onward.

object of negation (Tib. *dgag bya,* Skt. *pratiṣedhya*): That which is overcome by reasoning or meditation on the path (e.g., false conceptions of true existence).

other-emptiness (Tib. *gzhan stong*): A Middle Way view, mainly associated with the Jonang school, that claims that the ultimate truth (the content of authentic experience) is not empty of its own essence but is only empty of what is extrinsic to it (i.e., relative phenomena, or the content of inauthentic experience).

particular (Tib. *rang mtshan,* Skt. *svalakṣaṇā*): A phenomenon that is utterly unique in space and time. It is directly perceived (nonconceptually) in Dharmakīrti's presentation of valid cognition, in contrast to a universal, which is a conceptual construct.

pure vision (Tib. *dag gzigs*): An undistorted perspective of reality, which is the content of a sublime being's wisdom in postmeditation.

reflexive awareness (Tib. *rang rig,* Skt. *svasaṃvedanā*): Awareness's intrinsic feature of being aware of its own knowing (self-aware) as it knows an object.

relative truth (Tib. *kun rdzob bden pa,* Skt. *saṃvṛtisatya*): (1) The way things appear (equivalent to conventional truth); (2) the content of distorted experience.

Rongzom (Tib. *rong zom chos bzang,* ca. eleventh century): Important figure in the Nyingma tradition who, along with Longchenpa, was one of Mipam's main influences.

Śākyamuni: The historical Buddha.

samsara (Tib. *'khor ba*): A life of suffering perpetuated by ignorance.

Śāntarakṣita (Tib. *zhi ba mtsho,* ca. eighth century): Important synthesizer of the Yogic Practice School and the Middle Way.

Sarma (Tib. *gsar ma*): The traditions of the "new schools" of translation (e.g., Sakya, Jonang, Kagyü, Geluk) of Buddhist texts into Tibet, which developed from the eleventh century onward, as opposed to the old school (Nyingma) that traces its history in Tibet to the eighth century.

Secret Essence Tantra (Tib. *rgyud gsang ba'i snying po,* Skt. *guhyagarbhatantra*): The most important tantra in the Nyingma school.

self-emptiness (Tib. *rang stong*): According to Mipam, the Middle Way claim that nothing ultimately exists.

superimposition (Tib. *sgro 'dogs,* Skt. *samāropa*): A misconception of holding what does not exist to exist.

Sutra (Tib. *mdo*): (1) One of the three main sections of the Buddhist canon that contains discourses attributed to the Buddha; (2) a long path to become a buddha that contrasts with the faster path of tantra.

Sutra School (Tib. *mdo sde pa,* Skt. *sautrāntika*): Among the four philosophical systems, one of the Lesser Vehicle schools that asserts that irreducible particles of matter and indivisible moments of mind are substantially existent. Unlike the Great Exposition School, this tradition upholds reflexive awareness and attributes ultimate status only to functional particulars.

tantra (Tib. *rgyud*): (1) A genre of text attributed to the Buddha, or another enlightened being, that gives extraordinary teachings in mythological settings; (2) the Vajrayāna, a direct path to become a buddha that contrasts with the path of sutra.

terma (Tib. *gter ma*): "Treasure revelations" generally held to be eighth-century teachings of Padmasambhava that were hidden in the Tibetan landscape for future generations to uncover when the time was right for the particular teachings to be understood and practiced.

Tsongkhapa (Tib. *tsong kha pa blo bzang grags pa,* 1357–1419): Forefather of the Geluk school who is renowned for his distinctive interpretation of the Consequence School.

ultimate truth (Tib. *don dam bden pa,* Skt. *paramārthasatya*): The way things are, as opposed to the relative truth (the way things appear).

uncategorized ultimate (Tib. *rnam grangs ma yin pa'i don dam,* Skt. *aprayāya-paramārtha*): The genuine ultimate truth, which is nonconceptual.

universal (Tib. *spyi mtshan,* Skt. *sāmānyalakṣaṇā*): A common property shared by particular things. In Dharmakīrti's system of valid cognition, universals are simply unreal, conceptual constructs that are incapable of performing a function, in contrast to particulars.

universal ground consciousness (Tib. *kun gzhi rnam shes,* Skt. *ālayavijñāna*): A fundamental consciousness that serves as the repository of karma (actions) and latent potentials that manifest as embodied experience of a lifeworld.

valid cognition (Tib. *tshad ma,* Skt. *pramāṇa*): A correct means of assessing what is true or real. It is particularly associated with an influential system developed by Dharmakīrti.

Vinaya (Tib. *'dul ba*): One of the three main sections of the Buddhist canon that deals with moral discipline, especially for the monastic community.

wisdom (Tib. *ye shes,* Skt. *jñāna*): Nonconceptual awareness of reality.

Yogic Practice School (Tib. *rnal 'byor spyod pa,* Skt. *yogācāra*): A tradition that emphasizes that there is no reality independent of mind. Also known as Mind-Only.

Yogic Practice School of the Middle Way (Tib. *rnal 'byor spyod pa'i dbu ma,* Skt. *yogācāra-madhyamaka*): A school of the Middle Way that adopts a Middle Way view of ultimate truth and asserts the conventional truth as the Mind-Only School does.

BIBLIOGRAPHY

Translations of Mipam's Writings

Mipam. *Beacon of Certainty.* In *Mipham's Beacon of Certainty: Illuminating the View of Dzogchen, the Great Perfection,* translated by John W. Pettit, 194–240. Boston, MA: Wisdom Publications, 1999.

———. *Commentary on* Distinguishing the Middle and the Extremes. In *Middle Beyond Extremes: Maitreya's Madhyāntavibhāga with Commentaries by Khenpo Shenga and Ju Mipham,* translated by Dharmachakra Translation Committee. Ithaca, NY: Snow Lion Publications, 2006.

———. *Commentary on* Distinguishing Phenomena and Suchness. In *Maitreya's Distinguishing Phenomena and Pure Being,* translated by Jim Scott. Ithaca, NY: Snow Lion Publications, 2004.

———. *Commentary on the* Introduction to the Middle Way. In *Introduction to the Middle Way: Chandrakirti's* Madhyamakavatara *with Commentary by Jamgön Mipham,* translated by Padmakara Translation Group. Boston, MA: Shambhala Publications, 2002.

———. *Commentary on the* Ornament of the Middle Way. In *Speech of Delight: Mipham's Commentary on Śāntarakṣita's* Ornament of the Middle Way, translated by Thomas H. Doctor. Ithaca, NY: Snow Lion Publicatons, 2004; also in *The Adornment of the Middle Way: Shantarakshita's Madhyamakalankara with Commentary by Jamgön Mipham,* translated by Padmakara Translation Group. Boston, MA: Shambhala Publications, 2005.

———. *Commentary on* A Song on the View. In *Straight from the Heart: Buddhist Pith Instructions,* by Karl Brunnhölzl, 391–428. Ithaca, NY: Snow Lion Publications, 2007.

———. *Concise Summary of the Philosophies from the Wish-Fulfilling Treasury.* In *Buddhist Philosophy in Theory and Practice,* by Herbert Guenther. Baltimore, MD: Penguin Books, 1971.

———. *Fish King's Power of Truth: A Jataka Tale.* Retold by Lama Mipham. Berkeley, CA: Dharma Publishing, 1986.

———. *Fundamental Mind: The Nyingma View of the Great Completeness.* Translated and edited by Jeffrey Hopkins. Ithaca, NY: Snow Lion Publications, 2006.

———. *A Garland of Jewels: The Eight Great Bodhisattvas.* Translated by Yeshe Gyamtso. Woodstock, NY: KTD Publications, 2008.

———. *Gateway to Knowledge.* Translated by Erik Pema Kunsang (Eric Hein Schmidt). 3 vols.

Hong Kong: Rangjung Yeshe Publications, 1997–2002; also in *mKhas-'jug.* Translated by Richard Barron. Junction City, CA: Padma Publishing, 1998.

———. *Gem that Clears the Water.* In *Tibetan Treasure Literature: Revelation, Tradition, and Accomplishment in Visionary Buddhism,* by Andreas Doctor, 52–71. Ithaca, NY: Snow Lion Publications, 2006.

———. *Golden Zephyr: Instructions from a Spiritual Friend,* by Nāgārjuna and Lama Mipham. Translated by Leslie Kawamura. Berkeley, CA: Dharma Publishing, 1975.

———. *Great Gift and the Wish-Fulfilling Gem: A Jakata Tale.* Retold by Lama Mipham. Berkeley, CA: Dharma Publishing, 1986.

———. *Instructions on the Vision of the Middle Way.* In *Calm and Clear,* by Lama Mipham. Translated by Tarthang Tulku and the Tibetan Nyingma Meditation Center, 101–111. Berkeley, CA: Dharma Publishing, 1997.

———. *Lama Mipham's Commentary to Nagarjuna's Stanzas for a Novice Monk.* Translated by Glenn H. Mullin. Dharamsala, India: LTWA, 1978.

———. *Lion's Roar: Exposition of Buddha-Nature.* In *Mipam on Buddha-Nature: The Ground of the Nyingma Tradition,* translated by Douglas Duckworth, 147–80. Albany, NY: SUNY Press, 2008.

———. *Lion's Roar Proclaiming Extrinsic Emptiness.* In *Mipham's Beacon of Certainty: Illuminating the View of Dzogchen, the Great Perfection,* translated by John W. Pettit, 415–27. Boston, MA: Wisdom Publications, 1999.

———. *Luminous Essence: A Guide to the Guhyagarbha Tantra.* Translated by the Dharmachakra Translation Committee. Ithaca, NY: Snow Lion Publications, 2009.

———. *MO: Tibetan Divination System,* by Jamgon Mipham. Translated and edited by Jay Goldberg. Ithaca, NY: Snow Lion Publications, 1990.

———. *The Spontaneous Vajra Manifestation of Awareness and Emptiness.* In *Dzogchen Essentials: The Path That Clarifies Confusion,* compiled and edited by Marcia Binder Schmidt, translated by Erik Pema Kunsang, 91–94. Hong Kong: Rangjung Yeshe Publications, 2006.

———. *Treasure-Trove of Material Arts* (chapter 2). In "On the Manufacture of Ink." Translated by Cristoph Cüppers. *Ancient Nepal,* no. 113 (August/September 1989): 1–8.

———. *Ways of Enlightenment: Buddhist Studies at Nyingma Institute,* by Lama Mipham. Berkeley, CA: Dharma Publishing, 1993.

———. *The Wheel of Analytic Meditation.* In *Calm and Clear,* by Lama Mipham. Translated by Tarthang Tulku and the Tibetan Nyingma Meditation Center, 43–53. Berkeley, CA: Dharma Publishing, 1997.

———. *White Lotus: An Explanation of the Seven-Line Prayer to Guru Padmasmabhava,* by Jamgön Mipham Rinpoche. Translated by the Padmakara Translation Group. Boston, MA: Shambhala Publications, 2007.

The following texts by Mipam are available at www.lotsawahouse.org/mipham.html:
"The Great Cloud of Blessings: The Prayer which Magnetizes All that Appears and Exists"
"In Praise of Manjushri: Increasing Intelligence to the Full"
"In Praise of Manjushri: The Great Treasure of Blessings"
"Profound Instruction on the View of the Middle Way"
"Satirical Advice for the Four Schools"
"The Swift Fulfilment of All Wishes: Offering the Flag of Windhorse"

"The Sword of Wisdom for Thoroughly Ascertaining Reality"
"The Wheel of Analysis and Meditation"

ENGLISH WORKS ON MIPAM

Cuevas, Bryan J. "The 'Calf's Nipple' (*Be'u bum*) of Ju Mipam ('Ju Mi pham): A Handbook of Tibetan Ritual Magic." In *Tibetan Ritual,* edited by José Cabezón, 165–86. New York: Oxford University Press, 2010.

Dreyfus, Georges. "Would the True Prāsaṅgika Please Stand? The Case of 'Ju Mi-pham." In *The Svātantrika-Prāsaṅgika Distinction,* edited by Georges Dreyfus and Sarah Mc-Clintock, 317–47. Boston, MA: Wisdom Publications, 2003.

Duckworth, Douglas. "De/limiting Emptiness and the Boundaries of the Ineffable." *Journal of Indian Philosophy* 38:1 (2010), 97–105.

———. *Mipam on Buddha-Nature: The Ground of the Nyingma Tradition.* Albany, NY: SUNY Press, 2008.

———. "Mipam's Middle Way of Prāsaṅgika and Yogācāra." *Journal of Indian Philosophy* 38:4 (2010), 431–39.

———. "Non-Representational Language in Mipam's Re-presentation of Other-Emptiness," *Journal of Buddhist Philosophy* (forthcoming).

———. "Two Models of the Two Truths: Ontological and Phenomenological Approaches." *Journal of Indian Philosophy* 38:5 (2010), 519–27.

Goodman, Steven D. "Mi-pham rgya-mtsho: An Account of His Life, the Printing of His Works, and the Structure of His Treatise Entitled *mKhas-pa'i tshul la 'jug-pa'i sgo.*" In *Wind Horse: Proceedings of the North American Tibetological Society,* edited by Ronald M. Davidson, 58–78. Berkeley, CA: Asian Humanities Press, 1981.

Jikmé Phünstok. *Miracle Stories of Mipham Rinpoche.* Translated by Ann Helm, Nalanda Translation Committee, 2008.

Kapstein, Matthew. "Mipam Namgyel: The Lion's Roar Affirming Extrinsic Emptiness." In *Buddhist Philosophy: Essential Readings,* edited by William Edelglass and Jay Garfield, 61–72. New York: Oxford University Press, 2009.

———. "Mi-pham's Theory of Interpretation." In *Buddhist Hermeneutics,* edited by Donald S. Lopez, 149–74. Honolulu, HI: University of Hawaii Press, 1988.

———. "We Are All Gzhan stong pas." *Journal of Buddhist Ethics* 7 (2000): 105–25.

Khenpo Palden Sherab Rinpoche and Khenpo Tsewang Dongyal Rinpoche. *Opening the Wisdom Door of the Rangtong and Shentong Views.* Trout Creek, NY: Dharma Samudra, 2007.

Lin Shen-yu. "Tibetan Magic for Daily Life: Mi pham's Texts on *gTo*-rituals." *Cahiers d'Extreme-Asie* 15 (2005): 107–25.

Pettit, John W. *Mipham's Beacon of Certainty: Illuminating the View of Dzogchen, the Great Perfection.* Boston, MA: Wisdom Publications, 1999.

———. "Review of Altruism and Reality." *Journal of Buddhist Ethics* 6 (1999): 120–37.

Phuntsho, Karma. "'Ju Mi pham rNam rgyal rGya mtsho—His Position in the Tibetan Religious Hierarchy and a Synoptic Survey of His Contributions." In *The Pandita and the Siddha: Studies in Honour of E. Gene Smith.* Edited by Ramon N. Prats. Dharamshala, India: Amnye Machen Institute, 2007.

———. *Mipham's Dialectics and the Debates on Emptiness.* London: RoutledgeCurzon, 2005.

Thrangu Rinpoche. *The Middle Way Instructions of Mipham Rinpoche.* Boulder, CO: Namo Buddha Seminar, 2000.

Williams, Paul. "A Response to John Pettit." *Journal of Buddhist Ethics* 6 (1999): 138–53.

———. *The Reflexive Nature of Awareness: A Madhyamaka Defence.* London: Curzon Press, 1998.

PRIMARY SOURCES IN TIBETAN

Bötrül (*bod sprul mdo sngags bstan pa'i nyi ma*, 1898–1959). *Distinguishing the Views and Philosophies: A Lamp of Essential Points* [*lta grub shan 'byed gnad kyi sgron me*]. In *lta grub shan 'byed gnad kyi sgron me'i rtsa 'grel.* Sichuan, China: Nationalities Press, 1996.

———. *Ornament of Mañjughoṣa's Viewpoint: An Explanation of the Words and Meanings of "Distinguishing the Views and Philosophies: A Lamp of Essential Points"* [*lta grub shan 'byed gnad kyi sgron me'i tshig don rnam bshad 'jam dbyangs dgongs rgyan*]. In *lta grub shan 'byed gnad kyi sgron me'i rtsa 'grel.* Sichuan, China: Nationalities Press, 1996.

Gyeltsapjé (*rgyal tshab rje dar ma rin chen*, 1364–1432). *Commentary on the* Sublime Continuum [*theg pa chen po rgyud bla ma'i ṭīka*]. In *Gyeltsapjé's Collected Works* (*lha sa* ed.), vol. 3. Asian Classics Input Project, Release IV, S5434.

Jamgön Kongtrül (*kong sprul blo gros mtha' yas*, 1813–1899). *Stainless Light Rays of the Vajra-Moon: Teachings on the View of the Middle Way of Other-Emptiness* [*gzhan stong dbu ma chen po'i lta khrid rdo rje zla ba dri ma med pa'i 'od zer*]. In vol. 8, 581–611 *The Collected Works of 'Jam-mgon Kong-sprul* [*rgya chen bka' mdzod*]. Paro: Ngodup, 1976.

Jamyang Gyeltsen ('*jam dbyangs rgyal mtshan*). *A Short History of Kaḥtok* [*rgyal ba kaḥ thog lo rgyus mdor bsdus*]. Sichuan, China: Nationalities Press, 1996.

Kuchuk (*ku byug*). *Opening the Eye of Clear Intelligence: A History of the Transmission of the Middle Way View in Tibet* [*bod kyi dbu ma'i lta ba'i 'chad nyan dar tshul blo gsal mig 'byed*]. Beijing: China's Tibetan Studies Press, 2004.

Künzang Chödrak (*sa manta bhadra dharma kirti*). *Mipam's Essential Biography and Catalogue of Works* [*gangs ri'i khrod kyi smra ba'i seng ge gcig po 'jam dgon mi pham rgya mtsho'i rnam thar snying po bsdus pa dang gsung rab kyi dkar chag snga 'gyur bstan pa'i mdzes rgyan*]. In *Mipam's Collected Works*, vol. 8 (*hung*), 621–732. (Dilgo Khyentsé's expanded redaction of *sde dge* edition). Kathmandu, Nepal: Zhechen Monastery, 1987.

Longchenpa (*klong chen rab 'byams*, 1308–1364). *Precious Wish-Fulfilling Treasury* [*yid bzhin rin po che'i mdzod*]. In *Seven Treasuries* [*mdzod bdun*], vol. 7, 1–138 (Tarthang Tulku ed.). Sichuan, China, 1996.

———. *Treasure Trove of Scriptural Transmission: Autocommentary on the* Precious Treasury of the Expanse of Phenomena [*chos dbyings rin po che'i mdzod kyi 'grel pa lung gi gter mdzod*]. In *Seven Treasuries* [*mdzod bdun*], vol. 3, 83–765 (Tarthang Tulku ed.). Sichuan, China, 1996.

———. *White Lotus: Autocommentary on the* Precious Wish-Fulfilling Treasury [*theg pa chen po'i man ngag gi bstan bcos yid bzhin rin po che'i mdzod kyi 'grel pa padma dkar po*]. In *Seven Treasuries* [*mdzod bdun*], vol. 7, 139–1544 (Tarthang Tulku ed.). Sichuan, China, 1996.

Mipam ('*ju mi pham rgya mtsho*, 1846–1912). *Advice for Beginners* [*las dang po pa la 'dams pa*]. In *Dispelling the Darkness in the Hearts of Fortunate Ones: A Compilation of Mipam's Definitive Meaning Advice,* 186–87. Serta: Serta Buddhist Academy of the Five Arts, n.d.

———. *Banner Victorious Over All: An Interlinear Commentary on the* Treasury of Reasoning [*tshad ma rigs pa'i gter mchan gyis 'grel pa phyogs las rnam par rgyal ba'i ru mtshon*]. In *Mipam's Collected Works*, vol. 11 (*kha*), 549–752. (Dilgo Khyentsé's expanded redaction of *sde dge* edition). Kathmandu, Nepal: Zhechen Monastery, 1987.

———. *Beacon of Certainty* [*nges shes sgron me*]. In *nges shes sgron me rtsa 'grel*, 1–54. Sichuan, China: Nationalities Press, 1997.

———. *Brilliant Light of Reason: An Interlinear Commentary on the* Compendium of Valid Cognition [*tshad ma kun las btus pa'i mchan 'grel rig lam rab gsal snang ba*]. In *Mipam's Collected Works*, vol. 8 (*hung*), 473–619. (Dilgo Khyentsé's expanded redaction of *sde dge* edition). Kathmandu, Nepal: Zhechen Monastery, 1987.

———. *Mipam's Collected Works* (Dilgo Khyentsé's expanded redaction of *sde dge* edition). Kathmandu, Nepal: Zhechen Monastery, 1987.

———. *Commentary on the Wisdom Chapter of the* Way of the Bodhisattva [*spyod 'jug sher 'grel ke ta ka*]. Sichuan, China: Nationalities Press, 1993.

———. *Commentary on the Words of the Eighteenth Chapter* [of the *Wish-Fulfilling Treasury*] [*le'u bco brgyad pa'i tshig 'grel*]. In *Mipam's Collected Works*, vol. 21, 565–78.

———. *Concise Points of Bringing Illusion onto the Path: Advice for Practitioners* [*dge sbyong rnams la gtam du bya ba*]. In *Mipam's Collected Works*, vol. 23, 274–77

———. *Concise Summary of the Philosophies from the* Wish-Fulfilling Treasury [*yid bzhin mdzod kyi grub mtha' bsdus pa*]. In *Mipam's Collected Works*, vol. 21, 439–500.

———. *Difficult Points of Scriptures in General* [*dbu ma sogs gzhung spyi'i dka' gnad skor gyi gsung sgros sna tshogs phyogs gcig tu bsdus pa rin po che'i za ma tog*]. In *Mipam's Collected Works*, vol. 22, 427–710.

———. *Discourse on the Eight Commands* [*bka' brgyad rnam bshad*]. In *bka' brgyad rnam bshad dang spyi don 'od gsal snying po yang dag grub pa'i tshig 'grel bcas bzhugs*, 1–185. Sichuan, China: Nationalities Press, 2000.

———. *Dispelling the Darkness in the Hearts of Fortunate Ones: A Compilation of Mipam's Definitive Meaning Advice* [*'jam mgon mi pham rgya mtsho'i nges don gdams pa'i chos skor phyogs gcig tu bsgrigs pa skal bzang snying gi mun sel*]. Serta: Serta Buddhist Academy of the Five Arts, n.d.

———. *A Divination Manual That Delights Mañjughoṣa* [*a ra pa tsa'i mo yig 'jam dpal dgyes pa'i zhal lung*]. In *Mipam's Collected Works*, vol. 5 (*tsa*), 349–98.

———. *Elegant Discourse Introducing the Unmistaken Meaning of the Intended Meaning of the Victorious Ones' Mother: A Commentary on the Condensed Perfection of Wisdom Sutra* [*yon tan rin chen sdud pa'i 'grel pa rgyal ba'i yum gyi dgongs don la phyin ci ma log par 'jug pa'i legs bshad*]. In *Mipam's Collected Works*, vol. 24, 1–223.

———. *Eliminating Doubts* (*dam chos dogs sel*). In *dbu ma rgyan rtsa 'grel*, 498–563. Sichuan, China: Nationalities Press, 1990.

———. *An Elucidation of Various Difficult Points in the* Precious Wish-Fulfilling Treasury [*yid bzhin rin po che'i mdzod kyi dka' gnad ci rigs pa gsal bar byed pa*]. In *Mipam's Collected Works*, vol. 21, 501–64.

———. *Establishing the Three Vows as Essentially One* [*sdom gsum ngo bog cig tu sgrub pa*]. In *Mipam's Collected Works*, vol. 8 (*hung*), 137–55.

———. *A Feast on the Nectar of the Supreme Vehicle: Commentary on the* Ornament of the Great Vehicle Sutras [*theg pa chen po mdo sde'i rgyan gyi dgongs don rnam par bshad pa theg mchog bdud rtsi'i dga' ston*]. In *Mipam's Collected Works*, vol. 2 (*a*), 1–760.

———. *Flower Garland: Catalogue of Rongzom's Collected Works* [*rong zom gsung 'bum dkar chag me tog phreng ba*]. In *Rongzom's Collected Works* [*rong zom chos bzang gi gsung 'bum*], vol. 1 (*oṃ*), 1–22. Sichuan, China: Nationalities Press, 1999.

———. *Garland of Flowered Jewels: A Short Treatise on Letter Writing* [*yig bskur gyi rnam bzhag mdo tsam brjod pa me tog nor bu'i phreng ba*]. In *Mipam's Collected Works*, vol. 14 (*ca*), 929–40.

———. *Garland of Light Rays: Commentary on* Distinguishing the Middle and Extremes [*dbu dang mtha' rnam par 'byed pa'i bstan bcos kyi 'grel pa 'od zer phreng ba*]. In *Mipam's Collected Works*, vol. 4 (*pa*), 659–786.

———. *Gateway to Scholarship* [*mkhas pa'i tshul la 'jug pa'i sgo*]. In *mkhas 'jug*. Qinghai, China: Nationalities Press, 1994.

———. *Immaculate Crystal Rosary: Commentary on the* Introduction to the Middle Way [*dbu ma la 'jug pa'i 'grel pa zla ba'i zhal lung dri med shel phreng*]. In *Mipam's Collected Works*, vol. 1 (*oṃ*), 497–837.

———. *Inexhaustible Melody of Auspiciousness: A Commentary on Recollecting the Three Jewels Sutra* [*dkon mchog gsum rjes su dran pa'i mdo rnam par 'grel ba bkra shis mi zad pa'i sgra dbyangs*]. In *Mipam's Collected Works*, vol. 9 (*shrī*), 1–69.

———. *Intelligent Presence* [*gnyug sems 'od gsal ba'i don la dpyad pa rdzogs pa chen po gzhi lam 'gras bu'i shan 'byed blo gros snang ba*]. In *Mipam's Collected Works*, vol. 24, 411–566.

———. *Lamp Illuminating the Miraculous Knots* [*srid pa 'phrul gyi ju thig gi dpyad don snang gsal sgron me*]. In *Mipam's Collected Works*, vol. 16 (*tsa*), 1–814.

———. *Light of the Sun* [*brgal lan nyin byed snang ba*]. In *spyod 'jug sher 'grel ke ta ka*, 465–579. Sichuan, China: Nationalities Press, 1993.

———. *Light of Wisdom: Commentary on* Distinguishing Phenomena and Suchness [*chos dang chos nyid rnam 'byed 'grel pa ye shes snang ba*]. In *Mipam's Collected Works*, vol. 4 (*pa*), 609–58.

———. *Lion's Roar: Affirming Other-Emptiness* [*gzhan stong khas len seng ge'i nga ro*]. In *Mipam's Collected Works*, vol. 12 (*ga*), 359–78.

———. *Lily of Wisdom's Presence* [*ye shes grub pa'i utpal*]. In *Mipam's Collected Works*, vol. 27, 479–83.

———. *Lion's Roar: Exposition of Buddha-Nature* [*bde gshegs snying po'i stong thun chen mo seng ge'i nga ro*]. In *Mipam's Collected Works*, vol. 4 (*pa*), 563–607.

———. *A Logic Primer* [*bsdus tshan rtsod rig smra ba'i sgo 'byed*]. In *Mipam's Collected Works*, vol. 27, 285–354.

———. *Ornament of Rule: A Treatise on Kingship* [*rgyal po lugs kyi bstan bcos sa gzhi skyong ba'i rgyan*]. In *Mipam's Collected Works*, vol. 1 (*oṃ*), 1–157.

———. *Overview: Essential Nature of Luminous Clarity* [*spyi don 'od gsal snying po*]. In *bka' brgyad rnam bshad dang spyi don 'od gsal snying po yang dag grub pa'i tshig 'grel bcas bzhugs*, 381–605. Sichuan, China: Nationalities Press, 2000.

———. *Precious Crystal: Annotated Commentary on the* Treasury of the Abhidharma [*dam pa'i chos mngon pa mdzod kyi mchan 'grel rin po che'i do shal blo gsal dgyes pa'i mgul rgyan*]. In *Mipam's Collected Works*, vol. 3 (*ra*), 1–614.

———. *Precious Mirror: Catalogue of the Seven Treasuries* [*mdzod bdun spar du bsgrubs pa'i dkar chag rin chen me long*]. In *nges don rdzogs pa chen po'i man ngag phyogs bsgrigs zab don nor bu'i mdzod khang*, 7–44. Serta: Serta Buddhist Academy of the Five Arts, n.d.

———. *Precious Vajra Garland* [*gnyug sems zur dpyad skor gyi gsung sgros thor bu rnams phyogs gcig tu bsdus pa rdo rje rin po che'i phreng ba*]. In *Mipam's Collected Works*, vol. 24, 567–774.

———. *A Quintessential Instruction on the Vital Point in Three Statements* [*tshig gsum gnad kyi man ngag*]. In *Mipam's Collected Works*, vol. 27, 134.

———. *Sanskrit-Tibetan Dictionary* [*skad gnyis shan sbyar*]. In *Mipam's Collected Works*, vol. 26.

———. *Sea of Joy That Delights Sarasvatī: A Commentary on the* Mirror of Poetry [*snyan dngags me long 'grel pa dbyangs can dgyes pa'i rol mtsho*]. In *Mipam's Collected Works*, vol. 9 (*shri*), 185–640.

———. *Shedding Light on Thusness* [*gzhan gyis brtsad pa'i lan mdor bsdus pa rigs lam rab gsal de nyid snang byed*]. In *spyod 'jug sher 'grel ke ta ka*, 133–463. Sichuan, China: Nationalities Press, 1993.

———. *Song of the View* [*lta ba'i mgur ma*]. In *Mipam's Collected Works*, vol. 4 (*pa*), 821–67.

———. *Steps to Definitive Goodness: A Short Interlinear Commentary on the* Individual Liberation Sutra [*sor thar mdo yi mchan 'grel nyung ngu nges legs them skas*]. In *Mipam's Collected Works*, vol. 8 (*hung*), 1–130.

———. *Stillness, Movement, and Awareness in the Great Seal* [*phyag chen pa'i gnas 'gyu rig gsum*]. In *Mipam's Collected Works*, vol. 27, 22–23.

———. *Supplication Supplement for the Jonang Lineage* [*jo nang lugs kyi bshad pa'i brgyud 'debs kha skong*]. In *Mipam's Collected Works*, vol. 27, 279–80.

———. *Sword of Insight* [*don rnam par nges pa shes rab ral gri mchan bcas*]. In *Mipam's Collected Works*, vol. 4 (*pa*), 787–820.

———. *Sword of Intelligence: Method for Meditating on Bodhicitta* [*byang chub kyi sems sgom pa'i thabs blo yi ral gri*]. In *Mipam's Collected Works*, vol. 27, 491–94.

———. *A Talk to Monastics* [*dgon sde rnams la gtam du bya ba*]. In *Mipam's Collected Works*, vol. 23, 267–69.

———. *Treasure-Trove of Material Arts* [*bzo gnas nyer mkho'i za ma tog*]. In *Mipam's Collected Works*, vol. 10 (*ka*), 71–138.

———. *Treasury of Blessings* (*thub chog byin rlabs gter mdzod*). In *Mipam's Collected Works*, vol. 15 (*cha*), 1–8.

———. *Treasure of Jewels: An Interlinear Commentary on Padmasambhava's* Garland of Views [*slob dpon chen po padma 'byung gnas kyis mdzad pa'i man ngag lta ba'i phreng ba'i mchan 'grel nor bu bang mdzod*]. In *Mipam's Collected Works*, vol. 13 (*nga*), 417–63.

———. *Treasury Illuminating Elegant Discourse: A Clear Explanation of the* Commentary on Valid Cognition [*tshad ma rnam 'grel gyi gzhung gsal por bshad pa legs bshad snang ba'i gter*]. In *Mipam's Collected Works*, vol. 20.

———. *Trilogy of Innate Mind* [*gnyug sems skor gsum*]. In *Mipam's Collected Works*, vol. 24, 353–774.

———. *Vajra Essence* [*gnyug sems 'od gsal ba'i don rgyal ba rig 'dzin brgyud pa'i lung bzhin brjod pa rdo rje snying po*]. In *Mipam's Collected Works*, vol. 24, 353–410.

———. *Vajra Melodies: An Interlinear Commentary on Saraha's* Treasury of Songs [*dpal sa ra has mdzas pas do ha mdzod glu'i mchan 'grel gnyug ma'i rdo rje sgra dbyangs*]. In *Mipam's Collected Works*, vol. 12 (*ga*), 759–95.

———. *Various Categories of the* Compendium of Abhidharma [*mngon pa kun btus kyi rnam grangs sna tshogs bshad pa*]. In *Mipam's Collected Works*, vol. 12 (*ga*), 401–509.

———. *Verse of Auspiciousness* ['gro don bstan pa]. In *Mipam's Collected Works*, vol. 27, 742–43.

———. *White Lotus: Background for the* Treasury of Blessings [*thub chog byin rlabs gter mdzod kyi rgyab chos padma dkar po*]. In *Mipam's Collected Works*, vol. 15 (*cha*), 9–1010.

——. *White Lotus: An Explanation of the Seven-Line Supplication to Guru Padmasambhava* [*gu ru tshig bdun gsol 'debs kyi rnam bshad padma dkar po*]. In *Mipam's Collected Works,* vol. 19, 277–370.

——. *Wisdom Essence: The Method for Sustaining the Nature of Awareness* [*rig ngo skyong thabs ye shes syning po*]. In *Mipam's Collected Works,* vol. 27, 218–20.

——. *Words of Maitreya: Correlating the Sutra and Treatise from the Commentary on the Condensed Meaning, an Elegant Discourse Introducing the Intended Meaning of the Victorious Ones' Mother* [*sdud 'grel yum gyi dgongs don la 'jug pa'i legs bshad las mdo dang bstan bcos sbyar tshul ma pham zhal lung*]. In *Mipam's Collected Works,* vol. 24, 223–352.

——. *Words of Mipam: Interlinear Commentary on the* Sublime Continuum [*theg pa chen po rgyud bla ma'i bstan bcos kyi mchan 'grel mi pham zhal lung*]. In *Mipam's Collected Works,* vol. 4 (*pa*), 349–61.

——. *Words That Delight Guru Mañjughoṣa: Commentary on the* Ornament of the Middle Way [*dbu ma rgyan gyi rnam bshad 'jam byangs bla ma dgyes pa'i zhal lung*]. In *dbu ma rgyan rtsa 'grel*. Sichuan, China: Nationalities Press, 1990.

Nyoshül Khenpo (*smyo shul mkhan po 'jam dbyangs rdo rje,* 1931–1999). *Garland of Lapis* [*rang bzhin rdzogs pa chen po'i chos 'byung rig 'dzin brgyud pa'i rnam thar ngo mtshar nor bu baidurya'i phreng ba*], vols. 1 and 2. Thimphu, Bhutan: Indraprastha Press, 1996.

Rongzom (*rong zom chos kyi bzang po,* ca. eleventh century). *Secret Essence Commentary* [*rgyud rgyal gsang ba'i snying po dkon cog 'grel*]. In *Rongzom's Collected Works,* vol. 1, 33–253. Sichuan, China: Nationalities Press, 1999.

Sakya Paṇḍita. *Clear Differentiation of the Three Vows* [*sdom gsum rab dbye*]. In *A Clear Differentiation of the Three Codes,* translated by Jared Douglas Rhoton. Albany, NY: SUNY Press, 2002.

Sherap Gyatso (*shes rab rgya mtsho,* 1884–1968). *A Short Biography of Gendün Chöpel* [*mkhas dbang dge 'dun chos 'phel gyi rnam thar mdor bsdus*]. In *mkhas dbang dge 'dun chos 'phel gyi gsung rtsom phyogs sgrig,* 3–29. Sichuan, China: Nationalities Press, 1988.

Tāranātha (*jo nang rje btsun tā ra nā tha,* 1575–1634). *History of the Dharma in India* [*rgya gar chos 'byung*]. Sichuan, China: Nationalities Press, 1986.

Tsongkhapa (*tsong kha pa blo bzang grags pa,* 1357–1419). *Essence of Eloquence* [*drang nges legs bshad snying po*]. In *Tsongkhapa's Collected Works,* vol. 14. Lhasa, Tibet: Zhol spar khang. Asian Classics Input Project, Release IV, S5396.

——. *The Great Exposition of the Stages of the Path* [*lam rim chen mo*]. Qinghai, China: Nationalities Press, 1985, 2000.

——. *Thoroughly Illuminating the Viewpoint* [*dgongs pa rab gsal*]. Sarnath, India: Central Institute of Higher Tibetan Studies, 1998.

Yönten Gyatso (*yon tan rgya mtsho,* fl. nineteenth century). *Moonlamp: Commentary on the Precious Treasury of Qualities* [*yon tan rin po che'i mdzod kyi 'grel pa bden gnyis gsal byed zla ba'i sgron ma*], vols. 1–3. Bylakuppe, India: Ngagyur Nyingma Institute, n.d.

OTHER WORKS CITED

Ani Jinpa Palmo, trans. *Brilliant Moon: The Autobiography of Dilgo Khyentse.* Boston, MA: Shambhala Publications, 2008.

Bayer, Achim. "The Life and Works of mKhan-po gZhan-dga' (1871–1927)." Master's thesis, University of Hamburg, 2000.

Bötrül. *Distinguishing the Views and Philosophies: Illuminating Emptiness in a Twentieth-*

Century Tibetan Buddhist Classic. Translated, annotated, and introduced by Douglas S. Duckworth. Albany, NY: SUNY Press, 2011.

Dunne, John. *Foundations of Dharmakīrti's Philosophy.* Boston, MA: Wisdom Publications, 2004.

Dreyfus, Georges. "Where Do Commentarial Colleges Come From?" *Journal of the International Association of Buddhist Studies* 28, no. 2 (2005): 273–97.

———. *The Sound of Two Hands Clapping: The Education of a Tibetan Buddhist Monk.* Berkeley, CA: University of California Press, 2003.

———. *Recognizing Reality.* Albany, NY: SUNY Press, 1997.

Goldstein, Melvyn C. *The Snow Lion and the Dragon: China, Tibet, and the Dalai Lama.* Berkeley, CA: University of California Press, 1997.

Jackson, David P. *A Saint in Seattle: The Life of the Tibetan Mystic Dezhung Rinpoche.* Boston, MA: Wisdom Publications, 2003.

Klein, Anne. *Meeting the Great Bliss Queen: Buddhists, Feminists, and the Art of Self.* Boston, MA: Beacon Press, 1995.

Longchen Rabjam. *A Treasure Trove of Scriptural Transmission.* Translated by Richard Barron. Junction City, CA: Padma Publishing, 2001.

Ruegg, David S. *Three Studies in the History of Indian and Tibetan Madhyamaka Philosophy.* Vienna, Austria: Arbeitskreis für Tibetische und Buddhistische Studien, 2000.

Smith, E. Gene. *Among Tibetan Texts.* Boston, MA: Wisdom Publications, 2001.

Sperling, Elliot. "The Chinese Venture in K'am, 1904–1911, and the Role of Chao Erh-feng," *The Tibet Journal* 1, no. 2 (April/June 1976): 10–36.

Tashi Tsering. "Nag-roṅ mgon-po rnam-gyal: A Nineteenth Century Khams-pa Warrior." In *Soundings of Tibetan Civilization,* edited by Barbara Aziz and Matthew Kapstein, 196–214. Delhi: Manohar Publications, 1985.

Tulku Thondup. *Masters of Meditation and Miracles.* Boston, MA: Shambhala Publications, 1996.

INDEX

Printed in the United States
by Baker & Taylor Publisher Services